Magellan of the Pacific

Edouard Roditi

McGraw-Hill Book Company

New York   St. Louis   San Francisco

123456789BPBP79876543

FIRST AMERICAN EDITION

First published in 1972 by Faber and Faber Limited, London

Library of Congress Cataloging in Publication Data
Roditi, Edouard.
    Magellan of the Pacific.
    Bibliography: p.
    1. Magalhães, Fernão de, d. 1521. I. Title.
G286.M2B62 1973   910'.92'4 [B]   72-12759
ISBN 0-07-073754-1

Contents

7

Illustrations

MAP

Acknowledgements

The author wishes to express his gratitude to the Fundação Calouste Gulbenkian, of Lisbon, for its generous financial support of the research, in Portuguese libraries and archives and elsewhere, that preceded the writing of the present biography; to the library staff of Lisbon's justly famous Sociedade de Geografía, for its assistance and great courtesy; to Professor Armando Cortesão, of the University of Coimbra, for guidance in the complex history of sixteenth-century cartography; to Bay Şakir Eçzacibaşi, of Istanbul, and to the Curator of the Turkish National Naval Museum in Besiktaş, for information on Turkish naval history and on the artillery foundry of the Tophane Arsenal; to the Secretariat of College Five of the University of California at Santa Cruz and to Gregory Pearson, of Berkeley, and Bari Rolfe, of Los Angeles, for their help in typing a particularly difficult manuscript; to Larry and Justine Fixel, of San Francisco, for their friendship and encouragement; and to Justus George Lawler and George Woodcock, for their wise and patient editorial advice.

For their encouragement to pursue studies of some more specialized problems that could not be handled within the necessary limitations of the present volume, thanks are also due to the editors of *L'Arche* (Paris), *Ocidente* (Lisbon), *Judaism* (New York), and *European Judaism* (London), which have published the author's various essays on Jewish merchants who traded with Asia in mediaeval Europe, on ancient and mediaeval cosmography, on the Jewish

ACKNOWLEDGEMENTS

communities of India and on the influence of Magellan's voyage on Turkish navigational science.

For permission to reproduce the illustrations of the present volume, thanks are also due to: the editors and publishers of *Cartographia Portugallica*, Lisbon; the Archivo general de Indias, Seville; Kunsthistorisches Museum, Vienna; Museo del Prado, Madrid; John Howell Books, San Francisco, and the John Carter Brown Library, Brown University, Providence, Rhode Island; and the British Museum, London.

Introduction

Magellan's first circumnavigation of the Earth, though he died before his survivors returned to their point of departure, remains the most important voyage of exploration that man has ever accomplished on our planet. It proved four points: that the continent of America, like Africa, can be circumnavigated, that the circumference of the Earth at its Equator or along any of its meridians is greater than any geographer since Ptolemy in the second century A.D. had believed, that the Earth, on empirical evidence alone, is really a sphere, and that one gains a day by circumnavigating it as one follows the Sun from east to west.

This last observation alone, first noted by Antonio Pigafetta in his *Journal* of Magellan's voyage, provided the basis, during the next few centuries, for entirely new speculations in physics and metaphysics on the nature of time and eternity. Does time have a specific nature of its own, one and the same in every part of the universe and independent of whatever man may think of it? Or is time something which, according to a Socratic definition of language in Plato's *Cratylus*, may derive its nature only from a kind of tacit agreement in the minds of men who think in terms of time? In Magellan's day, orthodox philosophers and mathematicians viewed time and eternity in strictly geocentric terms and as entirely different concepts or realities. They thought that time must be the same throughout a finite created universe which, like the known world of antiquity in ancient maps, is surrounded by a kind of limitless ocean of eternity. By first posing in empirical terms the problem of the diversity or of the relative nature of time, Magellan's circumnavigation started a discussion that ultimately led to theories in which time and eternity become one and the same.

A relativistic conception of time, space, matter and the universe as something continuous which, infinite as a whole, remains everywhere and always a finite part of itself, has now made it possible to undertake extraterrestrial voyages of exploration too. Thus, as an ultimate consequence of Magellan's achievement, twentieth-century cosmonauts can leave our world and enter areas of the universe which are subject to other laws of time or of gravitation, but return from them to the Earth and its own laws of physics, no longer the only ones that we know.

The long record of Portuguese exploration that led up to Magellan's voyage had originally begun with discoveries off the north-west coast of Africa. Though the Canary Isles, and perhaps Madeira too, had been known to Phoenician navigators and even, if only as the legendary Isles of the Hesperides, to the Greeks of Homeric times, they were quite unknown to mediaeval Western Europe.

Thus Lancelot Malocello, a Genoese sailing in the service of Portugal, is generally reported to have been the first navigator to rediscover the Canary Islands around 1270, while a Norman from near Cherbourg, Jean de Bettencourt, was the first since the Phoenicians to establish a settlement, as a vassal of the King of Portugal, on one of these islands in 1402.

Is it a mere coincidence that Malocello's daring expedition into the Atlantic was undertaken less than a decade after Friar Roger Bacon shocked the orthodox world of Aristotelian scholasticism, when he sought to persuade his friend, Pope Clement the Fourth, to encourage empirical or experimental science and geographical exploration? Roger

Bacon indeed argued that the major policy aims of the mediaeval Papacy, such as the reconciliation of the Roman and Greek Churches, the conversion of the Tartars and the defeat of Islam, could be achieved only by developing Christendom's knowledge of the world and by discovering a westward sea-route to the Indies.

Madeira, however, was perhaps first rediscovered and briefly settled only in 1370, by Robert Machin, when he eloped from Bristol with Anne d'Arfet. The few survivors of his expedition are said to have returned to England in 1416, after their leader's death and that of his sweetheart. Reports of their discovery may have inspired some of Shakespeare's descriptions of Prospero's Isle in *The Tempest*. Two years later, João Gonzalez Varco and Tristão Vaz are known more reliably to have set out from Lisbon and occupied Madeira as a new Portuguese territory.

In 1431, the Canary Islands were finally occupied and settled by Spain, after having been repeatedly rediscovered and forgotten or merely abandoned because of the fierce resistance of their heathen stone-age Berber natives. Spain's claims to the islands conflicted with those of Portugal and both Kings appealed to the Pope, who granted the islands in 1435 to Portugal and shortly afterwards, when Spain appealed, reversed his decision in the latter's favour.

During the mid fifteenth century the tempo of exploration along the African coast intensified. Portuguese navigators reached Cape Blanco in 1441, Cape Verde in 1445 and, in 1446, the Cape Verde Islands. By 1470, the Portuguese had established trading posts all along the African coast down to the present area of Ghana and, soon after 1480, began to settle the islands of São Tomé and Principe. In 1484, Diogo Cão discovered the mouth of the Congo River; in 1485, a Portuguese fleet reached Cape Negro; in 1487, Bartolomeu

Dias at long last rounded the Cape of Good Hope and was thus the first navigator reliably known to have entered the Indian Ocean from the west.

The Portuguese were the first among Christian Europeans to persevere in systematic exploration of the areas south of Madeira. Arab navigators and traders, setting out from Ceuta, Tangier and other Moroccan ports, also sailed down the coast of West Africa, though never as far as Dahomey or the Congo. Instead, they generally traded with the Guinea Coast via Timbuctoo by using safer caravan routes across the Sahara. There they had been preceded, hundreds of years earlier, by Judaeo-Berber traders and nomads who influenced the Fulani language and culture. It was in order to avoid trading with Moslem intermediaries in the ports of Morocco, with which they were constantly at war, that the Portuguese preferred to face the greater risks of navigation along the stormy African coast, dangerous though it could be in areas where they found no natural harbours, for instance over considerable distances between Safi and Dakar. Such navigational perils explain why Portugal disputed so energetically, in the fifteenth and early sixteenth centuries, the Spanish possession of offshore bases in the nearby Canary Islands. In their repeated attempts to circumnavigate Africa in order to reach India, the Portuguese also found themselves obliged to establish small colonies, in the form of forts or 'factories', in most of the good natural harbours that they discovered along the coasts of Africa. There they could land safely to replenish the supplies of their tiny ships, which often carried too bulky a cargo of arms and trade goods to allow much space for water and other necessities.

An unbroken chain of Portuguese bases can still be traced by its ruined forts and other monuments, built at convenient distances, all the way from Ceuta, Tangier and Asilah in northern Morocco, along the coasts of Africa and Asia to India, Ceylon and the Malay peninsula, through Indonesia and on to Macao in southern China. These bases served the purposes of trade or colonial expansion, and offered facilities for obtaining supplies and for caulking and other necessary ship repairs.

Along the coasts of West Africa, Portuguese penetration at first met little resistance. Local African rulers were generally ready to trade with these newcomers, who found themselves in direct competition with the Arabs only if they penetrated inland to centres of trade reached by caravans crossing the Sahara. In East Africa, however, after they rounded the Cape of Good Hope, the Portuguese found Arab navigators and traders already well established throughout the Indian Ocean, as far south as the northern coasts of Mozambique and Madagascar. Here they had to wrest by force, from local Moslem rulers, nearly every suitable harbour where they needed to establish a new base.

In the age of Magellan, shortage of manpower prevented the Portuguese from attempting to colonize extensively the areas of Africa and Asia where they established their bases. So many of their men died of tropical diseases or infected wounds, were killed in battle or lost at sea, that their colonial expansion soon proved a great drain on the human resources of their metropolis. Ships built of European timbers rotted quickly in the Indian Ocean; after serving a couple of years there, many a vessel was unfit for the return voyage to Portugal. Shipwrecks were frequent on the way out, but much more frequent, with rotting keels and heavy cargoes, on the way back. To avoid wasting good Christian manpower on settling certain bases which, though strategically important, were considered economically unprofitable or too unhealthy, the Portuguese even preferred on occasion to send slaves or undesirables. In 1487 and 1493, they thus deported to the island of São Tomé several shiploads of Portuguese convicts and of Jewish children who had been separated by force from their parents.

As it was, emigration to the more temperate colonies, especially to Madeira, the Azores and later Brazil, drained many rural areas of Portugal of manpower that was needed there for agriculture. As early as the fifteenth century, African captives were already being imported to work on estates in the southernmost province of Algarve, which soon became the only area of Europe with a plantation economy based on negro slave labour. Gangs of Moorish prisoners of war also worked as slaves in the port of Lisbon and in the building trades which flourished with the rapid growth of the prosperous capital.

Though intolerant of religious differences at home, the Portuguese soon found themselves obliged by the same problems of manpower to allow the Inquisition less freedom to persecute heretics, Jews or other non-Christians in their colonies than at home. In India, when they made Goa their capital, they allowed only Catholic churches within the city, but tolerated mosques, Hindu temples and Parsee shrines beyond its limits. Whenever, especially in Tangier and other Moroccan bases, they were fortunate enough to find Jewish refugees from Spain or Portugal who could be useful to them as interpreters or intermediaries in trade with native Arab merchants, they were glad to employ them, not only as clerks but even as trusted agents. When Tangier was handed over to England in 1663, together with Bombay, as part of the dowry of Catherine of Braganza on the occasion of her marriage to Charles the Second, it was a member of a local Jewish family of bankers who drafted the agreement on behalf of Portugal.

Yet the history of European colonial expansion, especially in its early stages, remains on the whole a chronicle of terrible religious and racial intolerance towards the natives of territories explored and conquered. As one reads the many contemporary records of Portuguese and Spanish penetration of Africa, Asia and the Americas, one is soon shocked by their matter-of-fact accounts of ruthless massacre, of piracy and rapine, of cynical slave-trading and exploitation of native labour. Though all claimed officially to be bringing the benefits of Christianity to the benighted inhabitants of these other continents, very few sixteenth-century explorers approached them in such a truly missionary spirit as Magellan, who set out to convert them, especially in the Philippines, by offering them the example of his own unimpeachable behaviour rather than by using force.

The sixteenth century was Portugal's Golden Age. Spain was its only potential rival for the mastery of the oceans and of newly discovered lands. Grotius had not yet formulated the foundations of international law proclaiming the freedom of the seas. No power dared to claim that the open seas belonged equally to all who sailed them. Treaties were merely personal agreements between individual rulers, and no machinery of international diplomacy could be set in motion to seek a compromise when major interests came into conflict. In cases of the kind now referred, however ineffectually, to the Security Council or the General Assembly of the United Nations, wise monarchs then called upon the Pope to arbitrate their disputes.

After the return of Columbus from his discovery of the Americas, in 1494, the Treaty of Tordesillas in this way settled fairly effectively the dispute that had arisen some years earlier between the Kings of Spain and of Portugal concerning their respective 'spheres of interest' in newly explored lands or in territories that might yet be discovered. Ever since 1450, the Portuguese had sought to prevent Spanish penetration of their newly acquired spheres of interest along the coasts of Africa and in its offshore islands. Slicing the world, at last generally believed to be spherical, from north to south like an apple, Pope Alexander the Sixth, by a Bull issued in 1493, had drawn an imaginary line, a hundred sea-leagues to the west of the Azores and the Cape Verde Islands, which the Portuguese had already settled. All newly discovered territories west of this line were then assigned to Spain, which had financed the discovery of the Americas; but all territories to the east of this line were assigned to Portugal, which had already explored the coasts of Africa and rounded the Cape of Good Hope. The following year, at Tordesillas, King John the Second of Portugal achieved a considerable diplomatic victory when this imaginary line was shifted three hundred and seventy sea-leagues to the west, so that in 1500, when Pedro Alvares Cabral first landed near the future site of Rio de Janeiro, the bulge of Brazil was providentially almost all Portuguese territory.

Nobody could yet tell where this corrected imaginary line might pass through the unexplored other side of the globe. Would the legendary isles of Cipangu, now known as Japan, should they ever be reached by navigators coming from the Iberic peninsula, fall within the Spanish or the Portuguese 'sphere of influence'?

Because the calculations of the ancient geographer Eratosthenes, who in the third century B.C. estimated the world's circumference with astonishing accuracy at 25,000 miles, had later been amended incorrectly by Ptolemy, it was generally believed that the unknown expanse which later proved to be occupied by the Pacific Ocean was much narrower, and that the imaginary line of the Treaty of Tordesillas might well pass, on the other side of the globe, through the area of Borneo or Celebes instead of through that of the western part of New Guinea which is now the Indonesian province of Irian. According to this theory, the unattained Moluccas or Spice Islands, the unknown Philippines and legendary Cipangu or Japan, would all belong to Spain rather than to Portugal.

Most navigators and geographers moreover believed, at the time of the Treaty of Tordesillas, that the territories which Columbus had just discovered in the west were but outlying, less civilized and less wealthy areas of the East Indies or perhaps of Japan. Only a few unlettered fishermen in the ports of southern Spain had affirmed to Columbus, when he tried to recruit them for his fleet, that he would never reach the East Indies by sailing west. Somehow, they had already drifted to the West Indies and even beyond, returning to Spain with reports of a continuous coastline and of an unknown continent which later proved to be the eastern coast of Mexico. But nobody of consequence gave any credit to the gossip of such ignorant men.

The human mind, however sophisticated, tends indeed to imagine the unknown very much in terms of what it already knows: *nihil in intellectu quod non prius in sensu*. Because the geographers and navigators of antiquity knew only the closed seas that they could navigate, they assumed that the Indian Ocean, when it proved to be almost as easily navigable as the Mediterranean and certainly less dangerous than the Atlantic, must be also a closed sea. As Spanish and Portuguese navigators began to explore the Atlantic Coast of Brazil after the Pacific Ocean had first been sighted by Europeans when Balboa, in 1513, discovered and claimed it for the King of Spain, they similarly assumed, because it had already proved possible to circumnavigate Africa, that the vast land mass of South America could also be circumnavigated and that a passage somewhere in the far south must lead them from the Atlantic to the Pacific.

Maps and globes still depicted, in the early sixteenth century, vast unknown expanses of the Earth in what appears to us to be a very fanciful manner. Two of the earliest known globes, one made in 1492 by Martin Behaim before Columbus had discovered America and the other in 1515 by Johann Schöner before Magellan's expedition across the Pacific, offer us hypothetical versions of the geography of the whole Indian Ocean, of the Middle and Far East and of the Pacific. To a navigator, such globes and maps could be of little practical use once he sailed east of Aden on the Red Sea or west of the Azores or the Cape Verde Islands in the Atlantic.

Celestial maps, charting the stars that can be seen at night south of the Equator, were still unknown. In his *Journal* of Magellan's voyage, Antonio Pigafetta, who accompanied and survived him, notes and describes with wonder the presence of unknown constellations in the night skies of the Southern hemisphere. By such unknown stars, navigators could not usefully guide themselves, nor could they avail themselves of currents and winds of which they had no experience. The first Portuguese explorers of the Indian Ocean, for instance, had no knowledge of the monsoons, which can aid or hinder navigation, especially of sailing ships, according to the season and the direction of their course.

It required great courage to explore the waters and lands of the torrid equatorial zone or of any areas south of it. Ever since antiquity, men of the more temperate areas of the Northern hemisphere had firmly believed that the torrid

22

zone was uninhabitable and that the heat of the sun at its zenith would set fire to a man as if he were matchwood. The mediaeval maps of the great Arab geographer Edrissi, for instance, point out that all Africa, beyond where he believed the source of the Nile to be, was uninhabitable because of the heat.

This belief is clearly stated as an indisputable fact in 1375 by Ibn Khaldun. In the sixteenth century, Pigafetta, in his *Journal* of Magellan's voyage, still felt it necessary to refute, on the basis of his own observations of climatic conditions in the torrid zone, the belief that its air was always hot and dry.

Prehistoric man may have navigated for thousands of years in primitive barks on many seas, following their coasts or drifting from island to island with favourable currents and winds. But historical evidence of maritime exploration goes only as far back as ancient Egyptian chronicles reporting expeditions down the coast of East Africa to the land of Punt, some two thousand years before Christ. These ventures were followed by Minoan, Mycenaean and Phoenician expeditions in the Mediterranean and the Red Sea. But even after three thousand five hundred years of recorded maritime navigation, the available maps and charts of many areas of the world, around 1500, were still very fanciful and unreliable. Nevertheless, they inspired and guided Fernando de Magalhães, generally known as Magellan, on a voyage of world discovery that turned out to be man's first circumnavigation of the Earth.

'Of all the world's great heroes', Magellan remains, like the British Grenadier of poetry and song, one of those about whose character, psychology, personal appearance and private life we know the least and have the fewest reliable clues on which to develop a plausible biography. Of his place of birth, his parents, his childhood, adolescence and youth, we know practically nothing. Concerning the many years that he subsequently served in Africa or India, the historical records now available may well refer, in most cases, to other men of the same name. A mist of ambiguities shrouds his very birth, which is only presumed to have occurred in 1480, and the first thirty-four years of his brief life. After that he lived only seven more years, and his shadowy figure begins to emerge with a slightly clearer outline, against the general historical background of his age, only from the day when he is known to have been wounded in the knee in the course of a skirmish which occurred during a brief military expedition to Morocco. A couple of contemporary eye-witnesses reported briefly that Magellan was a man of short stature and unimpressive appearance and that he limped. But of such details as the colour of his eyes and hair, or the shape of his nose and chin, we know nothing.

Of his relations with women, we know only of his brief, shadowy, but advantageous marriage to an heiress of whom we have no portrait or written description. Of his relations with other men who accompanied him on his various ventures and expeditions, we know so little that we must conclude that Magellan must have been remarkably uncommunicative and that he could make enemies more readily than friends. Even Antonio Pigafetta, who saw Magellan almost daily from June 1519 until the great navigator's death in April 1521, has left us no physical description of Magellan, no revealing details about his private life and thoughts, in an otherwise ample and eloquent *Journal* of the first circumnavigation of the Earth. Even Pigafetta's observations of Magellan's character and behaviour are so laconic that we are left, after a reading of his *Journal*, merely with a vague impression of stern nobility and reticence, of an indomitable will, a rare obstinacy and singleness of purpose, and of a curiously passionate and apostolic Christianity. We know that Magellan was a strict disciplinarian, expecting as much of others as of himself; that he wept for joy and gratitude when finally vouchsafed his first view, from the Straits which he had just discovered, of the vast expanse of the Pacific Ocean, which he had so long been seeking to reach; also, that he could suffer great disappointment and hardship without complaining.

But even these few features of his character are revealed to us, in Pigafetta's *Journal* and the scattered testimony of a few other eye-witnesses, only by a bare minimum of laconically told anecdotes. In the final analysis, we know almost more about Juan de Cartagena, who mutinied against Magellan off the coast of South America, than about the Captain General himself.

Great actions often speak for themselves, but may lend themselves less easily to commentary and explanation than great books or great works of art. A man of action, Magellan was no artist or intellectual. His main hypothesis, in the field of cosmography, was proved by harsh experience to be false: that the estuary of the Plata River, in South America, was a strait that led from the Atlantic Ocean to the Pacific. Yet Magellan was stubborn enough to continue in his venture and finally to find a strait when he was almost ready to give up his search after failing again and again. Had he been a scholar rather than a man of action, he might have left us a treatise of geography on the fallacies of which future commentators would have found ample opportunity to expatiate. Instead, Magellan blazed a trail that is now clear, except for a few unimportant details, and that offers us little opportunity for conjecture or comment. It is indeed significant that some of Magellan's biographers have devoted almost more time and space to elucidating the ambiguities of the life and work of Martin Behaim, an obscure and unreliable cosmographer whose name Magellan is known to have mentioned only once, than to any aspect of Magellan's private life, to his thoughts and beliefs, or his behaviour towards those who associated with him.

Had Magellan survived his expedition and returned triumphantly to Spain, he might well have left an autobiography and, like Columbus, personal papers and a library with significant annotations in the margins of some of his books; there might also have been a wealth of anecdotes in the memoirs and letters of others, who would have boasted of their association with a man who had proved himself great. But Magellan's greatness was proved only after his death. During his lifetime, nearly all those who associated with him, except Pigafetta, remained remarkably unaware of his latent greatness and took little trouble to note or remember anything that concerned him. We are thus left with a detailed record of a great action, in fact a log-book that describes in detail the seas, the skies and the lands that provided its setting, but with only rare, ambiguous or shadowy details of the appearance, character and behaviour of the great captain who planned and accomplished it. Can we blame Pigafetta? He was only doing his duty: Magellan himself had commissioned him to keep a detailed journal of his expedition, not to write a biography of the man who captained it.

Part I

THE QUEST FOR MAGELLAN

I

Childhood and Youth

Fernando de Magalhães, known in Spanish as Magallanes and in most other European languages as Magellan, is believed by many scholars to have been born around 1480, on the outskirts of Sabrosa, a small town situated near Chaves in the mountainous and isolated province of Trás-os-Montes in northern Portugal. By other scholars, it has been affirmed that he was born in the city of Oporto or in its immediate neighbourhood and, in the contract that he later signed in Valladolid in 1518 with Juan de Aranda, Magellan indeed identifies himself as a citizen or native of Oporto. Though it appears unlikely that he was born in Sabrosa, nothing more is known of the circumstances of his birth and childhood in Oporto.

Magellan's father, Ruy de Magalhães, has been described as a *fidalgo* or noble of the fourth of five grades of Portuguese aristocracy, and as 'wearing armour and being of a line that bore a crest of nobility'. In a will some scholars believe Magellan drafted in 1504, shortly before setting out from Lisbon on his first venture overseas, he proudly boasts that his family is 'one of the most distinguished, the best and the most ancient in the Kingdom'. Other scholars give good reason to believe, however, that this will is a much later forgery. In his last will, a document of indisputable authenticity drafted in Seville in 1519 before setting out on the great expedition from which he never returned, Magellan certainly stresses his noble origins and insists that his heirs must bear his name and his arms, those of Magalhães de Sousa, but neglects to describe these arms. Various experts in Portuguese genealogies and heraldry have tried to identify them and to trace Magellan's claims. The difficulty of establishing exact information is illustrated by the fact that, in Magellan's own lifetime, the great navigator could easily be confused, in official documents, with a number of close relatives and of others who bore the same name. At least six others of the name of Magellan are known to have served in various capacities in Portuguese Asia while he was in India. Later, when he served on a military expedition in Morocco, he was accompanied by two namesakes, Fernão de Magalhães d'Eça and Fernão Gil de Magalhães.

Some writers have indeed affirmed that Magellan was descended from a French knight, reputed to have come to Spain in the eleventh century, when northern Portugal was still part of the province of Galicia, in the Spanish kingdom of León. This French knight was one of the paladins accompanying Count Henry of Burgundy, who became son-in-law of the King of León and was granted by the latter, as his vassal, the province of Southern Galicia, already known as Portugal, between the rivers Minho and Douro. Here Count Henry's line gradually established itself as independent sovereigns; no longer vassals of the King of León, his heirs adopted the title of Kings of Portugal and, unable to extend their boundaries to the north by reuniting the two halves of Galicia, increased their territories to the south by fighting the Moors. To Magellan's French ancestor, Count Henry is said to have granted an estate called Ponte de Barca, on the outskirts of Sabrosa, when he granted estates as rewards to other barons who had come with him from France.

Some time after the survivors of Magellan's great expedition had returned to Spain with reliable testimony of his death, an official enquiry was initiated to identify his heirs, as his wife and child had meanwhile died. Other bearers of his name were questioned, both in Spain and Portugal; among them, a Margalhães from Ponte da Barca, without claiming to be an heir, gave testimony which contributed to the recognition of a less distant relative as Magellan's next of kin and heir. It would thus appear that by the fifteenth century the estate in Ponte da Barca belonged to a collateral branch of the navigator's family. But, for lack of more reliable information, one may assume that Magellan's father, as a representative of one of the lower ranks of the landed aristocracy, lived on a very similar estate, probably near Oporto. Ponte da Barca can therefore be described only as the kind of place where Magellan was most probably born and spent much of his childhood.

With his brother Diogo and his sister Isabela, Magellan may thus have grown up in rural surroundings. The crusading tradition of warring against the Moors, and of profitable rapine under the blessing of the Church, appears to have been deeply rooted in his family. In Magellan's generation, it may have inspired several namesakes, who were not necessarily close relatives, to seek adventure and fight the infidels and their allies in the Orient or in Morocco. Pero Barreto de Magalhães fought in Ormuz on the Persian Gulf and Jorge de Magalhães perished in 1516 as a member of João de Machado's expedition to the Indies.

About Magellan's father, little is known or conjectured. His mother is said to have been Alda de Mesquita, the daughter of Martim Gonçalves de Pimenta and Inez de Mesquita. It is not clear, from any historical document, whether Diogo was Magellan's older or younger brother.

After his death and that of his wife and child, Magellan appears moreover to have left no heirs who could be traced, except a distant cousin, Lourenço de Magalhães, whose claims, considered doubtful at first, were finally recognized.

No other facts are known about Magellan's early childhood. But soon after he had reached the age of twelve, he was sent to Lisbon to perfect his education at Court as a page in the household of Queen Leonora. His brother Diogo was also sent there, as well as Francisco Serrão, who became his closest friend and may even have been a relative. Their names are cursorily mentioned at this time in lists of members of the royal household.

Sons of the less wealthy lower ranks of the nobility were nearly always sent to perfect their education and seek patronage and promotion by serving in a royal household. In addition to attending a few classes—at some courts, especially in humanistic Italy, a real College of Pages had already been established—such young provincials learned much from their more polished and sophisticated urban surroundings. They wore the colours or livery of the royal master whom they served, carried messages or made themselves otherwise useful, and generally improved their manners and minds by studying music, dancing, horsemanship, the niceties of falconry and other courtly accomplishments, perhaps even some Latin. The Portuguese court where Magellan gained his education was still relatively mediaeval in its simplicity, its feudal hierarchy and its Christian piety, but it was already feeling the humanistic influences of the Italian Renaissance.

In 1493, when Columbus sailed into Lisbon harbour aboard the battered *Niña*, on his return from his discovery of the Americas, young Magellan, as a page at the Portuguese court, certainly shared some of the excitement this great event caused throughout the city. Only four years later, in 1497, Vasco da Gama was destined to round the Cape of Good Hope and reach India by sea. Had Columbus sailing west into the unknown, beat the more cautious Portuguese navigators who had long been slowly venturing west of the Azores and progressing south down the coast of Africa in search of the same goal? Or were these Indies that Columbus had discovered part of an entirely new continent?

Nobody could yet answer these questions that haunted the minds of those with whom young Megellan came into contact at court or in the city. But, as we have seen, a year after the return of Columbus, King John of Portugal signed the Treaty of Tordesillas, which assigned to Spain the Indies since Columbus had discovered them on an expedition financed by its monarchs, and to Portugal all areas which its navigators had already discovered or were about to explore, with the exception of the Canary Islands.

A strange and unique mixture of motives inspired the Portuguese voyages of exploration and colonial expansion: adventurous curiosity, commercial greed, religious zeal and a hatred of Islam that was often more political than religious. Even in the minds of individuals, these motives that might easily conflict could combine at times in a code of behaviour which remains typical of that age and of Portugal and Spain. Magellan's own recorded behaviour in the Indies and especially in the Philippines illustrates perfectly this peculiar balance of qualities and motives that characterizes a kind of latter-day crusading spirit. While introducing Christianity to Asia, Africa and the Americas by the force of arms, it could tolerate, as its worst, ruthless massacres of practically defenceless non-Christians, piratical expeditions of sheer rapine and the sale of prisoners as slaves who, even if baptized, were not necessarily granted their freedom. At its best, it produced a few rare individuals, such as Magellan or Saint Francis Xavier, who stood out as exemplary exceptions among their contemporaries.

Their crusading tradition indeed inspired the Portuguese to be more persistent and systematic than the Genoese or the Norman navigators from Dieppe and Cherbourg in exploring the coasts of Africa and in attempting to circumnavigate the continent. Whereas others generally explored these unknown lands and waters only in search of trade and profits and were soon discouraged by the risk of heavy loss, the Portuguese, who before the First Crusade had fought the Moors in a mood of religiously inspired rapine on their own soil, continued to war against them in a similar crusading spirit, first in southern Portugal and later on the Moroccan coast, long after the last Crusade. Constant contacts with the Moors, whether as prisoners in times of war or as traders in rare intervals of peace, supplied them with information about western Africa which was not so easily available to other Europeans.

But the main early incentive in Portuguese explorations came from Prince Henry, the third son of King John the First of Portugal. At an early age, Prince Henry participated in the successful Portuguese expedition that in 1415 captured the Moroccan seaport of Ceuta. After distinguishing himself there and learning from Moorish merchants about countries that lay far to the south and with which they traded regularly by caravan routes across the Sahara rather than by sea, he returned to Portugal with only one ambition, to wrest from them this profitable trade in gold and other valuable wares. In Ceuta, he almost certainly heard of the travels and writings of Ibn Batuta, a native of nearby Tangier who had voyaged, only in the previous century, as far as China.

On his return to Portugal, Prince Henry, now governor

of the southernmost province of Algarve, remained responsible for the defence of Ceuta and for further operations against the Moors. From Algarve, in 1437, he launched a disastrous expedition against Tangier, much against the advice of his two older brothers. In the course of the expedition, his youngest brother was taken prisoner and kept as a hostage by the Moors, but Prince Henry stubbornly refused to give up Ceuta in exchange for the royal captive, who died miserably five years later in chains in Fez. Prince Henry finally withdrew in 1438 to his province of Algarve and established his residence at first in Lagos, then a few years later in Sagres, on a lonely promontory to the east of Cape Saint Vincent. There, he built up an almost monastic institution where he studied geography, astronomy, navigation and shipbuilding. From Lagos and Sagres, he launched repeated expeditions to explore the coast of Africa and the islands of the Atlantic, as far west as the Azores. As a knight of the Order of the Christ, of which he became Grand Master, he had taken oaths of celibacy and chastity and he never married. Before the Tangier expedition, he had already encouraged many voyages of exploration; after 1438, they became almost an obsession. Though he rarely went to sea, he has remained famous as Prince Henry the Navigator, because his patronage, as well as his theories and studies, inspired many navigators in his lifetime and for a century after his death, which occurred in 1460; Portuguese colonial and commercial expansion reached its furthest point in the Far East just a hundred years later, with the establishment in 1557 of a Portuguese settlement in Macao, on the southern coast of China, and with the attempted penetration of Japan, which was thwarted, because of Jesuit missionary activities, by the Tokugawa Shogun. Prince Henry is credited with having on occasion launched as many as three expeditions a year to explore the coasts of West Africa. For many years, he was constantly obliged to request additional funds for these ventures, over and above the vast income that he drew as Grand Master of the wealthy Knights of Christ.

While young Magellan was still one of the Queen's pages in Lisbon, the Portuguese capital was beginning to glitter with the vast profits which it was already reaping from so many dangerous and costly voyages of exploration. Lisbon had long been a prosperous port, both as a transit mart between the Mediterranean and the North Sea, and from its own huge exports of salt from Setúbal to Holland. From the coasts of the Gulf of Guinea, a large share of the gold trade which had previously reached the Arabs of Ceuta by caravan across the Sahara now came to Portugal by sea, together with malagueta, a West African substitute for pepper, indigo, brazil-wood and other valuable dyes, slaves and rich sugar crops from new plantations in Madeira and the Azores. When Vasco da Gama's fleet returned from the first successful European naval expedition to India, a mood like that of a gold-rush spread throughout Portugal. Out of a total population of just over a million inhabitants, it has been estimated that every fifth able-bodied adult man left Portugal within the next twenty-five years to seek his fortune overseas. In a single year, eight thousand men thus sailed for the Indies or elsewhere.

More populous than Portugal, Spain could more easily afford such manpower losses, and at times disposed of enough armed men to penetrate, as it did in Mexico and Peru, the hinterland of the coasts where it had established its first bases. But except in Brazil, where they met no armed resistance, the Portuguese generally had to be content with holding coastal forts.

Only Christians were allowed to take part in the Portuguese expeditions, on which they set out in great pomp, with religious ceremonies of much the same nature as those that once blessed armies of Crusaders setting out to liberate the Holy Land. The business of metropolitan Portugal's economy was thus left more and more in the hands of men who were unwilling or unable to venture overseas. These included, especially after the expulsion of the Jews from Spain in 1492 and the establishment of the Inquisition, a great number of Portuguese and Spanish Jews or recent converts who, after the forced baptism or expulsion of all practising Jews in Portugal too, were known as New Christians, closely watched and not allowed to leave the country, except when deported, for lack of other available settlers, to new colonies which were considered unprofitable, such as Brazil and the island of São Tomé.

To finance the purchase of their personal equipment or to raise money for goods which they hoped to barter profitably for spices and other valuables in the Orient, many Portuguese who were about to venture overseas had to sell or mortgage whatever they owned at home. All too many of these adventurers never returned, thus leaving their families despoiled. Others, like Magellan on his return from his first trip to India, had been shipwrecked and thus lost the precious wares with which they hoped to make a fortune in Lisbon, or had simply failed, in a spendthrift orgy of Oriental pleasures and extravagances, to save anything at all.

Such disappointed Portuguese voyagers would return to see that others, who had stayed at home, had meanwhile prospered without having assumed such heavy risks. Because so many wealthy landlubbers happened to be New Christians of Jewish origin, Anti-Semitism began to express itself in a new form, mainly in attempts to blackmail rich merchants

37

and, if they failed to respond, in denouncing them to the Inquisition so as to obtain prize money when it was proven, often by false testimony too, that the victim practised Judaism secretly at home, never bought pork from his butcher or kept his shop closed on the Sabbath. After the Spanish annexation of Portugal in 1580, the persecuted New Christians of the whole peninsula who had sought refuge in Portugal began to emigrate in greater numbers to more tolerant countries. By 1640, Portugal had again achieved its independence. But Portuguese Jewish refugees had meanwhile escaped in such large numbers to Amsterdam that they already contributed, with their wealth and experience, to the establishment of the Dutch East India Company and its great successes in ultimately driving the Portuguese out of Cochin, on the Malabar coast of India, out of Ceylon and all their possessions further east except Macao and their enclaves on the island of Timor.

In 1496, on the very eve of this great gold-rush, Magellan, his brother Diogo and his friend Francisco Serrão were promoted from the rank of page to that of squire. This led to their appointment as clerks in the Marine Department which King Manuel had set up soon after his accession to the throne. In their new jobs, these ambitious youngsters were kept busy outfitting the ships that older, more experienced and more influential men sailed to the lands where they hoped to amass great personal riches. A year later, with Vasco da Gama's return in 1497 from India, every clerk in Lisbon's Marine Department had but one ambition, to gain enough knowledge of seamanship or enough influence at court to be allowed to sail to the Indies and carve himself a personal fortune, however modest, out of the vast mass of Asia's glittering wealth.

The Christian kingdoms of the Iberic peninsula had

inherited, from the Goths who ruled there before the Islamic invasion, a feudal socio-economic class structure which almost ignored trade and was founded mainly on agriculture and land-tenure, the income from which supported throughout the Middle Ages the clergy and the nobility, with its tradition of bearing arms. An urban Christian middle class of craftsmen and merchants only gradually obtained some recognition by inserting itself in the feudal hierarchy. The latter continued for long to consist only of three classes: the clergy (*oradores*), the nobles or warriors (*guerreiros*) and the workers, whether farmers or fishermen (*lavradores* and *pescadores*), whose toil 'keeps the world alive'.

Because feudal Christianity, throughout the Iberic peninsula, despised trade, it was left mainly in the hands of the Jews, whose position was similar to that of those groups who were outside the traditional caste system of the Hindus. But the voyages of discovery brought about a social revolution in Portugal during the second half of the fifteenth century. From Madeira, the Azores, Africa and the Indies, warriors were now returning as rich traders. After 1470, Portuguese documents which, whether for purposes of taxation or of representation in *Cortes* or parliaments, divide the population according to its categories, offer evidence of a rapid expansion of the Christian merchant and craftsmen classes as well as of the appearance of a new class of slaves. In most of these documents, one finds no reference to the Jews, since they would not be represented in the *Cortes* or parliaments and, for purposes of taxation, would be handled separately, as outsiders who had no place in the feudal order.

One such document of the late fifteenth century reveals, for the district of Alenquer, the following class structure of the population: 42 per cent farmers, 23 per cent nobles and their vassals, squires and others attached to feudal households, 10·6 per cent merchants of the higher class, such as goldsmiths, 12 per cent craftsmen such as barbers, tanners, tailors or carpenters, and 12 per cent millers and other workers of various callings. Other documents, concerning claims for shipping losses due to piracy, show that the number of nobles engaged in ship-owning or financing overseas trade increased steadily throughout the fifteenth century. From all classes of Portugal's Christian population, ambitious men were flocking to Lisbon to seek an opportunity of being sent overseas. Portuguese settlements in the Orient, especially Goa in its heyday, soon offered a picture of incredible luxury, corruption and lawlessness. Many a Portuguese commander, to fill his pockets all the quicker, resorted to piracy in the Indian Ocean; great numbers of Portuguese deserters even joined the enemy forces of Islam or those of Hindu rulers for higher pay.

Magellan's own behaviour, as recorded in Pigafetta's *Journal* of his great expedition, offers no evidence of his having been attracted to the Orient by such baser motives. On the contrary, the strict discipline that he imposed on his officers and crews, the puritanical manner in which he always insisted that they respect native women, whether in South America or the Philippines, and especially the fervour with which he set about making converts to Christianity among the pagans with whom he had contact, all these reveal that he must have been one of the very few Portuguese who, in his generation, were still motivated by an almost obsolete crusading spirit. In a way, he appears to have behaved, when he was at last able to go overseas, as a kind of real-life Portuguese Don Quijote, inspired in his actions by the ideals of a bygone age of Christian chivalry.

But he was also inspired by a widespread new humanistic or empirical interest in geography and cosmography, no longer content with the obsolete teachings derived from the writings of Ptolemy. Ever since the days of Prince Henry the Navigator, there had been two new schools of thought on the question of how best to circumvent Islam and reach the Indies. Though classical Ptolemaic geography had long taught that the Indian Ocean was a closed sea, some believed, as Herodotus, Hanno and Eudoxus had explained in antiquity, that India could be reached by circumnavigating Africa, which Vasco da Gama proved to be possible; others, like Roger Bacon in the thirteenth century, that it could also be reached by sailing west, since it was already known, if only from the narratives of Marco Polo, that other seas and islands, beyond the Malay peninsula, still known as the golden Chersonese, extended as far as distant Cipangu or Japan and even beyond it. Did these unexplored seas then lead back to the Atlantic Ocean? According to the geographers of antiquity, all seas and oceans, even inland seas, communicate with a vast outer ocean by means of straits like those of Gibraltar.

Prince Henry, in his studies and speculations, never quite excluded this second hypothesis, though he tended to encourage more often and more persistently the less hazardous coastal explorations that were founded on the first. Towards the end of the fifteenth century, however, progress in shipbuilding and in the use of navigational instruments made it possible to test the second hypothesis more easily. It inspired Columbus, Amerigo Vespucci and perhaps Pedro Alvares Cabral who, in 1500, was first to discover and explore, on his way to India, the coast of Brazil.

But Prince Henry thought that Africa could not possibly extend as far south as Diaz discovered when the Cape of Good Hope was finally rounded; nor would he have believed that some other continent, unknown to him, could

41

extend even further south, as Magellan found later when he despairingly continued to sail towards the Antarctic, beyond the Plata estuary, until he discovered at last the straits named after him.

When Cabral, before proceeding on his mission to India, sent Gaspar de Lemos back to Lisbon to report the discovery of Brazil, named after its wealth of brazil-wood, Magellan had already been working four years in the Marine Department, and Cabral's discovery sowed in his mind the first seeds of a growing conviction that Vasco da Gama's feat of establishing a regular route to the Indies round the Cape of Good Hope could be emulated by seeking in the west a similar southern route to the same goal.

No contemporary portrait of Magellan in his youth or even later in life has come down to us. No documents or memoirs of any kind have yet revealed any details of his personal life as a page at court or as a clerk in the Marine Department. The few known eye-witness descriptions of his physical appearance and character are very brief and vague; besides they refer to him only as he appeared and behaved after his return from India. We can only presume that his tasks, during his early years in Lisbon, were those of any other page at court, then of any other clerk of his rank in the Marine Department. At most, he may have distinguished himself among his peers by being more serious-minded, more purposeful, more tenacious and perhaps also more puritanical, more devoutly and humanely Christian, than most other young nobles of his generation.

The years Magellan spent as a clerk in Lisbon's Marine Department certainly served to acquaint him, if only in theory, with many of the practical problems of navigation. His tasks included obtaining necessary supplies for ships preparing to sail forth on long and dangerous voyages. He thus became acquainted with the navigator's needs. From chandlers and other merchants, he had to obtain whatever might be required and to check the quality and quantity of deliveries. He may even have found opportunities to examine and test the few instruments then available for navigation as well as to study the maps and charts he was asked to supply to captains and pilots. The inventory of stores, ammunition, trade goods and other supplies that he later obtained in Seville for his own expedition reveals his thorough knowledge of a departing fleet's needs and of the tastes of the primitive natives of the areas he planned to explore; as gifts or trade goods, he took thousands of cheap bells and mirrors, mostly made in Germany.

Compared with the instruments, techniques and knowledge available to modern seafarers, air-pilots and cosmonauts, the basic instruments of sixteenth-century marine navigation were pitifully primitive. However fanciful or incorrect, maps of the known world, ever since Ptolemy's *Geographia*, had sometimes been divided up into squares by imaginary lines or points of reference known as longitudes and latitudes. The latitudes run horizontally across a map, so that navigators sailing due north or due south can calculate how many of these lines or degrees they have crossed. With the Equator estimated at zero degrees latitude and the North Pole at ninety degrees, navigators can roughly estimate their position by referring to the known stars in a clear night sky and, by day, by measuring the height of the Sun and then referring to a table of data concerning the position of the Sun in relation to what is known as the celestial equator. All this made it possible for them to guess roughly their ship's position in terms of latitude, but required, in addition to the compass, fairly exact and reliable instruments to measure the height of the Sun or of a given star.

Much has been written about the early navigational instruments which the great explorers of the late Middle Ages and the Renaissance may have known and used. Of the Vikings, we know for certain that they had no such instruments at all, but relied mainly on their knowledge of currents and winds and on observations of the flight of birds. If lost at sea, they liberated a caged bird and then followed the direction of its flight, presumably to the nearest land. The seaman's astrolable, a much simpler and less decorative instrument than the astrologer's planispheric astrolabe, was already described in the writings of Abulwefa, a ninth-century Arab astronomer. On the deck of a rolling vessel, even a skilled observer could obtain only very approximate and unsatisfactory results with such an instrument. One of the pilots of Cabral's fleet thus reports in his log-book that errors of four or five degrees in latitude were almost unavoidable. To obtain more trustworthy results, Vasco da Gama landed on the island of St. Helena to set up onshore a wooden astrolabe of larger dimensions on a tripod. Discouraged by misleading readings, many mariners soon abandoned the use of the astrolabe at sea. As their astrolabes were generally made of wood, they also reacted to changes of temperature and atmospheric humidity and easily became warped.

Though first described in 1342 as '*baculus Jacobi*' by Levi ben Gerson of Bañolas, in Catalonia, another instrument, the cross-staff, became of real practical use only after John Davis, a Devonshire mariner killed by the Japanese in 1605, had converted it shortly before his death into what became known as the back-staff. The original cross-staff consists of a staff along which a transom runs at right angles, with divisions of equal length marked along the staff and the transom. To measure the altitude of a star, the observer must place one end of the staff against his eye and then shift the transom until its lower end appears to rest on the horizon while its upper end seems to hit the star. Because the horizon at sea is often indefinite, the results thus obtained cannot be trusted. For taking the altitude of the Sun, the cross-staff is useless unless the eye is protected by smoked glass or the Sun

Fig. 1(a) *left* The Seaman's Astrolabe (b) *right* The Astrolabe of Regiomontanus, 1468

is seen but dimly through a screen of cloud. John Davis improved it in such a way that a seaman could use the backstaff with his back to the Sun.

To Magellan and other navigators of his age, two other instruments were also available: the meteoroscope and the quadrant. Invented in Nuremberg between 1471 and 1475 by the famous mathematician Johannes Müller of Königsberg, more generally known as Regiomontanus, the meteoroscope is a very delicate and complicated instrument which is practically useless on board ship as its orientation depends on an exact knowledge of the variations of its needle when using it to determine latitude and time by reference to extra-meridian altitudes of the Sun. The meteoroscope or armillary sphere has remained, however, the traditional symbol of

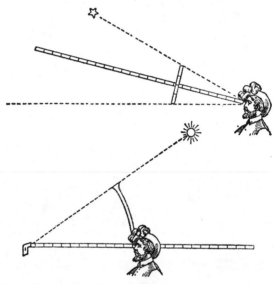

Fig. 2(a) *above* The Cross-Staff (b) *below* A Back-Staff

Portuguese navigation during the reign of King Manuel, which lasted from 1491 to 1521. Commonly but erroneously known to art historians as an astrolabe, the meteoroscope, armillary sphere or spherical astrolabe appears carved as a decorative detail on a great number of monuments of the Manueline style of architecture, which celebrates the great age of Portuguese explorations and discoveries. But one has good reasons to wonder how any navigator was ever able to use this strictly astrological or astronomical instrument

46

aboard a small sailing ship, unless he happened to be in a dead calm with time on his hands.

The quadrant and its even simpler version, the sundial, could be used more easily and were already widely known in Magellan's day. Such instruments gave only very limited and approximate readings. Generally, to correct these,

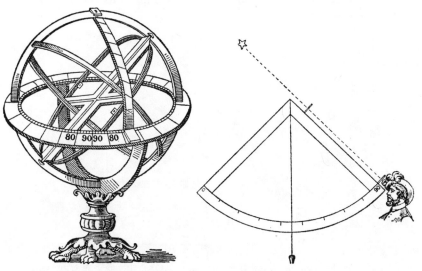

Fig. 3(a) *left* The Meteoroscope (b) *right* A Quadrant

pilots referred to a table of data concerning the declinations of the Sun, that is to say its various positions in relation to the celestial equator. After the publication in 1496 of Joseph Vizinho's Latin translation of the original Hebrew text of the astronomer Rabbi Abraham ben Samuel Zacuto's *Almanach perpetuum*, such tables, valid for at most three years, were widely compiled and even printed and sold. Graduated sailing charts, divided up by imaginary lines to mark longitudes and latitudes, then became more reliable and more popular. Earlier sailing charts or directories known as Portulans now appear to us very confusing, with their criss-cross network of loxodromic lines or rhumbs as indications of compass readings. But every sixteenth-century pilot knew their worth and could read them.

Both the seaman's astrolabe and the cross-staff or the improved back-staff can be used at night, to measure in

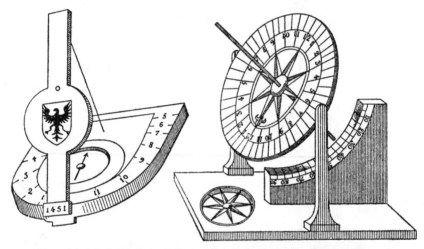

Fig. 4(a) *left* A Horizontal String Sundial, 1451 (b) *right* A Universal Equinoctial Sundial adjusted to Lat. 36° S.

degrees the altitude of the North Star. The latter reveals the ship's position in terms of latitude, since the degree of altitude of this star corresponds exactly to the latitude of the observer's position. As long as navigators remained within the Northern hemisphere where this star can still be seen, they could guide themselves by its position or by that of other familiar stars.

The most widely used navigational instrument in Magellan's age was the compass, which had been variously perfected in the intervening centuries since it was first known in Asia and the west. European poets and scholars began to describe it in the late twelfth and early thirteenth centuries, having learned of its use during the Crusades, from Arab navigators. But magnetic devices that point north are reputed to have been known even three thousand years earlier among the Chinese, who used them to guide chariots for travel and warfare in the vast deserts of Central Asia. In a thirteenth-century Arab treatise on rare stones, it is also said that navigators in the Indian Ocean had long been using a hollow iron fish that they attached to a line and threw overboard, so that it would point north and south in the water. The earliest known compass consisted of a metal needle that was rubbed with a lodestone and then thrust through a straw or cork which, set afloat in a cup of water, would point north.

By the fifteenth century, compasses with a movable magnetic needle set on a central pivot were already widely known. They are reputed to have been invented in 1302 by Flavio Gioia, a native of Amalfi, near Naples. Their frame was often divided according to degrees, when they formed part of an astrolabe or of the base of a portable sundial. The best such compasses appear to have been made in Germany, mainly in Nuremberg and Augsburg. At this time a knowledge of the magnetic pole and of the deviations of the compass began also to spread gradually.

The loxodromic lines or rhumbs, drawn radially across Portolan charts of the Mediterranean and the Black Sea from ornate compass roses or other points of intersection placed in different parts of the map, were intended to correct false scale or false orientation, which inevitably occurs on a plane representing a sphere or part of a sphere. These lines designate the course that a ship must sail, in order to reach a given coastal point, by always following one and the same direction according to the points of the compass as indicated in the rose or point of intersection from which the rhumbs radiate across the map.

Graduated maps divided into longitudinal and latitudinal squares, as in a Mercator projection, or by intersecting curves as in the plane representation of a sphere or a part of a sphere, became necessary only when navigators began to venture into oceans where coastal points of reference are less useful.

In the Atlantic Ocean, navigation by the height of the Sun or by the stars had to supplement mere use of the compass. But in the sixteenth century the astronomy of the Southern hemisphere was still unknown. Only in the middle of the eighteenth century did a young French churchman and astronomer, the Abbé de la Caille, draft the first reliable celestial map of the Southern hemisphere. From an observation post located on the Cape of Good Hope, he determined, in a year's work, the position of 9,766 stars, an unprecedented and unsurpassed feat of astronomy. In 1676, Halley had been able, on the island of Saint Helena, to determine only roughly the position of a mere 341 stars. South of the Equator, in the age of Bartolomeu Dias, Vasco da Gama and Magellan, navigators had practically nothing to guide them except common sense and extraordinarily good seamanship.

Though sixteenth-century navigators could roughly determine their latitudes in the Northern hemisphere, a ship's exact east–west position in terms of longitude could not yet be estimated. Firstly, as we have seen, the exact circumference of the Earth, though calculated fairly correctly by Eratosthenes in antiquity, was still a moot point among mathematical geographers, most of whom no longer accepted his figure of 25,000 miles, preferring Ptolemy's lower and inexact figure. It was known of course that the circumference of a circle or sphere represents 360 degrees or meridians, but the distance between any two of these degrees or meridians must depend on the extent of the circle or sphere's circumference. Throughout the sixteenth century, there was thus considerable disagreement about the exact measurement of a degree or of a marine league. The marine chronometer, an instrument that measures longitude, was invented only two centuries later.

Estimates of direction and speed allowed navigators in Magellan's age to guess their ship's position only very roughly in terms of longitude. Winds, familiar stars, the position of the Sun and common sense guided them in any estimate of their ship's course and direction, and they could determine their ship's speed only by tossing a floating object over the prow and then timing with a sandglass its drift to the stern. Spitting overboard, on a clear blue sea that was not flecked with foam, was their most primitive way of estimating speed.

As a clerk in Lisbon's Marine Department, Magellan could easily learn the theory of such a simple a science of navigation, just as, outfitting countless ships, he had learned what instruments, arms, munitions, supplies and goods for trade and barter would be needed for a major expedition. On March 25 1505, he was at last given his first opportunity to test this theoretical knowledge in practice: with his brother and his friend or cousin Francisco Serrão, he had been appointed *sobresaliente* or supernumerary aboard one of the twenty-two ships of the fleet of Don Francisco de Almeida, the first Portuguese Viceroy of the Indies, who sailed that day from Lisbon with fifteen hundred armed men, two hundred gunners, four hundred sailors and a staff of civilian administrators aboard twenty-one ships, to venture down the coast of Africa, round the Cape of Good Hope, and on to the Malabar coast of India. Though it was an official Portuguese expedition, it included, in addition to caravels and *naus* of the Portuguese fleet, three vessels chartered by the Nuremberg commercial firms of Imhof or Incurio, Hirschvogel and Hochstetter, in partnership with the Augsburg banking firms of Fugger and Welser. No contemporary historian of this great expedition mentions Magellan, his brother or Francisco Serrão. Their names are listed, however, in the records of the Casa da India among those of many other members of the royal household who accompanied the Viceroy's fleet.

II

To the Indies

In addition to the Germans and Flemings aboard the privately chartered vessels of the Nuremberg and Augsburg merchants, Almeida's fleet was manned by numerous other foreigners. Ever since the days of Prince Henry, Portuguese fleets had continued to rely to a great extent, especially for pilots and petty officers, on Genoese seamanship. Now they were beginning to use Negro slaves for much of the less skilled work aboard ship. Four years later, on the expedition against Malacca in 1509, Albuquerque reported to Portugal that his fleet was manned by a majority of Negro slaves recruited from the embankments of the Tagus in Lisbon.

Manpower shortages had indeed forced the Portuguese, both for *carabelas* or battleships and for *naus* or merchant vessels, to rely increasingly on foreign volunteers or slave labour. When Magellan was later recruiting for the great expedition that he commanded under the Spanish flag, he was glad to find, in addition to a majority of Spaniards and the small group of Portuguese officers and men on whose personal loyalty he relied, a number of Italians, mainly Genoese, a good dozen Frenchmen, Lowlanders, Germans or Englishmen, even a few Greeks from Rhodes or Nauplia in the Peloponnese.

Few questions were asked about the past of free men who volunteered in such motley crews. Many of them may have been seeking escape from the consequences of some crime they wished to keep secret, much as adventurers of the same nature, a few centuries later, sought anonymity in the French Foreign Legion. Some were even criminals, released from prison on condition that they accept duty in particularly dangerous or unhealthy outposts. Only one condition was imposed on volunteers: that they profess to be good Christians, meaning orthodox practising Catholics, not Jews or recent converts from Judaism or Islam. Forbidden to leave Portugal by a tangle of contradictory laws that were constantly revised under the pressure of manpower shortages, Jews and recent converts from Judaism and Islam or their descendants were closely watched by the Inquisition after its establishment. Some of them nevertheless found their way to India, where the Inquisition condemned a few in Goa, or to Brazil, whence New York's first Jewish community escaped in the days of Peter Stuyvesant.

In March 1505, a variety of motives thus inspired the men with whom Magellan sailed. Many were certainly hoping for personal profit and dreamed of making a fortune in the fabulous Indies. Only a few years later, Albuquerque, who replaced Almeida as governor, tried in vain to prevent his officers and men from enriching themselves in private ventures which were rarely honourable. His own example of piratical activities was scarcely likely, however, to encourage such discipline: on his raiding expeditions between the Persian gulf and Aden, whole shiploads of innocent Moslem pilgrims crossing the Indian Ocean on their way to or from Mecca were ruthlessly robbed and massacred. Each time, Albuquerque scrupulously reserved a large share of the prizes for the King of Portugal, who accepted these windfalls without demur.

Other volunteers sought adventure of an even baser kind.

Europe was already rife with rumours of a sexually more permissive Orient, where slaves and the women of conquered cities could satisfy the extravagant lusts of masters rarely as tender as the poet Camões in his exquisite lyric dedicated to a Negro slave girl. Within a few years, Portuguese Goa became a notorious centre of debauchery. Both there and in Lisbon, the Inquisition was kept busy for two hundred years with a constant flow of trials for sodomy and of other scandals involving even Catholic priests, nuns and monks. A few exceptional idealists sought in the Indies an opportunity to distinguish themselves as paladins of unusual courage: some good Christians were even inspired by a desire to convert the Mohammedans and pagans who inhabited these distant and benighted lands. But most Catholic apologists still condoned slavery: had not Joshua, in the Old Testament, quite properly massacred or enslaved the pagan inhabitants of conquered Canaan?

As supernumeraries in Francisco de Almeida's fleet, Magellan, his brother Diogo and Francisco Serrão were not members of the crew, but volunteers of gentle birth going overseas on military duty. No man could long remain idle, however, aboard a small but crowded Portuguese ship. Emergencies constantly arose in which all hands were needed, to maintain discipline in a hungry or thirsty crew that threatened mutiny, to take care of the wounded or the sick, to replace them or those who had died, or to help in urgent repairs. Any supernumerary who shirked tasks that might not seem to be included in his official duties could scarcely expect to lead an easy life on shipboard, especially on long voyages.

The Portuguese caravel, in the sixteenth century, was a ship with three masts, generally rigged with triangular or lateen sails. Its length was about one hundred feet and it sailed rather low on the water, so that its decks could easily be washed, above all if it were heavily loaded, by the waves of a stormy sea. Its hull was wider at the stern than at the bow and its burthen was rarely over two hundred tons. Some caravels, known as *carabelas redondas*, were rigged with square sails.

The Portuguese merchant ship or *nau* likewise had three masts, but its burthen rose to four hundred tons and sometimes more, so that it lent itself less easily to manœuvres in naval action. It used moreover a *mistic* or combined rigging that consisted of square sails on the mizzen and main masts and a lateen or triangular sail on the foremast. Bartolomeu Dias had sailed a *carabela redonda* when he first rounded the Cape of Good Hope; Vasco da Gama sailed a *nau* when he first sailed to India. English, Dutch or French navigators called the Portuguese or Spanish *nau* a *carrack* or *caraque*.

The hull of the caravel, being wider at the stern than at the bow, was moreover more rationally 'streamlined' than the hull of earlier European ships which, ever since the galleys of antiquity, had a symmetrical profile. Like the Chinese junk and the Arab dhow, it seems to have been inspired, in its construction, by the shape of birds that swim. The lateen rigging was also of Oriental origin, borrowed by the west, at the time of the Crusades, from the Arabs. According to Jean Amsler, a French naval historian, the first Portuguese caravels were built at Lagos, in the southern Portuguese province of Algarve, in official shipyards established, for experimental shipbuilding, by Prince Henry the Navigator when Don Pedro of Portugal returned from a long sojourn in Venice, where he had studied shipbuilding in its famous Arsenal. With the Majorcan naval expert Jafuda, or Jacob, Cresquez, son of the great Jewish cartographer Abraham Cresquez, Don Pedro prevailed on Prince Henry to put to the test this entirely new type of ship, the caravel, which assured Portugal the temporary mastery of the seas.

Whether a caravel or a *nau*, each Portuguese ship carried some fifty men aboard and, when armed, disposed of four or five cannon. On his first trip to India, Magellan sailed out of Lisbon aboard one of Almeida's caravels. Later, for his own expedition, he disposed of a fleet of five Spanish *naus*. On the great square sails of the caravels of Almeida's little *armada*, the red cross of the crusading Knights of Christ was painted. After an impressive religious ceremony performed just before they first set sail, daily services continued to be held aboard each ship. The Viceroy's mission was, however, more imperialistic than evangelical. Several centuries of wars against the forces of Islam had reduced the crusading spirit from its lofty ideals of saving souls by conversion to Christianity to the more worldly level of power politics. Almeida was not being sent to India with a shipload of catechistic literature and holy water to convert infidels or pagans, but with goods and arms, to establish trading posts or factories and forts which, along the coasts of East Africa and in India, would strengthen Portugal's new lines of communication leading to the major ports of the Malabar coast so as to wrest the profitable Asian trade definitely from the Venetians and their Egyptian and Turkish partners.

Down the coasts of West Africa, young Magellan sailed aboard one of the ships of Almeida's fleet, the greatest yet to follow Vasco da Gama's newly discovered course to India. On their way, they stopped for water and other supplies in a great number of Portuguese bases, in Madeira on March 30, then in the Cape Verde Islands and in various Portuguese forts all along the gulf of Guinea and as far south as the mouth of the Congo River, crossing the Equator on April 15. Beyond the Congo river, between the northernmost part of

Angola and the Cape of Good Hope, Portugal had not yet established, in 1505, any bases on the west African coast, so that in this region they would land wherever they found a suitable haven. Often, their appearance on shore led to skirmishes with hostile natives who were put to flight by their firearms. If captives were taken, they served as slaves to replace seamen who had succumbed to sickness or been otherwise lost.

Several ships of the Viceroy's huge fleet were left behind for repairs in Portugal's West African bases, with instructions to join him later as best they could. In a storm off the coast of south-west Africa, the bulk of the fleet was scattered and only half of it still followed Almeida's flagship when, to avoid further storms while rounding the Cape of Good Hope, he decided to sail much further south than usual. He was unfortunate in this decision, as the fleet ran into an antarctic blizzard. With snow on the decks of the ships and icicles in the sails and riggings, his men suffered much from the cold.

They found their way nevertheless into the Indian Ocean and rounded the Cape of Good Hope on June 26; moving closer to the shore, they made their first landing in East Africa in an area that may have been Zululand. It was very wild, almost uninhabited. The few natives they met were unfriendly. For this reason and because they saw there no prospects of profitable trade, they sailed further north and, after stopping again in Mozambique, finally found on July 22 in Kilwa, on the coast of present-day Tanzania, the first suitable place for the establishment of a fort or factory.

Kilwa, like Zanzibar, Mombasa and a number of other major East African offshore islands or natural harbours, was the capital of a small Moslem coastal kingdom that traded quite prosperously with the native Africans from the interior.

Vasco da Gama had already established friendly relations with its ruler some years earlier. The Portuguese now found that the city, with its terraced roofs, reminded them of places in Morocco and southern Portugal. Its inhabitants were relatively civilized, accustomed to urban amenities and luxuries which were unknown to the more rustic tribesmen of the countryside. Some of the Portuguese could speak Arabic and acted as interpreters for the Viceroy in his overtures to Kilwa's Moslem ruler. Contemporary Portuguese accounts of such early contacts with the Arabs of East Africa even use, in a modified form, certain Arabic words. They sometimes call heathen Africans 'Kafirs' rather than 'gentiles'; for those who were not urban but rural, they often use the Arab word *badawi* or bedouin.

After some fighting in which they deposed the local sultan, who had offended them, the Portuguese crowned a more friendly ruler in his stead, swore him in as a vassal of the King of Portugal to whom he agreed to pay annual tribute, and proceeded to build a fort. One account states that the deposed ruler had annoyed the Viceroy by failing to keep an appointment because a black cat had crossed his path that morning; being very superstitious, he felt that this would cast a bad spell on their proposed meeting. Having thus settled affairs in Kilwa, the Viceroy sailed on to Mombasa, which was taken by storm, sacked and destroyed on August 15. He then stopped in Melinde before crossing the Indian Ocean to the island of Angediva in the Laccadives, which he reached on September 13.

King Manuel's instructions to his first Viceroy of the Indies were to strengthen Portugal's communication lines with Cannanore and Cochin, where Cabral had established bases on the Malabar coast of India, by building and manning a number of similar posts at strategic points along the coasts of the Indian Ocean. Almeida chose Kilwa as the southernmost base in East Africa and left a number of men to build and man it. At first, such forts were built rather simply, with only timber stockades to defend them. Later, most of them became masonry monuments of military architecture; some have stood the tests of time and can still be seen. Almeida was in no hurry to reach India and spent some time selecting other strategic points of the African coast for similar bases. Melinde, where Vasco da Gama had found an Arab pilot to guide him across the ocean to the Malabar coast, then Sofala and Mombasa appear to have been his choices. Meanwhile, the stragglers of his fleet, which had been held up for repairs in West Africa or dispersed by storms, were catching up with him.

Some Portuguese chronicles suggest that Magellan was left to serve in the garrison of Kilwa; others, that he was sent back there from India a few months later, when Kilwa needed reinforcements. But records of Magellan's early activities in Africa or India are scarce, vague and contradictory. He was too young and undistinguished to be mentioned in official documents, and the rare documents where his name is actually mentioned may well refer to one of his several namesakes also serving in the Orient. Whether he was left in Kilwa now or sent there later, his duties in Africa could only have been those of any other junior Portuguese officer in these distant and isolated outposts. They would have included patrolling the coast in a light vessel to keep watch on the movements of Arab traders or pirates.

Arab fleets often attacked the Portuguese bases from the Red Sea, rousing the local Mohammedans and the native Africans to revolt. But Kilwa stood firm against all such attacks during these years. Portuguese officers who served in

East Africa have left scanty descriptions of their life there. Until gold and silver were later discovered near Sofala, most of their bases were not considered important for trade, except as a source of ivory and slaves. The Portuguese thus displayed at first very little interest in exploring the hinterland, except in occasional attempts to establish more permanent contacts with the Christian kingdom of Prester John in Abyssinia. It is true that, in the course of a long truce, after Nuno da Cunha had taken Mombasa by storm in 1528, they began to explore some of the hinterland of Mozambique and to exploit its silver and gold mines as well as those of Sofala. But this soon led them into conflict with the native ruler of Monomotapa, and they withdrew to their coastal bases.

Though Magellan saw little of Africa on his way to India and while he served in Kilwa, he was certainly kept too busy to feel bored or frustrated. In these small and understaffed Portuguese strongholds, there were always some members of the garrison who were sick or wounded, or who had died and not yet been replaced from Portugal. Every man was thus called upon at all times to face duties that were not necessarily his own. The whole community was moreover always on the watch for marauders, on the defensive when attacked, or busy pursuing enemies who had been repulsed. Little by little, especially under Albuquerque, who was appointed later to replace Almeida in the Indies, such Portuguese garrisons also began to engage in widespread piracy, attacking ships of Moslem pilgrims in the area of the Indian Ocean that lies closest to Aden and the Red Sea.

The number of Portuguese who were not mere transients in such a stronghold as Kilwa or Mombasa was never very great. When Mombasa was much later reoccupied by the Portuguese in 1594, its garrison consisted of only one hundred

Portuguese; because most of the defeated Moors had either been massacred or fled the city, an effort was made to re-populate it by bringing a bare score of Portuguese civilians, with their native wives and half-caste children, from other nearby strongholds, especially Zanzibar. In order to achieve a greater stability in the Portuguese civilian population, mixed marriages were soon actively encouraged in Africa and Asia by generous grants of lands and other privileges. Only after the establishment of a Portuguese capital in Goa did high-ranking officials begin to bring wives from Europe, but European women continued to be so scarce in the Indies that scandalous relationships and even run-away marriages often occurred between Portuguese officers and the European and Eurasian nuns of the Goanese convents.

From time to time, fleets came into such an African base as Kilwa from Portugal or India. Their officers were enter-tained while supplies and repairs had to be provided for the ships. As a former clerk in Lisbon's Marine Department, Magellan would then have been much in demand. With these fleets, news from India reached Kilwa. When Magellan, at long last, reached Cannanore and Cochin, the Portuguese bases which Cabral and Vasco da Gama had established on the Malabar coast, he must have known enough about India, however curious he might still be, to feel no stranger there. India had long haunted his imagination, whether in Lisbon or in Africa.

A clue to the time of Magellan's first arrival in India appears in a letter written by the Viceroy on December 26 1506, to the King of Portugal, reporting that an expedition had recently been sent from India to East Africa to strengthen the Portuguese bases in Kilwa and Sofala. Magellan's name is mentioned in the list of officers sent on this mission. It would therefore seem likely that Magellan originally reached

India in 1505 with the Viceroy, that he served in Africa in 1506, and returned from there to India at a later date.

The capital of a small and relatively peaceful Hindu kingdom, the port of Cochin lay south of Calicut, which was the main commercial centre of the whole Malabar coast. Though a vassal of Calicut's Zamorin or 'Emperor of the Sea', the Hindu rajah of Cochin was more friendly to the Portuguese than his overlord. He may have felt that these European newcomers, with their traditional hostility to Islam, might help him to avert the domination of their common enemy. After invading the Indian sub-continent some centuries earlier from Afghanistan, Mohammedan rulers were now extending their power in southern India over the many Hindu kingdoms which had come into being since the collapse of the great Dravidian empires.

Under its Zamorin, who exacted tribute from a great number of minor rulers up and down the Malabar coast, Calicut dominated most of the trade between Ormuz, on the Persian Gulf, and Malacca, on the Malay peninsula. Though a Hindu, the Zamorin was on very good terms with a number of Moslem states with which he traded. His hereditary admirals, the Kunjalis, were themselves Moslems, and he relied largely for military purposes on his Moslem subjects, the Moplahs.

On his first trip to India, Vasco da Gama had been well received by the Zamorin. Arriving with a fleet of merchant ships, he claimed to be only a peaceful trader. As such, he was denied no facility, whether to buy or sell. Calicut already had an important colony of foreign residents, among whom the most numerous were Moslem Arabs, from the Persian Gulf, Oman, Yemen, East Africa and even Egypt and Syria. All told, they numbered fifteen thousand, including residents and transients. Aware of the dire consequences of

63

Portuguese penetration and competition in Africa, these Moors viewed Vasco da Gama's arrival in India with suspicion and fear. But the Zamorin turned a deaf ear to their suggestions that he massacre the Portuguese intruders at once. Instead, he allowed the latter to dispose profitably of their own goods and, in exchange, to purchase and load peacefully the rich cargoes of spices and other valuables which dazzled Lisbon a few months later. As a result Portuguese traders began to sell successfully throughout Europe a popular novelty, the printed cotton goods from Calicut which were soon known as *calico*.

Yet there was some friction between the Arabs and Vasco da Gama's fleet in the port of Calicut; though the Zamorin denied any responsibility for what happened, the incidents led to reprisals and, as they continued over the next few years, to a state of constant tension, of intrigue, deceit and warfare, which came to an end only when Albuquerque finally conquered Calicut and destroyed the Zamorin's power.

In 1500, when he reached Calicut after accidentally discovering Brazil by sailing too far west in order to avoid the coastal doldrums off Cape Verde and in the Gulf of Guinea, Pedro Alvares Cabral was less fortunate than Vasco da Gama. This time, the Arabs instigated an outright attack on the Portuguese. Cabral was not taken by surprise and, after setting fire to the Arab ships, he retaliated by bombarding Calicut for two days. This marked the outbreak of open hostilities between the Portuguese and many of the native rulers and the Moslem communities which enjoyed considerable power in their seaports. For the next hundred years, Portugal was constantly at war in the Indian Ocean, and never at peace at any one time with all the rulers of its islands and coastal territories.

In Cochin and Cannanore, Cabral found friendly rulers

64

and in these two harbours he was able to establish Portuguese factories. On his return to Portugal, he left factors in charge of them, and he was accompanied by ambassadors of both these Hindu states, whose kings agreed to supply all their spices to Portugal. Two years later, Vasco da Gama sailed from Lisbon with these ambassadors on his second voyage to India, commanding a fleet of twenty ships. Five of these were to remain in India to guard Portugal's factories in Cochin and Cannanore and, in summer, to patrol the entrance to the Red Sea so as to prevent Arab ships from having access to the spice trade in the season when the monsoon was most helpful to vessels crossing the ocean. On his way out, Vasco da Gama stopped again in East Africa, in Mozambique, Kilwa and Melinde. It was then that the Moslem ruler of Kilwa agreed to become a vassal of the King of Portugal, to whom he would henceforth pay annual tribute.

In Calicut, Cabral had been forced to leave Portuguese captives in the hands of the Zamorin. Vasco da Gama now tried to obtain their release. Infuriated by the Zamorin's intrigues and delays, he finally seized hostages and executed them in the sight of the whole city, thus initiating a policy of reprisals and atrocities that characterized for a long while the warfare between the Portuguese and those rulers of the Indies who were unfriendly or openly hostile to their penetration of Asia. With the Rajah of Cochin relations continued to be very friendly, though the Rajah of Cannanore allowed himself, as a vassal of the Zamorin, to become involved in hostilities against the Portuguese. Further south along the Malabar coast, the Rani of Quilon, less sensitive to the pressures of the distant Zamorin, became, like the Rajah of Cochin, a staunch ally and vassal of the King of Portugal. From Cranganore, where a Jewish Rajah had ruled a community of his co-religionists for several centuries until

Moslem neighbours destroyed his principality, Vasco da Gama received, much to his surprise, a delegation of Indian Christians who appealed to Portugal for protection. They reported that they numbered some thirty thousand descendants of those whom Saint Thomas the Apostle had converted, and that their Bishops were Armenians.

Portuguese chronicles contain puzzled descriptions of these Indian Christians and of their customs and places of worship. Often their authors leave us wondering, as they wondered too, whether they were dealing with Christians or Hindus. In Calicut, the first Portuguese to land found a huge place of worship with doors of bronze. Before it stood a tall metal column, with a bronze bird like a cock on its summit. They were invited to enter the temple, and found its walls decorated with religious subjects painted in the Indian style, 'more frightening than pleasing'. The ceremonies they witnessed seemed to them both familiar and strange. Was it a church or a Hindu temple? In some churches they found images of Christ and of the Virgin Mary that appeared in their eyes to represent Hindu deities or devils. One of their reports describes a huge statue of Christ that appeared to be wrought of pure gold, with flashing eyes of jewels. Invited to enter these churches and worship, they accepted only with mental reservations, afraid to discover later that they had bowed down before idols and prayed to demons impersonating Christ, the Virgin Mary and the more familiar saints. Two centuries later, the Portuguese were more tolerant in such matters. In the cathedral and the other churches that they built in Goa, the Christian saints of their magnificent baroque altars were carved by Indian craftsmen who unconsciously gave them the traditional poses, gestures and features of Hindu deities.

After a touching, rather ceremonious and promising first

recognition scene, the Portuguese soon grew suspicious of these strange Christians who had no knowledge of Papal claims to jurisdiction over all Christendom. Within a few years of Vasco da Gama's first contacts with them in Calicut, Alfonso de Albuquerque, as governor of the Indies, was already suggesting to Lisbon that the Inquisition should be established in Goa. For the schismatic or heretic Christians and the Jews of the Malabar coast, Portuguese penetration of India thus heralded a new age of intolerance and persecution that lasted until the Dutch and the British allowed them again to live as peacefully as they had done, except in periods of warfare, for over a thousand years under Hindu rule. In Goa, the Inquisition continued to rage until it was virtually abolished throughout Portugal and its overseas territories by the Marquis of Pombal in 1774.

In the archives and contemporary chronicles of Almeida's four years of office as first Viceroy of the Indies, one finds very few references to Magellan and none to his older brother Diogo. On his arrival, in 1505, Almeida had been preceded by Vasco da Gama's two expeditions, by Cabral's *armada*, by a small flotilla sent out in 1503 under Albuquerque and, in 1504, by a great fleet of merchant ships under Lopo Soares. Though still understaffed, Portugal's few bases and factories of the Malabar coast were beginning to be a real threat to the Moslem traders with whom the Zamorin of Calicut, after much hesitation, had finally decided to cast in his lot, if only because he could not easily expel from his kingdom a colony of several thousand Moslem households that had lived and traded there for several generations.

In 1505 the Zamorin therefore, sent an embassy to Cairo, to seek an alliance and obtain naval and military support in his conflicts with the Portuguese. Soon after the Viceroy's arrival in India, his son, Don Lourenço de Almeida, was informed of this in Cannanore by a mysterious Italian who had recently witnessed in Calicut the arming of the Zamorin's fleet. Known to the Portuguese as Lodovico Romano, the bearer of this intelligence was actually a Venetian, Lodovico Varthema, who had been journeying ever since 1502, disguised as an Arab, in Egypt, Arabia, Persia, India and even the Malay archipelago. His knowledge of Moslem customs was so great that he could easily convince the Arabs that he was of their race and faith. Disguised as a pilgrim, Varthema is reputed to have been the first of the very few European Christians to penetrate the Holy City of Mecca. Though a Venetian, Varthema appears to have felt it was his duty as a Christian to warn the Portuguese of an impending Moslem and Hindu alliance to drive them out of India.

It would still take some time to prepare an Egyptian fleet and send it all the way to India, and the Viceroy therefore continued to follow King Manuel's instructions by strengthening Portugal's communication lines with India and its bases in Cochin and Cannanore. He had found the small Portuguese garrison in Cochin decimated by death, disease and desertion. But he soon improved the position there, as well as the Rajah of Cochin's prestige, which had been undermined by the Zamorin's intrigues and armed raids since Vasco da Gama's departure.

Because of the shortage of ships and men as long as reinforcements arrived from Portugal only once a year, when the monsoons were favourable to shipping, the Viceroy refrained from outright warfare with the Zamorin and, while testing the enemy's strength in a series of minor actions, preferred to follow a policy of great naval mobility and of establishing friendly relations with rulers of small kingdoms south of Cochin, where the influence of the Zamorin and his

Moslem allies and the fear of their reprisals decreased as the distances from Calicut increased. After signing treaties with the Rani of Quilon and the ruler of Travancore, Almeida sent his son on an expedition to explore Ceylon and the Maldive islands, where Portugal soon found new allies.

Magellan is reported by some later historians to have distinguished himself on this expedition, though no contemporary records have yet been found that mention him. Because Magellan, after 1517, became such a controversial figure, all Spanish and Portuguese historians of the latter part of the sixteenth century did their best to magnify his deeds or misdeeds in the Indies. Correa, in his *Lendas das Indias*, reveals a love for adventurous tales and accepts as gospel truth much colourful gossip. João de Barros, a less volatile Portuguese patriot, discovers the seeds of treachery in every rare mention of Magellan or of Serrão that he finds in the documents on which he based his history of the Indies. Magellan thus became a figure who served in turn to illustrate every historian's weaknesses and prejudices. Though most of these historians still had access to documents and eye-witness reports which are no longer available, one has good reasons to distrust nearly everything that they wrote about Magellan's years of service in the Indies. The fact remains that his presence and his activities there are scarcely at all recorded in any official documents.

On his return from East Africa to Cochin, probably in September 1507, Magellan is said to have begun investing his savings in business deals—presumably private shipments of small quantities of spices and other valuable goods to Portugal. Such savings came mostly from prize money, distributed to officers and crews after the capture of an enemy ship, from the sale of valuable loot after the sack of a captured city or from the personal gifts of grateful natives.

Whether officers or men, the Portuguese rarely received, when overseas, any regular pay. They had to cover their expenses by their own devices. Many of the men even sold their weapons and other equipment to natives. As capital of the Portuguese Indies, Goa was later infested with penniless soldiers in times of peace, when no loot was available; some of them begged by the porches of Goa's churches; others ranged its streets as armed robbers.

It is indeed known that Magellan had interests in legitimate trade. In June 1509, for instance, he received in Cochin a consignment of wheat as official prize money or pay. In 1510, he signed a contract in Cochin with Pedro Annes Abraldes, a Portuguese merchant who then failed to honour his commitments and whom Magellan had to prosecute later, on his own return to Portugal. In Cannanore, near Cochin, the great chronicler of Portuguese actions in India, Duarte Barbosa, into whose family Magellan later married in Seville, appears to have been factor or director of the Portuguese trading post. They became friends and Magellan may have been his associate in India in some private ventures.

Albuquerque was meanwhile engaging, under Almeida's nominal orders, in a series of lightning attacks on Arab ships and cities throughout the Indian Ocean, spreading terror far and wide. In Lisbon, King Manuel soon learned to rely, for the mounting expenses of his court and his building projects, on the prize money supplied by Albuquerque from piratical attacks on pilgrim ships and on protection money exacted by him from rich Moslem trade centres. The Viceroy's own activities in the Indies were less spectacular or profitable, though his wise policies of consolidation were slowly leading up to a crisis in which Portugal was destined to gain mastery of the Indian Ocean.

This crisis occurred between 1507 and 1509, when Al-meida's forces, concentrated in Cochin and nearby Cannanore, had their first decisive encounters with enemy fleets. From its bases, the Portuguese fleet set out to encounter a huge Egyptian fleet commanded by the Mameluk Sultan's chief admiral, the Emir Hüseyin, a Kurd from Anatolia. It had taken the Egyptians two years, since they received the Zamorin's embassy to Cairo in 1505, to prepare this expedition. Never very fortunate in his naval ventures, the Mameluk Sultan first appealed to Venice and the Sultan of Turkey for help. Venice supplied a vast quantity of timber, shipped from the Dalmatian coast to Alexandria, whence it had to be transported by land to new shipyards in Suez. Informed of this, the Portuguese Grand Master of the Knights of Rhodes attacked and destroyed some of these shipments and was then in turn besieged in Rhodes by the Turks.

From Venice, naval experts were also sent to advise on the building of the fleet in the new shipyards in Suez, where the Turkish Sultan Beyazit the Second had already delegated his admiral, Suleiman Reis, with a thousand Turkish shipbuilders and sailors, to organize the shipyards and build and man caravels instead of the traditional Arab dhows.

Information about the building and the progress of this fleet continued to reach Almeida. While it sailed down the Red Sea and across the Indian Ocean, stopping in Jeddah and elsewhere for water and other supplies, he was able to organize his own tactics. The Egyptian fleet was now commanded by another Turk, the Emir Hüseyin, who planned to join the Zamorin's small fleet in Calicut and, with its aid, to attack the Portuguese in Cannanore and Cochin.

Sailing out of Cochin well ahead of this planned attack, the Portuguese first defeated and destroyed the Zamorin's fleet between Cannanore and Calicut, then sailed north to encounter the Egyptian fleet. After a couple of minor skirmishes with the Emir's advance forces or Indian allies, the first decisive battle took place near Chaul, off the coast of Gujarat. The Portuguese force was led by Don Lourenço d'Almeida, the Viceroy's son, who was killed during the battle. In a fury of grief and revenge, the Viceroy attacked again, near Diu, with the bulk of his fleet.

The Emir Hüseyin's forces included numerous Venetians. The Adriatic republic was now Egypt's partner in the spice trade, and felt itself threatened by Portuguese ambitions in the Indian Ocean as well as by the gradual consolidation of the Ottoman Empire, which already controlled most of the land routes across Asia to the eastern Mediterranean. Genoa, Venice's greatest rival as a commercial and naval power in the Mediterranean, had already established good relations with both Portugal and Turkey. The Venetians had therefore invested huge sums in the Egyptian fleet, and provided not only the skill for the construction of its caravels but also some of the naval artillery that armed them.

In encounters with much larger Arab fleets, Portuguese naval tactics were founded on superiority in heavy artillery and on ability to manœuvre their few ships faster and more easily than the clumsier and more numerous dhows. The Portuguese captains thus made a point of keeping just beyond bowshot of the archers of the heavily overmanned dhows, and then aimed, with their cannon, mainly at the enemy's rudders and masts. The Arab dhow was not strong enough to carry heavy cannon and resist the shock of its backfiring. The collection of old pieces of naval and coastal artillery now exhibited in the Mendoubia gardens in Tangier reveals moreover that most Arab rulers, even at a much later date, acquired their heavy artillery from Spanish, Portuguese, French, Flemish, Dutch, English or Italian foundries. In the eastern Mediterranean, they could also obtain such guns from the Turkish foundries of Istanbul's Tophane Arsenal which, with the aid of Venetian or Genoese craftsmen, began to cast cannon as early as 1500, as can be seen in Istanbul's Naval Museum in Beşiktaş.

But the Emir's Turkish and Venetian officers, pilots, bombardiers and expert seamen were hampered on this expedition by Egyptian inexperience in the use and tactics of caravels and heavy naval artillery. The Emir's caravels were vastly outnumbered and constantly obstructed in their movements by the dhows which accompanied him and whose captains and crews pursued their own traditional tactics. If he used his heavy artillery, he risked hitting the dhows, which aimed at closing in with the enemy in order to outnumber him and then board his craft in hand-to-hand fighting. The Portuguese kept their distance, however, and disabled the dhows by bombarding them, then approached the enemy's caravels, caught in a tangle of helpless dhows, and bombarded them too.

The Portuguese also sought to attack the enemy, whenever possible, with the wind in their own rear, so that the dhows would not be able to head into the wind to grapple with their caravels. In a battle between two fleets of caravels, such tactics required expert sailing and great freedom of movement. In the battle of Diu, the Turkish admiral, however expert, was handicapped by his own forces.

Later chroniclers have claimed that Magellan was aboard the *Taforea Pequina* which, captained by García de Sousa, finally closed in with the Emir's heavily damaged flagship. Magellan may thus have been among the men who poured over its bulwarks and met the enemy admiral's bodyguard of mail-clad Turkish warriors in hand-to-hand fighting. García de Sousa was killed, as was the Emir Hüseyin himself. At the end of the battle, the victorious standard of Portugal was raised on the broken masthead of the defeated Egyptian flagship.

Whether off Cannanore or in Diu, Magellan was certainly wounded. Some of his biographers have claimed that he was sent back to Portugal for treatment. But the Portuguese had no hospital ships, and Indian surgeons and physicians were no less expert than those of Europe. In any case, we next hear of Magellan, barely a year later, taking part in the first Portuguese expedition against Malacca, which would scarcely have left him time for a round trip to Portugal.

Fought off the distant coast of Gujarat and rarely discussed at any length in contemporary European documents or in later works of history, the battle of Diu was a decisive point in the European penetration of the Middle or Far East. Had the Egyptians been victorious at Diu, they would soon have found enough allies, among Moslem and Hindu rulers, to drive the Portuguese out of their few bases on the shores of the Indian Ocean, and when Egypt, a few years later, on the death of its last Mameluk Sultan, became a dependency of Turkey, the Ottoman Empire would have inherited its power and might have ruled over most of Northern Africa, of Central Asia and India. For the next hundred years, however, the Portuguese remained in control of the Indian Ocean and managed to divert, round the Cape of Good Hope to Lisbon, a large share of profitable trade from more traditional routes, through the Red Sea or the Persian Gulf to Alexandria or Aleppo and ultimately to Venice.

But the Arabs and Venetians were not entirely eliminated from competition. Even at the height of their power, the Portuguese never disposed of enough men and ships to establish a real monopoly. Moreover, the waters of the Indian Ocean are infested with a marine micro-organism

74

that soon rots any timber except teak. Until the Portuguese
built ships of teak in Indian shipyards, they were constantly
handicapped by urgent repairs, by the wreck of leaking
hulls, and even the loss of whole fleets of overloaded ships
whose rotting timbers could no longer withstand, on their
return to Portugal, the buffeting of storms off the Cape of
Good Hope. The British East India Company finally solved
this problem when it began to build its own teakwood
clippers, in the eighteenth century, in the Bombay shipyards
of the Parsee Wadia family.

After their victory at Diu, the Portuguese had full control
of Calicut and of the coast of Gujarat in addition to their
original bases in Cochin and further south. But Arab
merchants continued to buy and sell there with the permission of the Portuguese, whose ships could not handle all
the goods which passed through these gateways to and from
Ceylon, the Bay of Bengal, the Malay peninsula, the East
Indies and the Far East. Each gateway along this route to the
Spice Islands and China exacted a heavy toll on transit
trade. It was Portugal's policy either to eliminate these
gateways or to control them. Now that she controlled the
major ports of Gujarat and the Malabar coast, her next
objectives were Ormuz, on the Persian Gulf, Aden, near the
entrance to the Red Sea, and Malacca, the fabulously
wealthy capital of a Moslem Sultan of the Malay peninsula.

In 1509, a Portuguese fleet of four armed merchantmen
was sent, under Lopez de Sequeira, to reconnoitre Malacca
while Albuquerque was still policing the north-eastern part
of the Indian Ocean. Magellan and his friend Serrão thus
found themselves, in September of that year, among the
first Portuguese to gaze, from the deck of their ship, on the
famed harbour of Malacca, crowded with every kind of
Asian craft, ranging from Arab dhows to Chinese junks,

from Siamese praos and Malay sampans to primitive cata-
maran outriggers of the kind that had originally served in
the great prehistoric migrations from this area through
Polynesia to Easter Island.

Beyond the harbour, the city rose in a maze of white
terrace-roofed houses, slim minarets and gilded or bright-
tiled domes of mosques and roofs of temples, towards the
sumptuous palaces of the Sultan and his court. These last
were built among gardens and palm groves on the heights.
Along the waterfront, huge warehouses dominated the
poorer quarters, where wooden shacks, often built on piles,
rotted in a network of stinking canals and backwaters
clogged with refuse.

From a lofty terrace of his palace that commanded a view
of the whole city and its harbour, the Sultan must have
watched the four Portuguese ships with as much curiosity as
its officers and men viewed his capital. He could see, like the
eyes of blind men staring fixedly at Malacca, the dark holes
of the ships' bulwarks from which, he had heard, their
deadly naval artillery could fire, at a moment's notice, from
far beyond the reach of his own army's weapons. He knew
that a decisive hour had struck. Moslem allies further west
had warned him of the wiles and the violence of these
dangerous intruders. He would be able to preserve his power
and wealth only if he managed to outwit and destroy them
utterly.

But the Sultan now saw a small boat being rowed from
one of the four Portuguese ships to the shore. An officer, in a
dazzling uniform and breastplate, sat there sweating in the
tropical sun, fanning himself desultorily with a stiff sheet of
parchment beneath the flying white flag which displays the
Cross of the Knights of Christ. Clearly, this was a peaceful
embassy, no feint to conceal an armed assault. When the

boat reached the shore, the exotically clad European officer landed and, followed by a small guard of armed men to mark his status rather than to defend him, approached a group of curious natives and asked his way to the palace.

The Sultan ordered his Vizir to receive this embassy in his stead. According to the traditional etiquette of Oriental courts, the monarch himself must remain mysteriously invisible until his wealth and power had been made fully manifest. His personal appearance could then be vouchsafed as a great and final honour, like a revelation of divine power after an arduous initiation. The Vizir was therefore instructed to impress these foreigners with every possible display of the Sultan of Malacca's wealth, power and magnanimity. The passages and halls of the palace where they passed were lined with splendidly armed guards. As guests of the monarch, the Portuguese were welcomed in great state; while their officers were regaled with a sumptuous banquet, their men were allowed to disperse freely in the haunts of the port where soldiers and sailors usually pursue their pleasures. If the Portuguese wished to trade, they were to be offered every facility to dispose profitably of their goods and to be granted priority, over other foreign traders, to purchase at fair prices whatever they had come to purchase. Malacca had goods in abundance in its warehouses, spices from the islands, ivory from Siam, precious stones from Pegu, pearls and porcelain from China, brocades from Japan, a rare choice of slaves of all races, even curiously contrived mummified mermaids made of the bust of a monkey or a human child and the hind quarters of a fish.

Here in Malacca, within the next few days, even Magellan, whose purse never allowed him much extravagance, was able to acquire a native slave, whom he named Enrique, because he had been purchased on Saint Henry's day.

Though slavery had once been forbidden or at least frowned upon throughout Christian Europe, it continued to be tolerated if the slave was not a Christian at the time of his purchase. Among the Portuguese, moreover, the ownership of a slave had become a status symbol, borrowed from constant contacts, whether in war or peace, with the Moors of the Iberic peninsula or North Africa. In their colonies in Africa and Asia, where manual labour of any kind was considered degrading by the native aristocracy, the Portuguese soon learned that a man of rank can lose face if he is seen even carrying in the streets some necessity that he has just purchased; he must be followed, at a respectful distance, by a bearer. As the master of Enrique, Magellan now acquired a new status even in his own opinion.

Enrique was destined to accompany Magellan back to India and Portugal, and on a campaign in Morocco, before following him to Spain and finally accompanying him on his great circumnavigation of the Earth. Somewhere he was baptized and taught to behave like a good Catholic. In the will Magellan signed in Seville in August 1519 on the eve of his departure for parts unknown, he promised to grant freedom to Enrique 'from the day of my death, thenceforth for ever'. But Magellan's will, in this and other respects, was not respected by those who survived him. On his death in the Philippines, Enrique was so frustrated, when his promised freedom was not granted, that he deserted his European companions to join the native ruler who had become their enemy.

Nothing more is known of Enrique's origins or of his subsequent fate. Though purchased on the Malay peninsula and therefore known as Enrique of Malacca, he appears to have come originally from Sumatra, further east. When Magellan first landed in the Philippines, Enrique understood immediately the Tagalog or Vizayan dialect of the natives and acted among them as the expedition's interpreter. After his desertion on the island of Cebu, did he find his way back to Sumatra or Malacca? If so, Enrique may well have been the first man ever to have circumnavigated the whole Earth and safely returned to his point of departure.

Sixteenth-century reports, based on documents now lost or on eye-witness accounts, give one a fragmentary, confused and often contradictory picture of Magellan's other activities during this expedition to Malacca. Among the earliest and most reliable Portuguese historians of the expeditions to the Indies, João de Barros contents himself with mentioning Magellan and Serrão briefly and somewhat disdainfully as future traitors to Portugal. Others, writing likewise after Magellan had become a controversial celebrity, attribute to him spectacular displays of gallantry and presence of mind which are not recorded in any official document that has survived. Many of his much later biographers allowed themselves great liberties in expanding these dubious accounts in their narratives of the part that he may have played in a dramatic sequence of events which occurred when the wily Sultan of Malacca decided to take the Portuguese by surprise and capture or annihilate their ships.

We know, at least, that Magellan was one of the few who were aboard the Portuguese ships when the attack took place. The Portuguese had been allowed to gain confidence and roam the city at their ease, and most of their men were ashore. Some officers or factors were busy supervising the purchase and loading of necessary supplies and of the valuable goods intended for export to Portugal. The seamen were scattered throughout the tea-houses and other pleasure resorts of this beguiling city.

The fleet's commander, Lopez de Sequeira, was aboard

his flagship, engaged in a leisurely game of chess in the shade of an awning spread above the deck. According to some historians, his partner was another officer; according to others, the son of Utimutiraja, one of the wealthiest and most powerful merchants in Malacca. João de Barros says that this young man had come aboard, apparently on a friendly visit, and stood watching the game, ready to strike Lopez de Sequeira with his Malay kris at a given signal from the Sultan's palace, but meanwhile idly conversing about the different rules of chess, as played in Malacca, compared with the game as he saw the Portuguese playing it.

Numerous native craft had surreptitiously gathered around the four Portuguese ships, ostensibly offering fish, fruit, vegetables and other delicacies or souvenirs to the idle men on the decks. The dark-skinned Malays who manned these boats, however, were not the usual crowd of petty traders who would normally include many older men, women and boys. These men were all powerfully built and in their prime. They were armed, but had concealed their weapons beneath their wares, pretending to trade as they awaited the signal for the attack.

Some romantically inclined historians relate that Serrão was informed of the impending attack by a kind of Malay Madame Butterfly with whom he was dallying in one of Malacca's more luxurious haunts. Abandoning his dark-skinned beauty to her tears and the self-destructive temptations of her own kris, he rushed through the crowded narrow streets to the strand and warned a few Portuguese companions whom he found loitering there or bargaining with waterfront traders. Together, they sent frantic signals to the ships at anchor offshore.

Magellan is likewise reported to have been, at this very moment, watching eagle-eyed from the maintop of his ship, and to have immediately reported to his captain these signals and the suspicious presence of the native craft. But all this seems scarcely likely. Officers were never assigned to watch duty on the maintop, especially if the ship was peacefully at anchor in an apparently friendly harbour. Magellan's captain, the legend continues, ordered him to report all this to the flagship. As fast as his men could row through the crowded native craft, busily selling melons, lumpia rolls, spiced shish kebab and curried fish to the idle Portuguese seamen, Magellan reached the flagship just in time, climbed aboard like Douglas Fairbanks playing the part of Magellan in a classic of silent movies, pushed his way through the crowd that stood watching the chessboard, and whispered breathlessly into the ear of Lopez de Sequeira: 'We've been betrayed!'

João de Barros tells the tale more credibly and somewhat less dramatically. His version says only that one of the ship's boys, on watch on the topmast of the flagship, suddenly became suspicious of the native craft crowding around it and shouted: 'We've been betrayed!' Whichever version of how Lopez de Sequeira was warned may be true, the captain rose promptly to his feet, upset the chessboard on Utimatiraja's son, who had drawn his kris, struck him and soon had him and the Malays who accompanied him overpowered. The few Portuguese who were still aboard their ships were called to arms just as the signal, a green flag flown from the Sultan's topmost terrace, was given for the attack. Before the armed men from the native craft that surrounded them could board their ships, the Portuguese were firing at them and, with their heavy artillery, at the city. Armed only with scimitars and kris, the Malays scattered in panic, heading for the open sea to avoid the bombardment of the shore.

Many of the Portuguese officers and the men of their

mixed crews, which included Indians and Africans, free men and slaves, were meanwhile being massacred in the city's eating-houses and brothels or pursued in the narrow streets that led to the waterfront. Some were captured alive and later held for ransom or sold as slaves. Serrão and his few companions however managed to reach the strand and escape in a rowboat, hotly pursued by enemy craft. Lopez de Sequeira sent a few armed men, including perhaps Magellan, in a rowboat to their rescue.

For three days, the Portuguese fleet waited off Malacca, hoping to obtain from the Sultan the survivors who were being kept as prisoners. Messengers hurried to and fro, but the Sultan, having failed in his original purpose of destroying the Portuguese fleet, felt that concessions would reveal weakness. Of the missing men, he returned no Europeans, but only three African slaves and one man from Madagascar. As a final gesture, he also sent a load of spices. To warn the Sultan that the Portuguese would return and avenge themselves by fire and sword, Lopez de Sequeira seized a man and a woman aboard a native craft and sent them ashore as messengers. The fleet finally set sail for India, pitifully undermanned. Its losses had been heavy: sixty Portuguese officers and fighting men, including the chief pilot of the fleet, to say nothing of the sailors, European, African and Asian, who had been killed or captured in Malacca.

The part that Magellan and Serrão actually played in the fighting in Malacca is scarcely recorded in official sixteenth-century accounts of the expedition. João de Barros only says that Serrão, with others, escaped to the waterfront and that Magellan was sent by Lopez de Sequeira to rescue them. Magellan and Serrão were still relatively young men, only junior officers, and it was not yet customary for military and naval commanders to mention, in dispatches sent home from battle fronts, the feats of individuals who would thereby be recommended for promotion through official channels. Advancement was often granted only orally in the field by the commanding officer, with no official record, while in India the Viceroy had the power to promote officers without consulting Lisbon, where such promotions were not necessarily noted. Magellan's later biographers have been at great pains to place him in the centre of the stage in Malacca, but it remains impossible to document the more romantic accounts of the part he may have played there. We know, however, that the undermanned Portuguese fleet, on its return from Malacca to India, engaged in skirmishes with Chinese or other vessels it met on the way. If only from spite, Lopez de Sequeira attacked any Asian vessel that crossed his path and it is difficult to decide, from the reliable accounts of these skirmishes, whether the Portuguese or their opponents were committing acts of piracy. In one such engagement with Chinese junks which may have been manned by pirates, Magellan is again said to have distinguished himself in a successful counter-attack. Whether for his bravery and alertness in Malacca and on the return voyage, or because of a shortage of captains after the heavy losses suffered in Malacca, Magellan now appears to have been promoted to captain one of the four merchantmen.

On his return to the Malabar coast, however, he had to face a discouraging situation. The first Viceroy's term of four years in office came to an end, and Francisco de Almeida, before returning to Portugal, handed the governorship of the colonies and factories to Affonso de Albuquerque. Jealous of his prerogatives as ruler, King Manuel followed a policy of dismissing in turn each successful commander so as to appoint a new one, and in this way encouraged the ambitions of all those who still hoped for advancement. Thus

Almeida was called back to Portugal, where he would probably have wasted his talents in disgrace or retirement, had he not died on the long return voyage. Vasco da Gama had already been dismissed and shelved in much the same manner.

During the last few months of his term of office, Almeida found himself again and again in conflict, over matters of policy, with his successor. As soon as the Viceroy left India, Albuquerque began to replace all those who had enjoyed Almeida's favour, and to promote his own men, who had fought under him in the Indies or had arrived more recently from Portugal. Magellan had enjoyed Almeida's confidence or that of lesser superior officers whose position was now precarious. Like many other veterans of the first Viceroy's administration, he was now pushed aside by Albuquerque's men. For a while, he was still kept busy in the new Governor's campaigns, which consolidated Portugal's power in the Indian Ocean by the capture of Goa, north of Malabar, of the rich city of Ormuz, which controls access to the Persian Gulf, of Malacca when a second Portuguese expedition avenged the humiliations of the first by sacking the city for six days, and finally of Aden. From Aden, Albuquerque even planned to attack the holy cities of Mecca and Medina and bring the Prophet's sacred remains to Lisbon in triumph.

After establishing the Portuguese administration of the Indies in the newly captured city of Goa, situated on a magnificent and easily defended bay, Albuquerque signed treaties with the kings of Ceylon and Pegu and, once Malacca had been captured, began to send out fleets to explore the islands of Indonesia as far as the Moluccas.

The policy Albuquerque continued to follow, when he was appointed Governor, thus differed radically from that which Almeida had tried in vain to impose. But Albuquerque's spectacular victories, and the huge sums of prize money and tribute he sent back to the King, impressed the latter more than Almeida's reliance on diplomacy to maintain as friendly relations as possible with native rulers while keeping control of sea routes and avoiding heavy manpower commitments on land. Instead, Albuquerque set out to smash every Asian coastal stronghold and establish a Portuguese empire on land as well. By a series of atrocious acts of piracy and of bombardments and massacres of the civilian populations of whole cities that his troops sacked, all the way from Aden, at the entrance of the Red Sea, to Ormuz, on the Persian Gulf, and Malacca, on the Malay peninsula, Albuquerque inspired terror throughout Asia.

The story of Albuquerque's first expedition against Ormuz, in 1507, when Almeida was still Viceroy, is in this respect significant. Appearing with a fleet of six ships before the wealthy island stronghold, he sent his interpreter to request an audience of its monarch. The latter replied by asking him what he wanted and what business had brought him there. Albuquerque answered haughtily that, as a vassal of the King of Portugal, the most powerful monarch in the world and lord of the Indies and the open seas, he had come to Ormuz to build a fortress and trading post and to sign with its ruler a commercial treaty which would assure him Portuguese protection against any enemies.

Such treaties demanded that all trade with the West be diverted from its traditional routes to Portugal. For centuries, caravan routes from Ormuz to Constantinople, Trebizond, Aleppo and Beyrouth had been provided with fortified halting places, like huge hotels, at regular distances of an average day's journey. One can still admire the ruins of those the Seljuk Sultans built in eastern Anatolia and parts of Iran. A wise monarch might well hesitate to disrupt at a moment's notice such a well-established trade route. The King of Ormuz asked for a delay of a few days to think it over, hoping to gain time and organize his defences.

A few days later, he ordered his ships to fire on the Portuguese, who responded with a regular bombardment of the city. Within a couple of hours, the King of Ormuz found himself obliged to request an armistice. Albuquerque's conditions included the immediate payment of the whole cost of his expedition and an act whereby the King of Ormuz declared himself a vassal of the King of Portugal, whose banner would henceforth be flown over his palace and to whom he would pay annual tribute. After thus exacting protection money from Ormuz, Albuquerque set about building there, mainly with slave labour from Malabar, a huge fort, which he manned with a garrison of five hundred soldiers and a hundred seamen who served in its fleet. It took Albuquerque over ten years to build this fortress, at a huge cost of manpower since many of his men died of fevers or deserted.

Under the first Viceroy, Magellan had received his training as a diplomat and trader, mainly on more peaceful expeditions, such as the mission to Ceylon of Almeida's son. Like many others who served under Almeida, Magellan felt that he had few chances of promotion under Albuquerque. He is even said to have made himself unpopular with the new Governor by openly criticizing his methods. In any case, Magellan now began preparing his return to Portugal. He had saved money and invested it in spices. Even if he would not be a spectacularly wealthy man in Portugal, he could hope to live comfortably, perhaps as a country gentleman on a family estate. He may even have planned to find enough capital in Portugal to return to the Orient as a private trader.

But Magellan was dogged by adversity. In the Indian Ocean, the ship that was bringing him back to Portugal, overloaded with precious goods and no longer very seaworthy after service in tropical waters, was grounded by a storm on the shoals of Padua, not far from Cannanore. The captain, crew and passengers escaped in a couple of boats to a nearby reef, but Magellan lost all his savings in the wreck.

Another Portuguese ship of the fleet was grounded and its survivors escaped to the same refuge. The senior captain, when the storm subsided, ruled that only officers and noble *fidalgo* passengers would row to the shore in the remaining boats, which could not accommodate all the survivors. A rescue party would then be sent to fetch the marooned crews.

The seamen who were to be left behind immediately mutinied and seized the water supplies. One of the more romantic accounts of Magellan's Indian years relates that he refused to leave with the officers and *fidalgos* because he was unwilling to abandon a friend, not of noble birth, marooned there with the crews. Was this friend his slave Enrique, all that was left to Magellan of his savings? Another such account relates that Magellan put an end to the strife between officers and mutineers by offering quixotically to remain, though a *fidalgo*, with the crews. As the boats full of officers and nobles were about to leave, Magellan is said to have been in one of them, receiving final instructions from the departing captain who was leaving him in command. A seaman suspected Magellan of planning not to keep his word and taunted him. Leaping from the boat on to the rock, Magellan exclaimed: 'Here I am!'

Be that all as it may, Magellan soon found himself back in India, where he tried in vain to recover his losses. There are few contemporary records of Magellan's participation in Albuquerque's subsequent expeditions, though it is reliably

known that he took part in the one that finally captured
Malacca. There is also evidence that Magellan was tactless
enough to fall into Albuquerque's disfavour. For one of his
many expeditions, for which he was always short of men and
ships, the new Governor proposed to seize privately owned
merchantmen and use them and their crews as reinforcements. Magellan is reputed to have pointed out to Albuquerque that in his opinion this was unnecessary, and
contrary to the royal charters granted to Portuguese shipping
exchanges. Besides, merchant ships would be more profitably used if allowed to sail back to Portugal with their goods
while the monsoon was still favourable, instead of accompanying Albuquerque on a mission that would delay their
return until the following monsoon, a year later.

In 1511, Malacca was besieged and bombarded for six
weeks. However out of favour Magellan may have been with
Albuquerque, the latter was too practical a leader to refrain
from availing himself of the experience of a survivor of the
earlier expedition. When Malacca capitulated and was
looted, the booty was enormous, though much of it was lost
in shipwrecks on the return voyage to India.

Possession of Malacca assured the Portuguese of freedom
of action further east. Albuquerque therefore appointed
three men, Antonio de Abreu, Simão Affonso Bisagudo and
Francisco Serrão, to explore the routes that lead to the
Moluccas. Their ships were light and scarcely armed.
D'Abreu continued to sail close to Serrão until they lost contact in a storm, while Bisagudo struck out on his own and
finally reached Banda, where he took on a cheap cargo of
spices and turned back to India without having yet reached
the Moluccas. Serrão was finally shipwrecked on the island
of Lucopino, where he was fortunate enough to be rescued by
a native vessel which, having unloaded its cargo of spices in

Malacca, was on its way back to Amboyna, one of the fabulous Spice Islands.

Serrão may have been the first European to reach Amboyna, which a later Dutch admiral described as a true earthly paradise, a fortunate island lacking none of the necessities of life. Serrão's charm and talents soon won him the confidence of the local rulers and earned him a reputation in the neighbouring isles. The Kings of two of them, Ternate and Tidore in the Moluccas, had been engaged for some years in desultory warfare, and they invited Serrão to arbitrate their differences. He proposed a treaty which the rival Kings found acceptable and sealed with a royal marriage whereby they became related, after which Serrão settled in Ternate. There he became a kind of Vizir, and he continued to live in Ternate until he died nine years later.

Magellan's biographers agree that he received letters from Serrão, describing Ternate and instructing him how to reach the Moluccas. Though no such letters are now available, the Portuguese historian João de Barros reports that Magellan's replies were found in Ternate by the first Portuguese to establish themselves there after Serrão's death. From a relative, Duarte de Resende, who read them in Ternate before they were lost or destroyed, João de Barros gathered that Magellan was led by Serrão to believe that the Moluccas were situated much further east than they actually are—in fact beyond the agreed line of the Treaty of Tordesillas and thus in the hemisphere granted to Spain; Serrão also described his discovery as a New World, suggesting that the Moluccas were closer to the Western shores of the Americas than to India. This contributed to Magellan's later insistence on the importance of reaching the Moluccas by sailing west from Europe rather than round the Cape of Good Hope.

Some of Magellan's biographers have affirmed that, in 1512, after his second expedition to Malacca, he ventured further east; it has even been suggested that, on this mysterious cruise, he failed to reach the Moluccas but discovered the Philippines. An anonymous Portuguese account of his great voyage, based on the reports of one of Magellan's companions, affirms that Magellan learned 'the arts of navigation and cosmography' from a relative, Gonzalo de Oliveyra, 'in whose company he had been to that land', meaning the Moluccas. But this manuscript, preserved in the library of Leyden University in the Netherlands, differs in many respects from Pigafetta's first-hand journal of the expedition; instead of solving any of our problems, it only poses new ones.

Whether this otherwise undocumented voyage east of Malacca ever took place or is purely fictitious, Magellan certainly disposed, before his return to Portugal, of intelligence about the islands east of Malacca. He may have acquired it in Malacca from native traders and seamen who plied between the Malay peninsula and the Moluccas. He may also have acquired it from his slave Enrique, who subsequently, in the Philippines, showed an understanding of dialects which are not those of the Malay peninsula.

On the way back from the conquest of Malacca to their Indian bases, Albuquerque's ships were so overloaded with loot and spices that several foundered off Sumatra and others off Cape Comorin. Albuquerque lost his flagship, with all the diamonds and other precious stones from the Sultan's treasury which he planned to send to King Manuel. If Magellan recouped from the looting of Malacca any of his earlier losses, he probably lost this hoard too on his way back to India. Yet soon after his return to Cochin, having terminated his years of duty in the Indies, he finally set sail for Portugal.

These years spent in Africa, India, Ceylon and Malacca were decisive in the history of Portugal's penetration of the Orient. The Portuguese had first settled peacefully in Cochin, where a tolerant Hindu ruler allowed them to build a Catholic church. In Calicut they were involved in armed conflicts with the Zamorin and his Moorish allies, but their first contacts with Ceylon were peaceful and friendly. Albuquerque's new policy was to waste no time on friendly contacts and embassies, but to strike first, to crush the enemy, and then to impose his own terms on the terrified neutrals.

Everywhere, the Catholic Church established itself as soon as the Portuguese had implanted a colony. The Jesuits and other monastic orders soon appeared, followed by the Inquisition. Often, the first Catholic church was built, as in Ormuz, Goa and Diu, on the smouldering ruins of a once-prosperous city that had just been sacked and most of whose inhabitants had been massacred. In Goa, the churches were built of stones quarried from a magnificent Hindu temple that the Portuguese demolished on a nearby island with a vandalism that shocked the humanistic Italian traveller Andrea Corsali: 'It was built with wonderful skill, with ancient figures carved in a black stone with great perfection, many of which were left standing there damaged or destroyed, because the Portuguese attach no value to them.'

One wonders how many of their crimes of violence, rapine and fraud some of the Portuguese confessed in their new churches, where, during the great heats, slaves fanned them diligently through High Mass. In spite of the violence and corruption of Portuguese imperialism in India, sparks of the crusading spirit still survived. Slaves and free men continued to be converted to Christianity, though their baptism posed social, economic and legal problems, and a whole series of laws, constantly revised, concerns itself with the conversion of slaves: a Moslem, Jewish or Hindu master must sell his converted slaves to a Christian; a converted slave must be liberated after a period, even by a Christian master. But these laws were revised so often that one must conclude that they could not be easily applied and all too often were evaded.

Little is known of the reasons that finally led to Magellan's return to Portugal in 1513. Those who believe that Magellan had already explored, from Malacca, the regions further east, as far as the Moluccas or even the Philippines, have suggested that, on his return from this expedition, he again fell into disgrace with Albuquerque. This time, Magellan is said to have defended too openly his conviction that the much coveted Moluccas lay beyond the longitude specified in the Treaty of Tordesillas and therefore belonged to Spain, not to Portugal. However honest this conviction may have been, Albuquerque and King Manuel of Portugal would have considered it disloyal. Magellan certainly expressed this view later, when he proposed to reach the Spice Islands by circumnavigating the newly discovered Americas, on an expedition financed by Spain. But there is no evidence that he ever stated any conviction of this nature as long as he was in the service of Portugal or could still hope to undertake his expedition to the Moluccas on behalf of his own native land and its sovereign.

III

The Slough of Despond

Magellan had spent eight years in Africa, India and other parts of Asia when he returned to Portugal in 1513. Far from having distinguished himself or made a fortune in the Orient, he was an obscure veteran, not much richer or more influential than when, so full of hopes of advancement and wealth, he had first set sail in 1505.

Lisbon meanwhile had become a great metropolis, bustling with trade and, in its wealthier sections, full of splendid new palaces, churches, convents and other buildings in the conspicuously ornate Manueline style which still illustrates so eloquently the King's love of display. In his public appearances, indeed, King Manuel had adopted the style of living of a legendary Oriental satrap. Elephants, camels and leopards, with Indian, Moorish and African slaves as their drivers or keepers, now accompanied him when on special occasions he rode through the streets of his capital.

But Lisbon's slums, with their narrow streets winding in a tangle of staircases and blind alleys up the steep and rocky slopes from the harbour on the banks of the Tagus to the fortress, had kept the mediaeval character of an old Moorish *medina* that enchants tourists in the Alfama even today. During the early decades of the sixteenth century, famine and plague were almost endemic in Lisbon's slum population, which repeatedly invaded the rest of the city in riots and pogroms such as those of 1506, when some three thousand Jews were lynched or burned alive in three days while all other Jews were forcibly baptized. Even in times of relative quiet, few of Lisbon's streets were clean or safe. Women of any standing refrained from going on foot in the city. Men went around armed and always on the alert. Portugal's national archives are full of pardons granted by its Kings to respectable citizens who had committed manslaughter in self-defence.

In the new building that housed the central offices for the administration of Portugal's expanding overseas trade with Africa and the Indies, a veteran like Magellan who came to seek promotion without powerful influence was granted a summary audience by the busy, corrupt and haughty bureaucrats. Magellan was told that he might expect promotion from his rank as squire of the royal household to that of a mere gentleman-in-waiting, *moço fidalgo*, with a small purse of a thousand *réis* per month.

Though his personal needs were modest, he was too proud to be content with such slight advancement after so many years of faithful service overseas. Besides, he appears to have been in financial straits: a document dated December 7 1513 reveals that he prosecuted in Lisbon a debtor named Pedro Alves who, since the clerk who drafted it was very careless in his spelling, was probably the merchant, Pedro Annes Abraldes, with whom Magellan had signed a commercial agreement some years earlier in Cochin, and who was now arrested and imprisoned for debt in the tower of Moncorvo. It has even been suggested that Magellan had relied on the recovery of this sum to provide capital for a private commercial expedition to the Moluccas, where he would have joined his friend Serrão in the spice trade. Invested in trade goods to be sold or bartered against spices in the Moluccas, such capital would have been increased tenfold on each return to Portugal. But Magellan was dogged by misfortune. Pedro Annes Abraldes died, presumably in prison; Magellan then prosecuted his debtor's father and heir, who fled without paying.

Magellan perseveringly applied to the King for a higher rank, that of *cavaleiro fidalgo*, but obtained no immediate satisfaction. Only a year later was this second request granted, in 1514, with a monthly purse of one thousand two hundred and fifty *réis*; by that time, Magellan had probably obtained the aid of a powerful sponsor. But he was offered no employment, though he was luckier than some other veterans of Portugal's overseas campaigns whom he saw begging in Lisbon by the porch of the city's splendid new churches, built with the profits of the trade they had helped divert from Venice and its Moslem partners. A few years later, the great poet Luis de Camões, on his return from the Indies, admitted that he was forced to send his slave out to beg in the streets in order to support himself and his master. Magellan still had his slave Enrique, whom he had purchased in Malacca, and was wealthy enough, while awaiting a reply to his petition, to fit himself out with weapons and a horse in order to volunteer, unaccustomed as he was to idleness, for a military expedition to Morocco. From a document listing the names of officers to whom bread rations were distributed in Morocco, it appears that Magellan may have been accompanied by his brother. It was in Morocco that Magellan now met the famous Portuguese pilot João de Lisboa, whose knowledge of the Atlantic and of the coastline of South America was still unsurpassed.

Portugal was almost constantly at war in Morocco, defending against Arab or Berber raids one or other of the string of coastal strongholds which it managed to capture and hold, sometimes only for a few months, all the way from Ceuta and Tangier, on the Mediterranean, down the Atlantic coast as far as Safi and Agadir.

East of Ceuta, Portugal agreed that the Barbary coast was a Spanish sphere of influence. Melilla was thus captured by Spanish troops in 1497 and Piñãl de Beles in 1508. From such coastal fortresses, Portuguese or Spanish raiders sallied forth, looting villages and towns, taking prisoners who were held for ransom or sold as slaves, seizing crops or horses and cattle, and making a business of warfare so as to supplement with rapine the meagre pay of their troops. In brief periods of peace, the Spaniards and the Portuguese traded legitimately with the Moors, generally through Genoese or Jewish agents. From the rich coastal plains of the Gharb and the Doukala, all the way from Larrache to Safi, the Portuguese thus obtained wheat to satisfy their huge needs of ship's biscuit or to supply their offshore island colonies and their African bases on the Gulf of Guinea.

When Magellan volunteered, a punitive expedition was being launched against Azzemour, a semi-independent Moroccan city which had appealed a few years earlier for Portuguese protection and agreed, as vassal of King Manuel, to pay him yearly tribute. Torn by internal dissensions between rival factions in its municipal politics, Azzemour had failed for two years to pay its tribute and had become involved in acts of piracy on Portuguese shipping. A preposterously demonstrative force of 13,000 men and 2,000 horses, aboard no less than 500 ships, was gathered to offer a striking picture of Portuguese power. In Rome, the Pope was informed that the infidels were about to be roundly defeated and that all bells should be ready to peal so as to celebrate a great Christian victory. Don Jaime of Bragança, the son of a royal bastard and destined to be the ancestor of

Portugal's last royal dynasty, led the Portuguese forces. In an access of madness, he had cruelly murdered his young wife. To rehabilitate himself after his recovery, he agreed to outfit and lead the whole expedition.

It landed in Mazagan, which was already a Portuguese base, and marched north on Azzemour, where its approach caused such a panic that eighty people were crushed to death in the city's narrow gates as they tried to flee into the wooded upstream areas of the countryside. After some skirmishing and a very brief siege, the city surrendered. Using it as a base, the Portuguese began to sally forth on a series of raids. In the course of one of these, Magellan's horse was killed and, on March 29 1514, he filed a petition in Lisbon for compensation. In another skirmish, he was wounded in the leg by an enemy spear. He had already been wounded at least twice in India, but this new injury marked him for life with a limp which, with his small stature, remains one of only two physical characteristics ever recorded by any of those who knew him.

Don Jaime soon returned in triumph to Lisbon, where he may have used his influence to obtain the promotion Magellan had requested. In Rome, Don Jaime's great victory was celebrated with appropriate ecclesiastical pomp. As a victorious crusader, the conqueror of Azzemour no longer needed to fear that anyone might remind him of such youthful errors as murdering his wife.

João Soarez, under whose orders Magellan now found himself in Azzemour, suggested that he be invalided and returned to Portugal, but Magellan refused. He was then appointed *quadrilheiro das presas*, or provost marshal in charge, with another officer, Álvaro Monteiro, of the prisoners, horses, cattle and other booty captured from the Moors. After the battle of Tidouest, where the rulers of Fez and of Meknes were defeated, this booty was enormous: two hundred thousand head of cattle and three thousand horses and camels.

The responsibilities of handling these important prizes involved Magellan in one of the most confused and humiliating episodes of his whole life. Very summary inventories of such booty were generally kept, and the officers appointed as provost marshals were expected to avail themselves of such opportunities to line their own pockets. An appointment as provost marshal was a reward for services rather than a real responsibility.

But Magellan was a provost marshal of embarrassing integrity, and soon found himself accused of corruption. The exact nature of these charges has never been clearly specified. Some sources suggest that he was suspected of selling horses and cattle back to the enemy whose villages had been raided; others, that some inhabitants of Azzemour, who had helped the Portuguese capture the city in the hope of trading with them, now complained that he had not granted them their share of the booty. The population of such coastal cities of Morocco, in the early sixteenth century, was often very ambivalent in its loyalties. Composed to a great extent of *moriscos*, more or less christianized Moors or islamized Christians who had been driven out of Spain or Portugal, it both posed problems to the Portuguese commander and his officers, and offered them many opportunities for corruption. The archives of the Inquisition in Tangier, for instance, contain numerous appeals of wealthy *moriscos* to be allowed, after giving financial guarantees and providing witnesses who may have been bribed, to return to Portugal as good and loyal Christians. Whatever Magellan's responsibility in this particular scandal may have been, several hundred head of captured cattle disappeared one night and found their way back to the Moors.

The accusations seem fantastic, in the light of our knowledge of Magellan's integrity, as later reported and illustrated in Antonio Pigafetta's *Journal*. It would appear more likely, though none of Magellan's biographers has yet suggested it, that he was the slandered victim, in Azzemour, of a brother officer's spite. Magellan may indeed have sought to prevent Álvaro Monteiro, who shared his responsibilities as custodian of prisoners and booty, from lining his pockets; and Álvaro Monteiro may have avenged himself by accusing Magellan of doing what he himself had done or tried to do.

Don Pedro de Souza had meanwhile replaced João Soarez in command of the Portuguese forces in Azzemour. Without asking his commander's permission, Magellan sailed to Lisbon on the first available ship and, to clear himself of these accusations, requested an audience with the King. Don Pedro de Souza immediately sent a furious message to the King, warning him that Magellan was absent without leave and giving his own version of the charges.

In the royal palace, glittering with riches from three continents, an embittered, battle-scarred and limping veteran, waiting nervously for an audience, must have appeared like a bird of ill-omen to the crowd of fawning and splendidly dressed courtiers. It was even whispered that his limp was an affectation intended to inspire sympathy. When Magellan was at last received by the King, he lacked the elaborate manner and the eloquence that might have gained him a willing ear for his case. Since he had been a page of the queen's household, the Portuguese court had abandoned the relative simplicity of mediaeval manners in favour of greater pomp and ceremony. Its new etiquette smacked of the kind of flattery which characterizes absolute monarchy by divine right as opposed to the feudal relationship between a suzerain and the noble vassals who remain to some extent his peers. Instead of giving a decision in Magellan's favour in the proceedings which had been started against him in Morocco, and of placing him, as he requested, in command of a caravel, King Manuel reprimanded him sourly for abandoning his military duties without official permission. Magellan could only return to Azzemour and doggedly appeal there. Finally, he won a verdict that cleared his name of slander and he obtained leave to seek a second royal audience in Lisbon. On his arrival there, it was refused. King Manuel had not forgotten his reprimand and remembered Magellan only as a dissatisfied and troublesome subject.

In spite of two years of rebuffs, frustrations, humiliations and misfortunes, Magellan was not to be discouraged. If King Manuel refused him a personal audience as a noble, he would humbly try his luck when the monarch next granted a collective audience to a crowd of commoners. It was almost without precedent that a proud Portuguese *fidalgo* should thus humiliate himself, and one can imagine the contemptuous surprise and curiosity of his peers when they heard his name and title announced at court after the long list of commoners who preceded him.

Again, Magellan asked for the captaincy of a caravel, this time specifically to sail to the Moluccas. He may well have referred to information about these islands received from his friend Serrão who was still in Ternate and with whom he is known to have kept up correspondence. But Serrão too was in disgrace. His failure to return from his mission to the Moluccas branded him as a deserter, if he were indeed still alive.

Moreover, King Manuel and his naval and military commanders were jealous of information about the geography of areas they had explored or were planning to explore. Other European monarchs went to great expense to obtain stolen

Portuguese maps and charts through secret agents. In Italy, in Modena's Biblioteca Estense, one can admire a veritable classic of early sixteenth-century Portuguese cartography that the Duke of Modena obtained from a secret agent named Cantino. Duke August's library in Wolfenbüttel in Germany exhibits another fine early Portuguese map of Asia which may also have once been stolen from Lisbon.

Portuguese officers who claimed to have private intelligence about geographical matters and failed to report it to their superiors were thus looked upon with suspicion. In 1504, King Manuel decreed the death penalty for any of his subjects who communicated abroad any secret information about Portuguese discoveries. Lisbon's National Archives still contain the reports of Portuguese ambassadors who kept a close watch abroad, especially in Spain, France and England, on the activities of some Portuguse mapmakers who were living in exile. In Paris, the Portuguese ambassador, in 1568, went so far as to instigate an unsuccessful attempt on the life of the somewhat suspect or disloyal cartographer André Homem. In a letter reporting the incident to the King of Spain, the Spanish ambassador states that three shots of an arquebuse were fired, 'but none touched him in the flesh, only in the cloth'.

Thus, if Magellan was tactless enough, in his last audience with King Manuel, to mention secret information received privately from Serrão, this might explain why the moody, ostentatious and suspicious monarch met his request for a caravel with a blunt refusal. In any case, the King obviously disliked Magellan, who in turn was too proud or too tenacious to accept such a refusal without further ado. In an almost rebellious mood, he now made an unbelievable request for permission to go abroad and serve some other monarch.

King Manuel replied with impatience and disdain that he cared little where Magellan might go or what he might do. In his *Lendas da Índia*, the historian Gaspar Correa adds here one of his typically dramatic pieces of gossip: he claims that Magellan bowed to kiss his sovereign's hand, but that the King refrained from offering it. Free to seek for his ventures whatever other patrons he might find, Magellan took his leave and soon withdrew from Lisbon, where he had experienced too many humiliations, to Oporto, closer to his home. He appears to have spent the next two years mostly in Oporto, with occasional trips to Lisbon, living in obscurity and associating with other disappointed subjects of King Manuel, of whom there were many both in Portugal and abroad. Unlike some of his forebears, King Manuel never achieved much popularity except among his flattering courtiers. He suspected and despised all who showed real ability or initiative, and humiliated many of his most gifted subjects, including Vasco da Gama, Almeida and Magellan.

In Oporto Magellan met Ruy Faleiro, the astronomer and geographer whose theories were to play such an important part in his plans for the expedition without which his whole life would have remained obscure and insignificant. But Magellan also had access, as a noble and an officer, in spite of his being in disgrace, to the Lisbon archives of the administration of Guinea and the Indies. Maps, globes, navigation charts, celestial maps, log-books and rare nautical instruments were kept here as official secrets. When he released Magellan to serve any other power, King Manuel neglected to forbid him access to this valuable mine of information and misinformation.

On his visits from Oporto, Magellan probably spent many hours studying there. If one is to believe, with most of Magellan's biographers, a brief and ambiguous passage in

Pigafetta's *Journal*, he was particularly influenced, in his plans for the circumnavigation of the world, by a world globe or a map of South America believed to have been designed by a dubious German cosmographer, Martin Behaim von Schwarzbach, a native of Nuremberg.

Pigafetta's one mention of Behaim has inspired a vast amount of speculation about him. In the transactions of a meeting of the American Philosophical Society held in Philadelphia in 1786, one can even read a letter written by a certain Otto, a German residing in the United States, who claimed that, before Columbus, Behaim had been the real discoverer of the Americas. Benjamin Franklin felt that this claim deserved serious attention and had Otto's letter printed in the Society's transactions.

Born around 1435 of a patrician family of Nuremberg merchants whose ancestors had come from the village of Schwarzbach in Bohemia, Behaim received a commercial training at home and in Flanders. His adventurous character is revealed by the fact that, in March 1483, he was condemned by a Nuremberg court for having attended a Jewish wedding and danced there on Ember Day in Lent. A friend who was a maker of compasses also attended the wedding, but refrained from dancing and was acquitted. Letters from Behaim's more respectable brothers, preserved in the family's archives, suggest that he later embarrassed them on several occasions, probably because of his failure to pay debts.

Martin Behaim's forebear, Albrecht Behaim, was a grocer who, in 1342, was elected burgomaster of Nuremberg. His father, also Martin, was a general merchant whose business interests once took him to Venice, the main European market for spices. In Antwerp, in 1484, the future presumptive discoverer of America is known to have purchased nine sacks of galls. But young Behaim also speculated in Flanders on raw cloth imported from England, which he converted at his own expense by having it dyed and finished for export to Nuremberg. All these activities explain how he appeared soon after 1484 in Lisbon, which imported cloth from England and Flanders and already competed with Venice as a centre for the spice trade. He may also have brought to Lisbon, a likely market for such gadgets, some novel nautical compasses, astrolabes or sundials made by friends in Nuremberg, which was already known as a centre for the manufacture of precision instruments. A few years later, one of Behaim's brothers, Wolf Behaim, is known to have failed to sell in Portugal some novel Nuremberg clockwork timepieces.

In Lisbon's scientific circles, young Behaim claimed to be a disciple of Johannes Müller of Koenigsberg who, as we have seen, invented the meteoroscope. Actually, Behaim was in Flanders when Müller was in Nuremberg. Yet the Portuguese historian João de Barros, who had access to documents that may have later been lost in the Lisbon earthquake, states that Behaim became a member of the *Junta dos Matemáticos*, appointed by the King of Portugal in 1484. A special committee of astronomers and mathematicians that included Joseph Vizinho, pupil and translator of Abraham Ben Samuel Zacuto, the Junta was called upon to lay down simple rules for determining a ship's latitude from meridian altitudes of the sun, because the Pole Star, traditionally used for that purpose in the Northern hemisphere, was no longer visible south of the Equator. It was also consulted on the probable feasibility of all the more ambitious expeditions proposed to the King, such as that of Columbus, which it turned down as less likely to be profitable than the known route to the Indies around the Cape of Good Hope. Behaim may have appeared before the Junta with some similar proposal.

Be that as it may, Behaim seems to have enjoyed for a while credit at court and in scientific circles in Lisbon, on the basis of his claims to have been a pupil of Müller and of his inability, as a German, to communicate his presumed knowledge very clearly in Portuguese.

In 1486, Behaim was on the island of Fayal, in the Azores, where he married the daughter of Jobst van Hurter, a Flemish settler married to a Portuguese heiress from Madeira who held Fayal in fief from the King of Portugal. Behaim's marriage failed to put an end to his adventurous wanderings or to bring real stability in his life. In 1491, he was back in Nuremberg, where he impressed his fellow citizens with tall tales of his adventures, claiming to have accompanied the great Portuguese explorer Diogo Cão on his expedition down the coast of Africa beyond the island of São Thomé. Funds were raised to commission him to draft a map of the world, and to supervise the construction of a terrestrial globe, a rather beautiful and mysterious object which he completed in 1492 and which remained for over four hundred years in the possession of his family until they deposited it, as a national treasure, in Nuremberg's Germanisches National-museum. On this globe, Behaim calls the island of Annobom, close to São Thomé, Martin's Island, thereby claiming to have discovered it himself.

Behaim's vast and controversial reputation as an explorer and a cosmographer now rests mainly on the evidence of this globe and of two lines in Pigafetta's *Journal* where Magellan is said to have known of a passage from the Atlantic to the Pacific, through the continent of South America, 'from a map is the Treasury of the King of Portugal by that excellent man Martin Behaim'. But no such map is now known and Behaim's globe, constructed before the return of Columbus from his discovery of America, does not depict the New World at all. When Behaim died in Lisbon in 1515, he enjoyed no reputation there and had no friends. In fact, he died as a pauper in a hospital.

It has been proved that Behaim could not have accompanied Diogo Cão, as he claimed, on any of the Portuguese navigator's expeditions to Africa. He may, however, have followed him a few months later on a private commercial expedition that is not officially recorded. This might explain the many detailed references to trade that appear along the African coast on Behaim's globe.

In spite of the artistic qualities of its workmanship, which can be attributed to the skilled Nuremberg craftsmen who helped him as much as to Behaim himself, this globe proves to be, when compared with other fifteenth-century maps, in many respects less well informed. On Andrea Bianco's map of 1448, for instance, one already finds the newly discovered Azores replacing the mythical island of Antilia which Bianco had depicted on his earlier map of 1436. Drafted in London after a visit to Lisbon on his way from Venice, Bianco's map of 1448 shows all recent Portuguese discoveries in Africa as far as Cape Verde, first sighted only three years earlier. Historical Portuguese records mention only three islands in the newly discovered Azores. Only in 1449 does a deed mention seven. But Bianco's map already shows seven and, on the far edge of the map, south-west of Cape Verde, also depicts on the other side of the Atlantic a coastline, designated as an 'authentic island', which suggests that some navigator may already have sighted the coast of Brazil as early as 1447. Although he had lived in the Azores, from where these earlier unrecorded expeditions which sighted the coasts of America most probably started, Behaim, unlike Bianco, offers us on his globe no indication of an awareness of the American coast.

In spite of Portuguese attempts to guard discoveries as official secrets, reliable reports of them appear to have spread very fast to Venice, London and perhaps Flanders and Germany too. These leakages may have been due to the numbers of foreign pilots and other seamen, mainly Genoese and Flemish, whom the Portuguese employed and on whom they could scarcely impose secrecy unless they prevented them from ever returning to their homes. In addition to official Portuguese expeditions, there were also private adventurers and fishermen exploring the Atlantic; only rarely were any reports of their purported discoveries kept, so that one now finds occasional evidence of some knowledge of the Azores or of the American coastline that precedes by a few years the recorded date of an official discovery.

Though ignorant of America, Behaim proves to be, according to his globe, relatively up to date in his knowledge of the African coast. But his knowledge of the Asian coasts of the Indian Ocean and of the Far East is very deficient, if one compares his globe to the better maps produced in the decade that preceded 1500. East of the Persian Gulf, he still relied mainly on the writings of Marco Polo and depicts, for instance, a vast imaginary promontory east of a dwarfed Golden Chersonese that is supposed to be the Malay peninsula. This promontory, which one finds also on many earlier maps, appears to be a kind of fictional residue of the legendary coast of Asia which, according to Ptolemy, curved here to the south and west in order to enclose the Indian Ocean by joining Africa. In a few other maps of about 1500, this promontory is called Gatigara or Cattigara.

If Magellan indeed quoted Behaim as the source of his geographical knowledge, it would appear that he either mentioned his name at random, to conceal his real source in official Portuguese secrets, or had mistaken a later map by another German, Johannes Schöner, for one by Behaim. In 1515, Johannes Schöner produced another globe, in an attempt to bring Behaim's up to date. Printed in Nuremberg without the author's name and in the form of paper gores which could be cut out and mounted on a globe, Schöner's new work is much closer to geographical reality than Behaim's and may have reached Lisbon very soon after its publication. Because it was anonymous and also came from Nuremberg, Magellan may well have attributed its authorship to Behaim, whose name and globe were not unknown to him.

Between a continental mass which he calls America and another one, south of it, that he calls Brazil, Schöner's globe indeed reveals a strait leading from the Atlantic to the Pacific. But Schöner's knowledge of the American coasts is still so vague that his map also suggests the existence of another strait leading from the Gulf of Mexico through Central America. In any case, Schöner also published in Nuremberg a Latin text explaining the use of his printed gores and the advantages and improvements which his globe offered. It is entitled 'A most delicious description of the whole earth' and appears to rely not only on Behaim's work but also on recent reports of explorations contained in a German publication, *Copia der neue Zeytung aus Presily Land*, a printed version of a long newsletter sent from Madeira by an agent of the great Augsburg Welser family of bankers and traders.

Based on the remarks of a Portuguese pilot, this German text is the only one to record an otherwise unknown private expedition, possibly fitted out by Don Nuno Manuel, controller of the royal household, and the merchant Cristóbal de Haro in 1514. It is reported to have reached, before the official Spanish expedition led in 1515 by Juan Díaz de

Solis, points on the Atlantic coast of South America as far south as the fortieth parallel, and to have discovered in that area a gulf so vast that the explorers navigated for two days without ever sighting its ultimate shore-line. A storm-drove them back into the Atlantic before they could verify whether these waters might be a strait leading to the Pacific. The pilot who gave the information to the Welser agent in Madeira may have been João de Lisboa, with whom Magellan had been in Morocco and from whose descriptions Magellan's pilot later recognized Cabo de Santa Maria in South America. Cristóbal de Haro was to be one of the financial backers of Magellan's expedition and must later have confirmed to him whatever theory about this gulf, estuary or strait Magellan had formed in Lisbon from his studies of available maps and log books.

The controversial gulf appears to have been the estuary of the Plata River, first officially discovered in 1515 by de Solis, who perished there at the hands of cannibals. After witnessing from the decks of their ships how their leader and his companions were beheaded, cooked and devoured on shore, the terrified survivors of his expedition fled back to Spain without bringing conclusive evidence of the real nature of these waters. It was thus left to Magellan to explore their inland reaches and to discover fresh water instead of a salt-water strait leading to the Pacific.

A world map of 1519, attributed to the Portuguese cartographer Lopo Homem and now in the Marcel Destouches collection in Paris, also reveals an estuary, on the Atlantic Coast of Patagonia, which might be a strait leading, beyond the circular edge of this hemispheric map, to the Pacific, depicted in its twin circular hemisphere. Rewarded in 1521 by the Portuguese governor of Azzemour for feats performed there 'and because he served me with arms and horse in my said city of Azamor for two years', Lopo Homem may have known Magellan, who had also served there eight years earlier, and have communicated to him some cartographical information.

Like the mapmakers themselves, Magellan derived his knowledge and his theories from a great many sources, sometimes too from personal convictions about how to solve their contradictions. Behaim, or else Schöner remembered as Behaim, was but one of these many mapmakers and geographers who influenced him in his final belief that the Spice Islands could be reached by sailing west.

And, however much he may have studied the available globes, maps and log-books in the archives of the Lisbon's House of the Indies and of Guinea, Magellan had only the legendary and traditional evidence of antiquity, concerning a limitless outer ocean bathing the farthest shores of the known areas of a flat world, to lead him to believe that the earth's continents, even Europe, Asia and Africa before they were separated artificially by the Suez canal, are really vast islands which can all, in theory, be circumnavigated. Here, though all of the maps available to Magellan were incorrect, his own experience of navigation and his instincts were right.

Magellan's other major source of information or misinformation, in addition to the somewhat misleading maps that he studied, was the astronomer and astrologer Ruy Faleiro, whom he had met in Oporto. Though now considered, by some Portuguese historians, one of his nation's greatest cosmographers, Faleiro enjoyed little credit among his contemporaries and appears to have fallen into disfavour, at the time he met Magellan, in the eyes of King Manuel.

Faleiro is reported to have known four different methods of determining the exact longitude of any point of the

Earth's surface. Had his methods been correct, Faleiro would have been able to solve the major navigational problem of his age and would thereby have proven himself a truly great mathematical geographer. Unfortunately, his methods seem to have been founded on an incorrect estimate of the Earth's diameter, an error which led him and his disciple Magellan to believe that the Pacific Ocean was much less wide than it actually is, and that Japan, then known as Zipango, would be much closer than it is to the western coasts of North America.

Behaim, Schöner or some other cartographer led Magellan to believe that he could circumnavigate continental South America without having to sail as far south as the straits that bear his name. Faleiro led him to believe that, by crossing the Pacific, he could reach the Moluccas or Spice Islands much sooner and more easily than his survivors actually did, after Magellan's own death in the Philippines.

Faleiro's beliefs may have been the cause of his disgrace. Because of his miscalculation of the Earth's diameter and of the extent of the Pacific Ocean, he must have come to the same conclusion as Magellan: that the controversial latitude of the Treaty of Tordesillas, on the other side of the globe, would leave the Moluccas, to say nothing of the unknown Philippines, the coasts of Cathay and Japan, in the agreed sphere of influence of Spain. However much it might conform to contemporary geographical articles of faith, according to which the whole Earth was about one quarter smaller than it actually is, such an opinion was contrary to Portugal's vital interests; to voice it would be considered traitorous in Lisbon, where any new, however incorrect, estimate of the extension of a degree or of a nautical mile was accepted as proof that Malacca or the Moluccas fell within the official Portuguese sphere of influence.

Faleiro was in any case a disappointed man. Before even voicing such opinions, he had applied in Lisbon for the position of royal astronomer in succession to the famous Rabbi Abraham Ben Samuel Zacuto, who had been a professor of mathematics in Salamanca before coming to Portugal in 1492 as a refugee. A rival who enjoyed more favour at court than Faleiro was appointed.

Common misfortunes led Magellan and Faleiro to seek a common solution to their enforced idleness and impecunious condition. If Portugal refused to avail itself of the rare opportunity of using their talents, the other power that might be interested was Spain, especially as their theories were compatible with Spain's new imperial ambitions. Ever since Columbus had returned from his first successful expedition to what proved to be, contrary to his own convictions, a somewhat unprofitable New World rather than an outlying area of Asia, Spain was sending out one expedition after another to find a strait through this new continent or a way of circumnavigating it. Magellan certainly knew of the voyages of Amerigo Vespucci, who discovered that America is a continent and not an Asian promontory with a few off-shore islands, to say nothing of the expeditions of many less famous navigators financed by Spain.

At this point, fate was at last favourable to Magellan. In India, as we have seen, he had become friendly with Duarte Barbosa, clerk of the Portuguese trading post in Cannanore and later the author of a book of travels and observations which even today reveals a rare understanding of the Orient. Duarte Barbosa was another Portuguese veteran of the Indies who felt that he had been slighted by King Manuel. But he was a man of wealth, acquired through private deals which came his way as official clerk of the Cannanore factory, and he had powerful relatives and friends. Diogo Barbosa, a former Portuguese navigator whom King Manuel had also offended and who emigrated to Spain and became Alcalde or Governor of the Alcazar in Seville, was either Duarte Barbosa's father or his uncle, a detail about which historians still fail to agree.

Magellan now chanced to meet Duarte Barbosa again in Portugal. In Seville, the former clerk of Cannanore had recently heard, from the Alcalde of the Alcazar, that a group of wealthy Spaniards, after sending out one private expedition to explore the Atlantic coast of South America, was planning to send another to seek a westerly route to the Moluccas. One of these enterprising Spaniards happened to be Cristóbal de Haro, heir to a great merchant house with extensive interests in Antwerp and Lisbon as well as in Spain, where the Haro family had originally come from Burgos. After conducting his business for many years from Lisbon, Cristóbal de Haro had recently withdrawn from Portugal to Spain because King Manuel refused him compensation for losses suffered by some of his ships which, while sailing under the Portuguese flag, had been attacked by pirates. From Spain, Haro then sent out, in partnership with Don Nuno Manuel, Controller of the King's household, the private expedition that first sailed up the Plata estuary. Its pilot, João de Lisboa, had later expressed in Madeira his belief that this estuary was perhaps a strait which might lead to the Pacific in accordance with Johann Schöner's representation of the coastline of South America on his 1515 globe.

Magellan appears to have discussed his own theories and plans with Duarte Barbosa, who hastened to recommend him to Diogo Barbosa, the Alcalde of Seville, and his Spanish friends. On his return to Portugal from another trip to Spain, Duarte Barbosa proposed to Magellan that he come to Seville to discuss the possibilities of reaching the Moluccas by circumnavigating the American continent.

The reception accorded to Magellan on his arrival in Seville has led some historians to believe that his plans to circumnavigate the world had been known there for some time and that Duarte may have been a secret Spanish emissary, sent to Portugal for the sole purpose of persuading Magellan and Faleiro to come and discuss their plans with interested Spanish sponsors.

In the summer of 1517, Magellan was in his late thirties, no longer a young man according to the standards of his age, which enjoyed a much lower average life expectancy than ours. Battle-scarred, prematurely aged by the years spent without any effective medical precautions in Africa and Asia, he was also an embittered man who had failed to achieve his ambitions in the service of his country. He did not hesitate to accept the new chance that was offered him. Leaving Faleiro for the time being in Portugal, he went to Seville, never to return.

Much has been written about Magellan's 'disloyalty' in thus shifting his allegiance from Portugal to Spain. But he was only one of many Portuguese, disappointed by King Manuel's haughty indifference to the merits of those who had served him well, who were now seeking their fortunes abroad. Our modern notions of citizenship and loyalty are founded on laws rarely as much as two hundred years old. In sixteenth-century Europe, a man was bound to his nation and his sovereign only by a personal oath. An Italian, for instance, could serve in Italy under half a dozen different local Italian sovereigns in turn. In the Iberic peninsula, Spain was a relatively new nation, composed less than a century earlier of older kingdoms among which Portugal, once a mere province of the Spanish kingdom of Leon, was the only one to have retained independence and achieved national identity. In any case, King Manuel himself had released Magellan from any obligation to serve Portugal and no other nation.

IV

Farewell to Portugal

When Magellan took his decisive step in October 1517, he was destined to live less than four years more. But he was now about to play a leading part in the historical drama of man's exploration of the planet on which we live. Though he had never remained idle for any long period, his activities in the years that preceded his great venture are recorded only sparsely and at random in the few historical documents available to us. Like the submerged mass of an iceberg that reveals only its small peak above sea-level, nearly all Magellan's life up to 1517 will never be known to us except in outline. He was still merely one of a great number of Portuguese soldiers, adventurers and navigators whose individual feats, in Africa, the Indies or elsewhere, were not considered important enough to be recorded systematically. From now, however, Magellan's life was noted in detail by many of his contemporaries. These witnesses included officials and accountants of the Spanish monarchy, Portuguese spies and jealous rivals; above all, he was fortunate enough, in Seville, to meet Antonio Pigafetta and to allow this alert young Italian to accompany him on his voyage of exploration.

Others, while Magellan was discussing the terms and details of his expedition with the interested Spanish authorities, were already watching and reporting his every action. Followed and spied upon, especially in Seville, by Portuguese agents, he was an object of suspicious interest in the eyes of King Manuel, who now, in spite of his earlier disdainful reply to Magellan's request for freedom to serve another monarch, was concerned with what the disgruntled exile did and where he went.

In Seville, Magellan found an impressive *Casa de Contratación*, very much like Lisbon's *Casa das Índias e da Guiné*, with which he was already familiar. Housed in one of the wings of the Alcazar, it served not only as a secret central depository for maps, charts, log-books and other valuable information concerning newly discovered lands and those soon to be explored, but also as a kind of Chamber of Commerce which centralized the administration and government-sponsored trade of Spain's overseas territories. Here all official Spanish expeditions were planned, mainly by shipowners and financiers who were to assume the monetary risks and expected a big share of the profits.

A new King had recently acceded to the Spanish throne, nineteen-year-old Charles the First, later, as Charles the Fifth, elected Holy Roman Emperor. Educated in Flanders, Charles was not yet familiar with Spain, its language or its problems. After landing in Santander, he established his court in Valladolid; only later during his reign was Madrid to become Spain's permanent capital.

Magellan was anxious to obtain an audience to propose his project to the young monarch. But, from his bitter experiences at the Portuguese court, he knew that such audiences must be well prepared, with the support of powerful patrons. Nor did he yet dare approach the authorities of Seville's *Casa de Contratación*: here too, to obtain a favourable hearing, he needed friends who could vouch for him.

Through Duarte Barbosa, he first met Diogo Barbosa, a former Portuguese navigator who, in 1501, had sailed under João de Nova, the discoverer of the Atlantic island of St. Helena. Diogo Barbosa was one of the many Portuguese who, slighted by King Manuel on their return from overseas service, sought their fortunes abroad. As Alcalde of Seville's Alcazar, he was in a position of considerable authority. Within a short while, he and Magellan became such close friends that the latter moved into the Alcazar and, a few months later, married Diogo Barbosa's daughter Beatriz. The marriage was celebrated in the chapel of the Alcazar in November or December 1517. According to Magellan's last will and testament, dated August 24 1519, his bride's dowry amounted to 600,000 maravedis. This corresponds to fifteen thousand pounds, or fifty thousand dollars, and, in an age when even the wealthiest never kept much ready cash because bank accounts were still practically unknown, it represented a considerable sum of capital.

As the wealthy son-in-law of the Alcalde of Seville's Alcazar, Magellan became overnight a man of position and influence in Spain. Though the marriage proved very useful, we have no reason to suspect that he contracted it as a mere stepping stone to success. Nothing in Magellan's life and career suggests that any of his actions was inspired by motives of self-interest not compatible with his high ideals of integrity. His last will and testament seems to indicate, on the contrary, that his brief marriage was happy and that he had every intention of founding a family. No portrait or contemporary description of his wife is known; but, though Magellan has left us no letters expressing any love or affection for her, she remains the only woman with whom he is known to have had any relationship, whether sentimental or purely physical.

With his father-in-law's support, Magellan was assured a favourable hearing when he decided to submit his project to the powerful board of directors of the *Casa de Contratación*. But, though well prepared in every other respect, Magellan failed to reckon with the intrigue with which the administration of Spain's overseas interests was already rife. The great Arab philosopher Ibn Khaldun, considered the true father of modern sociology, had already suggested in 1378, in his *Al Muqaddima*, that it takes at least three generations for an empire's élite to become utterly corrupt. In Spain, they appear to have improved on this: within less than a generation after Columbus had first discovered the Americas, its *Casa de Contratación* was already a perfect illustration of what Lord Acton meant much later when he stated that power tends to corrupt and that absolute power tends to corrupt absolutely. Greed, inspired by the legendary wealth of the Indies, appears to have corrupted Spain even faster than power.

The *Casa de Contratación*'s board consisted of three directors, who listened to Magellan's project with great interest, especially when he quoted from experience the low cost of a cargo of spices at their source in the Moluccas and the profits that could be expected on its arrival in Spain, if one could circumvent all those intermediaries, in Malacca and elsewhere, who exacted their dues on goods which passed through such gateways of trade. Yet these directors finally turned Magellan's proposal down, without discussion.

The very next day, however, he was invited to visit the chairman of the *Casa*'s board, Juan de Aranda, in his home. It turned out that Aranda had rejected Magellan's proposal in the name of the *Casa* because he found it so lucrative that he wished to finance it himself, in order to secure an even larger share of its profits. A few years later, the *Casa* was actually to sue Aranda for repeatedly availing himself, for his own personal profit, of confidential information that reached him as a member of its board. In the course of this trial, Aranda made some curious statements which suggest that he may have been the prospective sponsor whose secret agent, Duarte Barbosa, had originally persuaded Magellan and Faleiro to leave Portugal and propose their great expedition to him and his friends in Spain.

Magellan was forced to accept Aranda's proposal of a partnership, perhaps because it seemed his last chance of success, perhaps because Aranda had originally brought him to Spain. But Aranda first wanted references concerning Magellan himself and Ruy Faleiro. He enquired of Cristóbal de Haro, who still had good connections in Lisbon. Haro was able to give satisfactory assurances concerning the professional competence and honesty of both the navigator and the cosmographer. As he himself had been slighted, in his interests, by the Portuguese court, Haro was not shocked by the fact that they were in disfavour in the eyes of King Manuel.

Meanwhile, Ruy Faleiro had also arrived in Seville, accompanied by his brother Francisco. Magellan and the cosmographer began to discuss their project with Aranda almost daily and in great detail. But Aranda was too inquisitive, in the opinion of Faleiro, who was jealous of his own knowledge and theories. Faleiro soon lost his temper and accused Magellan of speaking too freely of their common secrets. The two partners, never at odds in Portugal, were beginning to quarrel in the atmosphere of intrigue and personal greed that reigned in Seville. Faleiro's suspicions and hesitations may also be attributed to the fact that he had never really abandoned hope of returning to Portugal. Unlike Magellan, he had no family ties in Spain. After their final quarrel, he was indeed foolish enough to return to his native land to see his parents. King Manuel had him arrested and he was finally released from a Portuguese prison only through the efforts of the King of Spain, whose subject he had become as a commander of the Order of Saint James of Compostella. Mentally deranged, Faleiro finally died in Seville.

In January 1518, only a month after his marriage, Magellan left Seville for Valladolid, accompanied by Faleiro. The roads in Spain were very insecure, especially in Andalusia. Moors, Gypsies and Jews, persecuted by the Inquisition and too poor to seek refuge abroad, had taken to the hills and joined the ranks of the outlaws and brigands who, throughout the Middle Ages and even as late as the nineteenth century, continued to infest Spain and, as an endemic expression of popular unrest, enjoyed the support of the disgracefully exploited peasantry in a common struggle against landlords, the authorities and the Church.

For safety, Magellan and Faleiro joined the train of Beatriz de Pacheco, Duchess of Arcos, who was travelling with an armed escort. Juan de Aranda went ahead of them, to prepare an audience with the King as well as to obtain a reply to a letter which had previously been sent to the monarch through the *Casa de Contratación*'s special courier. In Puerto del Herrado, as they were crossing the mountain pass of the Sierra de Guadarrama, Magellan and Faleiro met a messenger sent by Aranda from Valladolid, to bring them news of the King's favourable reply. Aranda arranged to meet them in Medina del Campo, where they spent the night discussing their plans in an inn. The next day, in Puente del Duero, they were already at odds when Aranda began to demand, as payment for his services as go-between, a larger share of the profits of the expedition they were planning.

Painfully, after many angry scenes with Faleiro and many threats of disrupting the partnership, they at last agreed on a figure: Aranda would be given one-eighth of the profits. Only he, through his connections, could persuade the King and council to arm a fleet for Magellan. The contract, between Magellan, Faleiro and their powerful go-between, was signed and notarized on their arrival in Valladolid, in the first week of February. It was in this contract that Magellan stated that he was a citizen or native of Oporto, not a native of Sabrosa or a resident of Lisbon. The contract, however, was never honoured: after Magellan's death, neither his heirs nor his two partners were able to collect their full share of the profits of the expedition.

In Valladolid, Aranda offered to lodge Magellan and Faleiro as guests in his palace, but they preferred to move to a nearby inn. It would thus appear that, in spite of their notarized contract, Magellan still found it difficult to keep peace between the greedy Spaniard and the suspicious and moody Portuguese cosmographer.

A few days later, they were received by the King's Council. It consisted of four members, one of whom was Adrian, cardinal-archbishop of Utrecht, a Dutchman and a close friend of Erasmus. A few years later, he was elected to the Papacy as Adrian the Sixth, the last Pope not to be an Italian.

The Council included two more Netherlanders, William of Croy, the young King's tutor, and Sauvage, head of the Chancellery of State. The fourth member, a Spaniard, was Cardinal Fonseca, bishop of Burgos. The three foreign members of the King's Council were far more interested in territorial conquests on the European continent, to consolidate the young King's position in his rivalry with King Francis the First of France, than in risky expeditions overseas. The latter demanded a crusading spirit of a kind which had become obsolete in humanistic Renaissance Europe and now survived only in Portugal and Spain, where the Moors remained traditional enemies and, as neighbours, a constant threat. The Bishop of Burgos, though more open-minded in matters which involved overseas expeditions and possible conflicts with the Moors or with distant pagans, was reputed to be over-cautious. He had been opposed, for instance, to Spain's financing of the expedition which led Columbus to discover the Americas. Perhaps because Bishop Fonseca later became convinced that his opposition had been a mistake, he subsequently gave his approval to other expeditions that set out to explore the Americas and encouraged Cortez to conquer Mexico and Juan Díaz de Solis to explore the coasts of South America as far south as the Plata estuary. He even discussed later with the Genoese navigator Sebastian Cabot a project to sail north of Newfoundland and the coasts of Labrador, still known as *Tierra de los Bacalaos* or Codfish Land, to discover a north-west passage that might ultimately lead to the Pacific Ocean and the Spice Islands.

Some historians have interpreted this change of mind, in Fonseca, as a mere attempt to save face, after his mistake in failing to encourage Columbus. But Fonseca's change of mind can be attributed to more rational motives of policy. Until Columbus discovered the Americas, Fonseca may have been a firm believer in an eastward route to the Indies. Even if Columbus had now failed to chart a practicable westward route, the islands and the continent that he had discovered might well prove profitable to Spain, as indeed they became. On the other hand, the Treaty of Tordesillas offered Spain few chances of profitable discoveries to be made by further exploring, through waters |controlled by unfriendly

Portuguese fleets, an eastward route to the Moluccas, at least until one knew where the agreed line dividing the two spheres of influence might cut through the Indies on the other side of the globe. On this side of the globe, however, any lands discovered west of that line would clearly belong to Spain.

Because of his favourable attitude to westerly explorations, Fonseca came to be known within a short while as the most knowledgeable of the young King's councillors in matters concerning the Indies, for which the other three and the King himself generally relied on his judgement and advice. Magellan and Faleiro therefore knew that their task would consist mainly in convincing Fonseca.

Did Magellan appear before the Council with, in addition to his charts and maps, a beautifully tooled, though geographically incorrect, leather globe of the world, like the one still in Nuremberg's Germanisches Nationalmuseum? Did he bring the letters that his friend Serrão is reputed to have sent him from distant Ternate? Bishop Bartolomé de las Casas, in his *Historia de las Indias*, indeed describes Magellan, whom he met in Valladolid in the office of the High Chancellor, as a man of small stature and undistinguished appearance who limped and had 'a well-painted globe on which the whole world was depicted', when he came there, with Fonseca, for his first audience with the King. To the High Chancellor and las Casas, Magellan indicated on this globe the route that he proposed to take. Las Casas asked him what he proposed to do, should he fail to find a strait leading to the Pacific where he anticipated finding one, presumably in the area of the Plata estuary. Magellan then replied that, if he failed to find a strait, he would follow the Portuguese route to the Indies, crossing the Atlantic again and rounding the Cape of Good Hope.

Whatever he and Faleiro may have shown or said to the cautious, knowledgeable and enterprising Fonseca, they managed to convince him of the validity of their project. He backed them with all his power and revealed to them the secret reports brought back to him, only a few months earlier, by the survivors of the expedition of Juan Díaz de Solis. In discussions with Aranda and Cristóbal de Haro, Fonseca even defended Magallen's and Faleiro's financial interest in the expedition's profits. In the long run, Fonseca thus proved to be Portugal's most dangerous political enemy in the struggle to control the unknown seas and lands that were then being explored.

No minutes or other record of this historical council meeting have survived. All published descriptions of it belong in the realm of historical fiction. Peter Martyr of Anghiera, who in 1518 became a member of the Supreme Council of the Indies, was instructed by the King to collate, on the return of the survivors of Magellan's expedition, their testimony and other relevant documents. His manuscript, together with the supporting documents, was sent to the Pope, and was lost or destroyed in 1527 when the Eternal City was sacked by the mercenary troops of the Emperor Charles the Fifth. But Peter Martyr also included in his own book, *De Orbe Novo*, a summary of his findings. Here he states clearly that navigators or explorers always relied on Fonseca's knowledge and support in their dealings with the Council.

Now that he had won Fonseca's support, Magellan began to face other difficulties. On the one hand, Faleiro was proving increasingly suspicious and cantankerous. On the other hand, Álvaro da Costa, Portugal's ambassador to Spain, had obtained information of the Council's favourable decision and reported it to his King. Nothing could be more intolerable to King Manuel than the idea that a Spanish expedition, under the leadership of a Portuguese navigator, might reach and claim the Spice Islands and deprive Portugal of the ultimate goal of its explorations and campaigns in the Indies. Álvaro da Costa was therefore instructed to spy on the whole project and do his utmost, through his numerous agents, to sabotage it. Everything should be attempted to prevent Magellan's expedition from ever materializing.

Soon after the Council's favourable decision, Magellan and Ruy Faleiro were received by the King. In the course of this royal audience, their first with the young monarch, they were awarded the insignia of Commanders of the Order of Saint James of Compostella; this made them members of the Spanish nobility and, as such, vassals of the King of Spain, to whom they swore loyalty in the course of the ceremony which granted them this honour.

Magellan's next step was to obtain ratification of the contracts which set forth in writing all that had been agreed. This was all the more easy now that Cristóbal de Haro had decided, should the *Casa de Contratación* and the Spanish treasury fail to back Magellan's expedition officially, to finance it privately, with his own funds and those of his associates in Antwerp, Amsterdam and Hamburg, and with his own ships, since he was one of the wealthiest shipping magnates of his age. Fonseca, seeking to regain for Spain some of the advantages King John of Portugal had obtained through the Treaty of Tordesillas, had already exploited Haro's differences with King Manuel to persuade him to abandon Lisbon as his base of operations and establish himself in Spain. The wily bishop may well have used him now as a pawn in his own intrigues within the Council; the threat that Haro and Aranda might privately finance

Magellan's expedition and reap the profits may even have convinced the Council that it should expedite the contract it had promised.

Magellan could scarcely hesitate in his choice between the two offers. Sailing officially under the Spanish banner, with the vast resources of the Spanish treasury to back him, he would be in a much stronger position, even as a Portuguese renegade, if he came into conflict with Portuguese authorities in the course of his expedition, than if he were to sail with private backers, however wealthy and powerful these might be.

On the Council's request, Magellan and Faleiro drafted a detailed memorandum in which they proposed their own conditions and justified in great detail their belief that the Moluccas lay in the Spanish hemisphere of influence according to the Treaty of Tordesillas, though 'it might happen that the King of Portugal should wish, at some time soon, to claim that the islands of the Moluccas are within his area of the line of demarcation and to send an expedition to explore them'. Magellan and Faleiro offered the King of Spain the following alternatives: he could either share in the financing of the expedition, in partnership with their proposed private backers, or assume the full financial responsibility of providing the ships, their equipment, their supplies etc.

The King chose to finance the whole expedition and, on March 22 1518, signed the agreement in person. His youthful imagination was perhaps fired by Magellan's personality, as a veteran of so many campaigns in the Indies, and by the extraordinary nature of his daring venture. Within the next few months, the King repeatedly gave Magellan his full support, in every conflict that arose between him and any Spanish authority or officer.

When Fonseca, for instance, tried to reduce, probably for reasons of security, the number of Portuguese seamen whom Magellan would be allowed to sign on, the King quadrupled their number. When one of Magellan's Spanish captains was insolent to him, the King sent a chilling rebuke. The final contract commissioned Ruy Faleiro and Ferdinand Magellan 'to seek, in that part of the ocean which is under Our Sovereignty, islands, mainlands, spices, and other things by means of which We shall be advantaged and which will benefit Our land'. The King moreover undertook, during the next ten years, not to authorize anyone 'to go in quest of discoveries on the same route and in the same regions as yourselves'. This curious clause constitutes, in an age when the protection of intellectual and industrial properties was practically unknown, an almost unprecedented legal innovation in that it grants, for a period of ten years, a kind of patent on Magellan's proposed discoveries, whether of a new route to the Spice Islands or of territories as yet unknown.

Magellan and Faleiro were assured 'a tenth part of the proceeds and gains from all the lands and islands that you will have discovered, and shall besides receive the title of Viceroys of these lands and islands for your sons and heirs for all time ... Of the islands which you will have discovered [meaning only the ultimate goal, the Spice Islands], after six of them have been selected for Us, you may choose two from the remainder, of whose income and profit you shall have a fifth part, after deduction of costs.' Over and above this share of gross profits, the King finally granted them also a fifth part 'of the net profits which you bring us ... after deduction of the costs of the fleet'.

As for the costs which the King assumed, they were likewise clearly defined in this remarkable agreement: 'I promise to outfit for you five ships: two each of 130 tons, two each of 90 tons, and one of 60 tons, equipped with crew, food and weapons and munitions for two years, including 234 men, with the captains, able seamen and ordinary seamen necessary for the operation of the fleet, and with whatever other persons are needed . . .'

Early in the spring of 1518, with this contract in hand, Magellan returned to Seville and began to busy himself with the material preparations for his expedition. He met obstacles, however, at every turn. Faleiro's increasingly pathological suspicions were inevitably leading to their final break and were meanwhile a constant source of difficulties. The Portuguese representative in Seville, Sebastião Álvarez, followed his ambassador's instructions and kept a strict watch on Magellan's activities, stirring up trouble whenever he could. Nor was this difficult: rivalry between Spain and Portugal was so open, in an age when the interests of these two nations were clearly in conflict, that the Spaniards could barely help being suspicious of the activities of Magellan, Faleiro and their few Portuguese associates, even though these activities were now financed and encouraged by the King of Spain.

The reports that Álvarez wrote from Seville to King Manuel of Portugal have survived. From these, we gather that Álvarez was often better informed than Magellan about Spanish intrigues that sought to hamper the navigator's progress. Álvarez thus reports the arrival in Seville of Cristóbal de Haro and Juan de Cartagena, 'chief factor of the Fleet and captain of a ship, and the treasurer and clerk of his fleet'. He points out that, in the regulations that they now bring concerning the preparation and management of the expedition, 'there are clauses contrary to the instructions of Magellan . . . seen by the accountant and factors of the

Casa de Contratación', with the express purpose of stirring up trouble with Magellan. Among other objections, the representatives of the *Casa de Contratación* argued that Magellan had already signed up too many Portuguese, 'and that it was not well that he should take so many'.

Magellan answered this objection by pointing out that his contract allowed him a free hand. After much argument, the factors 'ordered pay to be issued to the seamen and men-at-arms, but not to any of the Portuguese' whom Magellan and Faleiro had signed on. The factors, to justify their action, at the same time sent a courier, reporting all this to the King.

Before the courier's return from the court, Álvarez visited Magellan in his lodgings, 'where I found him packing hampers and chests of victuals, preserves and other things. I pressed him, feigning that, as I now found him thus busied, it seemed to me that the undertaking of his evil design was settled, and that, as this would be the last conversation I might have with him, I wished to recall to his memory how many times, as a loyal Portuguese and as his friend, I had spoken to him in order to dissuade him from the great mistake he was about to commit . . .'

Magellan was surprised that Álvarez knew so much. Always ingenuous and truthful, he told him about his difficulties with the *Casa*'s factors and accountants and that he was now awaiting the courier's return with the King's decision, all of which Álvarez feigned not to know. Magellan added that he would under no condition abandon his project, even if the King's reply were not in his favour, unless of course the *Casa* deprived him of 'anything which had been assigned him by his contract'. He stated, however, that 'he first had to see what Your Highness would do', which suggests that Magellan still feared, on the part of King Manuel, some direct action that might prevent the whole expedition.

Álvarez argued with Magellan that 'he thought he was going as Captain-major, whilst I knew that others were being sent in opposition to him, whom he would not know of except at a time when he would not be able to defend his honour'. He warned Magellan moreover to distrust 'the honey, which the Bishop of Burgos put to his lips'. Finally, Álvarez suggested that Magellan 'should give me a letter to Your Highness, and that I, out of friendship for him, would go to Your Highness to act on his behalf'. In conclusion, Álvarez reported to King Manuel that Magellan had assured him 'he would not say anything to me until he saw the message which the courier brought'.

The King of Spain finally solved the conflict with the *Casa de Contratación* entirely in Magellan's favour and allowed him to sign on as many Portuguese companions as he wished.

Álvarez went on to report his two meetings with Ruy Faleiro, who seemed to him 'like a man deranged in his senses' and repeatedly asked 'how could he do anything against the King his lord, who did him such favour?' In the opinion of Álvarez, 'if Magellan were removed . . . Ruy Faleiro would follow whatever Magellan did'. The rest of the report gives details of the material preparations for the expedition. The five ships, in the opinion of Álvarez, 'are very old and patched up'. He had already seen them beached for repairs eleven months earlier: 'they are now afloat, and they are caulking them in the water. I went aboard them a few times . . . and I would be ill inclined to sail in them even as far as the Canaries, because the wooden braces supporting their timbers are already rotten.' Their artillery consisted only of eighty guns, 'of a very small size'. On Magellan's ship only, the largest of the fleet, 'there are four very good cannon'. It would be unwise, however, to attach too much importance to these derogatory remarks. Flushed with the pride of their own successes, the Portuguese were all too often contemptuous of Spanish shipping and seamanship, and refused for many years to admit that any other sea power could vie with them. Besides, such remarks were sure to flatter King Manuel.

Álvarez also reports the conflict about the pay to be given to the Portuguese who had been signed on. Apparently, they were offered a thousand réis, which may have been less than their Spanish comrades received, and refused to accept it until Magellan promised them an increase. They were now awaiting the courier's return with the King's reply to their petition.

The fleet, Álvarez assured King Manuel, carried provisions for two years. Magellan himself was to captain the first ship; Faleiro, the second. Juan de Cartagena, chief factor or accountant of the whole fleet, was to captain the third; Quesada, 'a dependant of the Archbishop of Seville', the fourth; 'the fifth goes without any known captain, but Carvalho, a Portuguese, goes in her as pilot and it is said here that, as soon as they are out of the mouth of the Guadalquivir river, Magellan will appoint Álvaro de Mesquita, of Estremoz, as captain'. Magellan seems to have hesitated to set sail officially with three Portuguese captains out of five. Álvaro de Mesquita, a Portuguese reputed to be related to Magellan on his mother's side, was already in Seville.

Álvarez even listed the trade goods that Magellan's fleet carried: 'copper, quicksilver, common cloths of colours, common coloured silks, and jackets made of these silks'. The official lists of all these supplies, munitions and trade goods have survived: they include thousands of cheap bells, made in Germany, and of mirrors to dazzle and delight the natives of primitive lands. Copper was a valuable article of trade and barter in the East Indies; Serrão in his letters from the

Moluccas may have advised Magellan to bring copper as payment for spices.

Though the fleet was expected to start down the river at the end of July, Álvarez scarcely expected it to leave before the middle of August. Its proposed course was to sail straight to Cape Frio, near the present side of Rio de Janeiro, and to keep the coasts of Brazil to the right 'until they reach the line of demarcation' agreed in the Treaty of Tordesillas, and then to navigate to the west and west-north-west until they reach the Moluccas. Álvarez points out that, from Cape Frio to the Moluccas, 'there are no lands laid down in the maps which they carry with them'. He concludes by wishing: 'Please God Almighty that they may make such a voyage as did the Cortereals,' two brothers whose ships had disappeared off the coasts of North America in 1501 and 1502, 'and that Your Mighty Highness be at rest, and forever be envied, as You are, by all princes . . .'

On the subject of Magellan's maps, Álvarez reported to King Manuel, in July 1519, detailed intelligence. Its significance has been pointed out by cartographical scholars, but is generally neglected by Magellan's biographers. Álvarez stated that he had 'seen the land of the Moluccas put on the globe and chart that the son of Reinel has made here, which was not finished when his father came here to fetch him, and his father finished it all and put these lands of the Moluccas [on it] for all the other charts which are made by Ribeiro, and [the latter] makes the compasses, quadrants and globes, but he does not go with the fleet nor does he want more than to earn his bread through his skill'.

In one breath, Álvarez names here three contemporary Portuguese cartographers whose maps are known to us: Pedro Reinel, his son Jorge Reinel and Diogo Ribeiro. However, in the detailed account of the moneys paid out for supplies for Magellan's fleet which can still be consulted in the Archives of the Indies in Seville, we find a well-known Spanish cartographer, Nuño García de Toreno, listed instead of Diogo Ribeiro for payment for thirty-two charts. As Professor Armando Cortesão, a world authority on Renaissance cartography, has pointed out, Nuño García was too well known to be expected to produce in his own hand as many copies of master charts as Magellan's fleet might need. But he certainly ran a workshop that was organized to handle such large orders. Since Diogo Ribeiro was then a young man and not yet known as an expert cartographer, he was probably employed at that time in García de Toreno's workshop.

If one consults surviving charts known to be the work of some of the cartographers mentioned by Álvarez in his report to King Manuel, one discovers in the British Museum a chart which Pedro Reinel probably drafted in 1522, immediately after the return of the survivors of Magellan's expedition, and which depicts the Far East and the Indian Ocean exactly as they were then known. Munich's military museum, until it was bombed during the last war, possessed a parchment planisphere of 1519 by Jorge Reinel, in which the controversial longitude of the Treaty of Tordesillas was depicted incorrectly as passing, in the unexplored area on the other side of the world, exactly where Magellan argued that it passed, leaving the Moluccas, the Philippines and Cipango or Japan in the Spanish instead of the Portuguese half of the world. Moreover, this chart leaves a blank for all the coasts of South America still unexplored when Magellan set out on his expedition.

No other known map by a Portuguese cartographer makes this mistake, which was contrary to vital Portuguese interests and would have been considered disloyal to Portugal. Yet this map, lost in an Allied bombing of Munich, was in the unmistakable style, in decorative details as well as geographical knowledge, of the famous Reinel cartographers. Was it a map made for Magellan, according to his instructions, to be shown to the King of Spain? Though a mere map, is it the 'globe' mentioned by Bishop de las Casas and by Álvarez?

The references to a globe in the Álvarez letter to King Manuel and in the *Historia de las Indias* of Bishop de las Casas may allude to the lost Munich planisphere, which indeed depicted the world in the form of a globe projected on a plane and may therefore have been described in both texts as a globe, especially as Álvarez uses this term so loosely that, when it crops up again in his letter, he appears to refer to something quite different, in a list of instruments that include compasses, quadrants and, most probably, spherical astrolabes too.

One can reasonably conclude that the lost Munich parchment planisphere was the original or a contemporary copy of Magellan's very controversial 'globe', also described as having been of leather, which may well mean parchment; indeed, a later Spanish historian, Bartolomé Leonardo de Argensola, in his *Conquista de las Islas Molucas*, published in Madrid in 1609, specifically states that Magellan showed Charles the Fifth a planisphere, meaning a map representing the globe projected as a plane, and not a globe. Writing some eighty years later, Argensola may have seen with his own eyes, preserved in the library or Archives of the King of Spain, the original planisphere which Magellan had given to the King and which may later have somehow found its way to Munich. Though not as ornate as some of his father's masterpieces of cartography or some he himself later produced, Jorge Reinel's Munich planisphere was obviously one of those sumptuous portolans which were destined for the libraries of great patrons rather than for practical use aboard ships. From such a map, prepared according to Magellan's specifications by Jorge Reinel and to which the latter's father, Pedro Reinel, put the finishing touches, Diogo Ribeiro certainly made, in the workshop of García de Toreno, the many practical charts that were needed for Magellan's fleet. Both Pedro Reinel's map of South America in the British Museum and his son's planisphere illustrate, with great accuracy and a minimum of fantasy, all that was really known of the areas depicted, between 1519 and 1522. Surely Magellan relied far more on such up-to-date maps than on any Martin Behaim might have drafted at least twenty years earlier, since there is no evidence, though Behaim died in 1515, of his having engaged in any carto-graphic activity after producing his famous and outdated globe of 1492.

Meanwhile, the Portuguese Ambassador to the Spanish court was doing his best to dissuade King Charles from implementing his agreement with Magellan. It would appear that an offer had now been made to Magellan that he undertake his expedition officially on Portugal's behalf; but Magellan, loyal to his contract with the King of Spain, had refused. Plans were afoot for the latter's sister Leonora to marry the King of Portugal. The Portuguese Ambassador argued that the financing of Magellan's expedition would be considered, in Portugal, a hostile act which might wreck this project to unite the two royal families by a marriage ensuring peace between the two nations. In his report to the King of Portugal, after his audience with King Charles, Álvaro da Costa even states that he spoke of Magellan's expedition very energetically to the young monarch: 'I pointed out to him that a sovereign did himself disservice and

136

violated good usage and customs by taking into his service the subjects of another sovereign, against the latter's formally expressed wish ... I begged him to consider that this was not a good time to risk offending Your Highness, especially for a venture that is so foolish and so unlikely to succeed ... Finally, I begged him to agree, in his own interest and in that of Your Highness, to either of two solutions: to allow Magellan and Ruy Faleiro to return to their own country or to delay the whole expedition for another year.'

King Charles was not yet twenty years of age, but already he revealed his ability to handle difficult situations without committing himself. He advised the Portuguese Ambassador to discuss the whole matter with the Cardinal of Utrecht and other members of his Council of Advisers. Álvaro da Costa understood that this was but a dilatory device concealing a rejection of his pleas and arguments. Since official steps met with no success, he now took to more devious ways of sabotaging Magellan's expedition.

On October 22 1518, a crowd of curious idlers was gathered in the harbour of Seville watching the preparations for Magellan's *armada*. Magellan himself could be seen on the stern deck of the *Trinidad*, his flagship, which had just been repainted. Proud and hot-tempered Andalusians had long been smarting under the shame of seeing a Spanish fleet preparing to set sail under a Portuguese commander. Suddenly, someone in the crowd pointed out that the flag which flew from the topmast of the *Trinidad* bore Portuguese arms. Immediately, a mob attacked the ship. Magellan was unarmed. In the emergency, he summoned the harbour guards. Their officers explained that the Portuguese arms on the flag of Magellan's flagship were only his own, not those of Portugal. As an Admiral, he had the right to fly his personal flag and the royal banner of Spain would of course be solemnly unfurled on the ship's stern when the fleet officially set sail. The mob withdrew as the Alcalde of the Alcazar came to the rescue with his armed escort. According to some reports, however, Magellan himself was struck and wounded by the mob, though not seriously, in the course of the strife which Sebastian Álvarez had managed to stir up.

The Portuguese Ambassador or his agent in Seville may even have been responsible for Magellan's final disagreement with Faleiro. In any case, Faleiro soon decided that he would not accompany Magellan on his expedition. Instead, he remained for a while in Seville with his brother, Francisco Faleiro, who later wrote and published a treatise on navigation. From the King of Spain, Faleiro obtained a pension and the promise that he would soon head a second expedition of the same nature as Magellan's. By a royal decree signed in Barcelona on July 26 1519, Magellan was finally appointed Commander of the expedition; Ruy Faleiro was ordered to stay in Seville for reasons of health, and Juan de Cartagena was appointed Magellan's *conjuncta persona* or deputy. Magellan was none too pleased with this latter decision, especially as he was also ordered to dismiss seventeen Portuguese apprentice seamen whom he had just signed on and whom he was now told to replace by Spaniards. Magellan's reply quoted the earlier agreement of May 5 1519, which authorized him to sign on all persons of his own choice, 'since he, Magellan, was the only one who had full powers in such matters'. Finally, Magellan agreed to accept Juan de Cartagena instead of Ruy Faleiro on condition that the latter's brother Francisco captain one of his ships, and that Ruy Faleiro communicate to him and to the officials of the *Casa de Contratación* his secret method of observing east–west longitudes, together with the corresponding reference tables. Ruy Faleiro was thus obliged to part with his precious theory for estimating longitude by the inclination of the compass as it points to the magnetic pole instead of the true north, but Francisco Faleiro preferred not to captain a ship and finally stayed in Spain.

It would not in fact have been easy for Magellan to comply with the King's orders and man his fleet, as popular prejudice also demanded, exclusively with Spanish officers and seamen. Barely a quarter of a century earlier, Columbus had failed to arouse much enthusiasm when he tried to enlist Spaniards; finally, he too had been forced to sign on a considerable number of foreigners. Intrigues and technical problems also contributed towards delaying Magellan's departure, as Sebastian Álvarez had expected in his letter to King Manuel. During these delays, many of the seamen Magellan had originally signed on simply vanished, after receiving their first pay. When his fleet finally left Seville on August 10 1519 for San Lucar, situated further downstream, it was manned by a motley crowd in which Spaniards and Portuguese constituted the majority, but which also included at least fourteen Frenchmen, a number of Italians, mostly Genoese, a couple of Flemings, three men who were perhaps natives of the island of Rhodes, two Englishmen, a German, 'Nicolas of Naples', known as 'the Greek' and actually a native of Nauplia, and of course Magellan's faithful slave Enrique of Malacca. Most of the men of his crews are listed, in the records, only under given names and places of origin. The family names of the officers are, however, nearly all listed.

Magellan's last few months in Seville were not devoted exclusively to the solving of problems raised by intrigues and technical difficulties. Shortly before he finally set sail, a son, Rodrigo Magalhães, was born to him and Doña Beatriz Barbosa. Before finally setting sail from San Lucar, more than a month later, on September 20 1519, he returned to Seville to draft and sign, on August 24, his last will and testament, a remarkably pious and charitable document. He willed there, 'if I die in this city of Seville', that his body be buried in the church of Santa María de la Victoria, in the city's neighbourhood of Triana; but, 'if I die on this said voyage', that his body be buried in a church dedicated to Our Lady, in the nearest place to that where he might happen to die.

To the orders of the Holy Trinity and of Santa María de Merced, both of Seville, he bequeathed, to each, the sum of one *real* in silver, 'in aid of the redemption of such faithful Christians as may be captives in the country of the Moors'. On the day of his burial, he requested that his executors clothe three poor men, 'so that to each may be given a cloak of grey cloth, a cap, a shirt and a pair of shoes, that they may pray to God for my soul'.

His will also acknowledged the receipt of his wife's dowry of 600,000 maravedis and requested that, 'before anything else', Doña Beatrix be repaid this full amount from his estate, 'together with the arras', or tapestries, which he had given her. His next bequest was to his slave Enrique, 'that from the day of my death thereafter for ever the said Enrique may be free', and that 'of my estate there may be given to the said Enrique the sum of ten thousand maravedis in money for his support; and this manumission I grant because he is a Christian, and that he may pray to God for my soul'.

Finally, Magellan ordered that 'all and everything of the said possessions which may remain' over and above his other bequests 'be had and inherited' by his son Rodrigo, 'and by the child or children of which the said Doña Beatriz is now pregnant'; and if, 'which God forbid, the said my son, or child to be born of my wife, die before attaining the proper age for the succession . . . that the said Doña Beatriz . . . may inherit my estate'.

Doña Beatriz died a few months after Magellan's departure, while giving birth to a still-born child, thus frustrating her husband of the hope of further issue expressed in his will. Their only surviving child, Rodrigo, died soon. Within the three years that followed the drafting and signing of his will, Magellan and all the direct heirs whom he mentions had died; nor had his provisions for his slave Enrique been respected, on Magellan's death in the Philippines.

After the return of the *Victoria* with reliable testimony of Magellan's death, the King of Spain ordered an enquiry to discover in Spain or Portugal the navigator's residual heirs. On the testimony of a great number of persons who had known Magellan or happened to bear his name, the claims of a distant cousin, Lorenzo Magalhães, were finally recognized. Among the documents preserved in Seville's *Archivo General de Indias*, one also finds a great number of claims filed with the Spanish authorities, for payment of arrears of pay, pensions, or financial losses, by survivors of the expedition or their heirs and by Cristóbal de Haro and others who had invested in it, including the Fugger bankers in distant Augsburg.

From these claims and other documents, one gathers that 107 members of the expedition drew salaries, and that Magellan himself, at the time of his death in Mactan on April 27 1521, had earned a total of 116,533 maravedis, from which one has to deduct an advance of 47,000 he had drawn in Seville before his departure. Because of the other claims, Magellan's share of the net profits of the expedition itself could never be calculated; besides, the Spanish authorities, even when they recognized some of the claims after years of costly litigation, were either slow to make any payments or deliberately failed to do so. As for the clauses of Magellan's contract concerning his share of the future income of all territories that he might discover and claim for Spain, these proved to be of little value. The Philippines were colonized and profitably exploited by Spain only much later, and the Moluccas, which Magellan failed to reach before his death, remained a Spanish territory only for a short while and then had to be ceded to Portugal, which lost them later to the Netherlands.

From the documents preserved in Seville it would thus appear that Magellan's residual heir, Lorenzo Magalhães, inherited, when he settled in Spain to collect it, only what was left of the navigator's back pay.

Part II

MAGELLAN'S QUEST

FERDIN · MAGELLANVS · SVPERATIS
ANTARTIC'   FRETI · ANGVS
TIIS ·   CLARISS·

1 (a). Imaginary portrait of Magellan, anonymous and painted in Spain shortly after the return of the survivors of his expedition. (By courtesy of the Kunsthistoriches Museum, Vienna.) A similar portrait of Magellan can be seen in the collections of the Academia San Fernando in Madrid and a later copy is also exhibited in Seville.

(b). Magellan's autograph. (By courtesy of the Archivo General de Indias, Seville.)

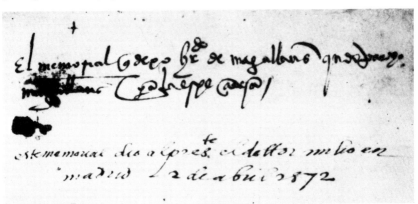

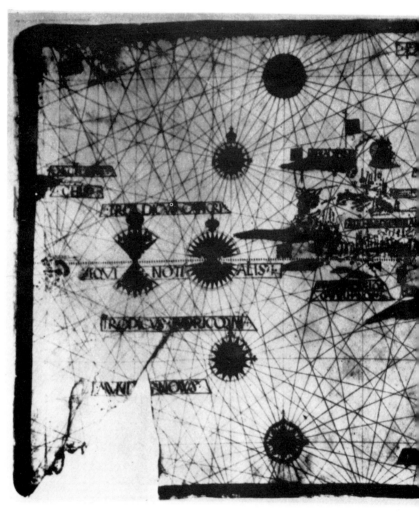

2. Map of the world, anonymous but attributed to Jorge Reinel who is known to ha
been one of Magellan's cartographers in Seville. Formerly in the Collections of t
Military Museum in Munich and believed to have been designed in 1519, it depicts t
whole world as it was known or believed to be until the survivors of Magellan's expediti
returned to Spain. Because it is the only known map in which the imaginary line of t

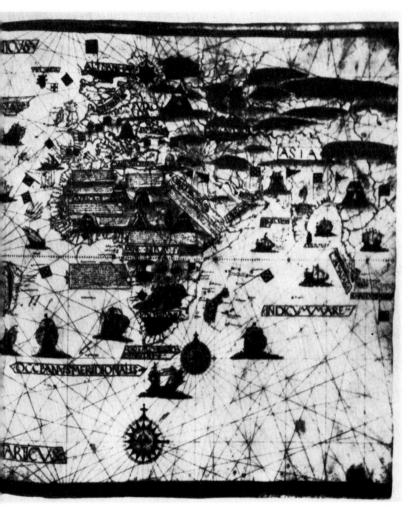

Treaty of Tordesillas clearly leaves the Moluccas in the area thereby granted to Spain, it may actually be the map that Magellan showed to King Charles in Valladolid. Lost, destroyed or looted when Munich's Military Museum was bombed during World War II, it is now reproduced from *Cartographia Portugallica* with the permission of its editors and publishers, by courtesy of the Fundação Calouste Gulbenkian, Lisbon.

3. First page of the original of the Treaty of Tordesillas. (By courtesy of the Archivo General de Indias, Seville.)

4. *Naufragio* (Shipwreck) by Juan de Toledo (El Capitan) who was born in Lorca, Murcia, in 1611 and died in Madrid in 1665. Oil on canvas. (By courtesy of the Prado Museum, Madrid.)

5. Details from the Abraham Cresquez map of the world. (By courtesy of the Bibliothèque Nationale, Paris.)

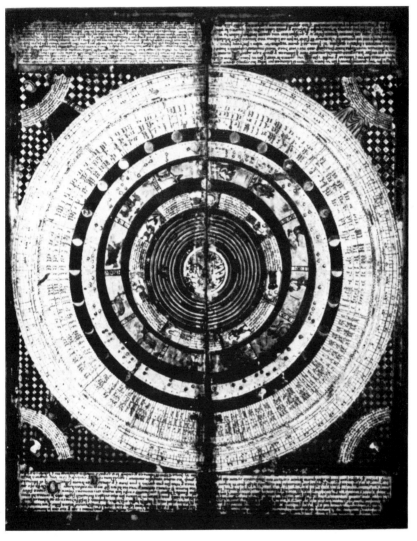

(a) *left* depicts parts of Asia, (b) *above* depicts the Ptolemaic concept of the Universe.

anber alweg der klainer dem gewalcigen zynßpar sein. Sol
liche zinß geben sy allain/zü ainem zaichen/ der gehorsam in
schlechtem werd/etlych bryngen dem andern fürsten je har/
die andern ain lauß von jrem herren/vnd alles so dise herren
beschliessen vol ziehen die vnderthon/von stund an/onn alle
hynderuus.

⁋ In disen allen ist fast hoch scharpf gepürg vnd grosse kelte
tin / der massen das man vom halben october biß auf halbn
Marcio vor grosser kelein/ vnd scharpffen winden der selby
gen aue nie schiffen mag.

⁋ Es wonen auch jnnerlichen hohen gepürgen die gegen dem
ast vnd weßt winden ligen ryfen/welche so groß seynd/dz jre
pain vom knye/hinauff fünff spañ lang sein/vnd die propor
cion jres gantzen leibs darnach machen/achten sy so hoch
als ainer gen ainem rayß oder schweitzer spieß/ das leichtig
klich zü gelauben.

⁋ Dañ ich hab ain solichs ryfen bain/das dem grossen kätz
ler geschenckt gesehen/welliches allain was/ vom knye über
sich/ist mir von der erd biß an die weich gangen.

⁋ Von disem bürg ferrer hinein/sol als man sagt/ain grosß
hauß wie ain kloster gepaut/vnd darin ain mechtige fraw
sey/die Castilianer die frawen von Sylber haissen/welliche
fraw so vil sylber hat/das die pfeyler jres hauß/durch aus
lettig sylber sey.

⁋ Sunst hat die Ray. May. am.r.tag Augusti jm. M.D
rix. Jar/ain ander Armata mit schiffen/vnd damit Aynn
haupeman Wagelanus genant mit.iiij. Hundert personen
außgeschickt der geleichen new land zü suchen/daruß am.vj
tag Septembris difes.xxij. Jar/nur ains mit. xviij. persone
wider komen/vnd der selb Wagelanus/ Vnd noch ainer so
nach m haupeman gemacht mit namen Seranus send in
diser reiß vm komen/ welches sy als glauwbwirdig bericht

6. Second page of an anonymous German newsletter printed in Augsburg presumably
in 1520 and containing the first known published report of Magellan's expedition.
Magellan is mentioned twice as Wagelanus and Serrão as Seranus. (By courtesy of
John Howell Books, San Francisco, and the John Carter Brown Library, Brown
University, Providence, R.I.)

V

Discipline and the Rumblings of Revolt

Antonio Pigafetta, to whose lively pen we owe a detailed day-by-day account of Magellan's great voyage, was an observant and communicative young nobleman, a native of the beautiful city of Vicenza, in Northern Italy, not very far inland from Venice. Little is known of Pigafetta's life before he met Magellan in Seville, and his last years are likewise shrouded, after his return from his circumnavigation of the Earth, in an obscurity that still puzzles many scholars.

Magellan was fortunate to meet, shortly before setting sail from Seville, this faithful and talented reporter. He immediately signed Pigafetta on as *Criado del Capitán y sobresaliente*, aide to the admiral and supernumerary. In addition to the duties which might be imposed on him as *sobresaliente* in an emergency when all hands were needed, Pigafetta was the official historian of the expedition. He survived Magellan and was one of the few who returned to Seville aboard the battered *Victoria* three years later.

As we have seen, the scattered details of Magellan's biography, from his birth until shortly before he finally set sail on his great expedition, must be collated or conjectured from readings of a great number and variety of conflicting sources. But from the moment that Pigafetta began writing his account of the expedition, he kept a reliable and systematic day-by-day account of its progress, though we still find

Magellan himself described or discussed there only some-what sparingly.

A Genoese pilot whose identity remains doubtful also wrote a brief record of part of the expedition, but kept it only until his ship reached the Moluccas, whence his captain decided to return, aboard the *Trinidad*, across the Pacific to the Americas, instead of venturing with the *Victoria* round the Cape of Good Hope to Seville. But the *Trinidad* failed to find its way across the Pacific to Mexico and had to turn back to the Moluccas, where its starving survivors were arrested by the Portuguese garrison and then languished for many years in Portuguese prisons. Francisco Albo, another pilot, also kept a brief and factual log-book of the whole expedition and returned to Seville with Pigafetta aboard the *Victoria*. After their return, Charles the Fifth, who was anxious to collect and preserve all documents and any useful testimony concerning Magellan's voyage, had one of his secretaries, Maximilian of Transylvania, write and publish in Latin, in 1523, *De Moluccis insulis*, a treatise on the Spice Islands which contains some otherwise unrecorded facts about Magellan's voyage. A son-in-law of Cristóbal de Haro's brother, Maximilian also provides some useful insights into the complex arguments whereby King Charles was first persuaded to take an interest in Magellan's project.

From these fragmentary sources and from the scattered documents that have been discovered in Spanish and Portuguese archives, it would be impossible, however, to extract a detailed history of Magellan's expedition. Pigafetta thus remains the most important source, though he deliberately avoided telling the full story of some of Magellan's difficulties with Juan de Cartagena and other Spanish officers. As a neutral Italian, Pigafetta tactfully refrained, though always loyal to Magellan, from bearing witness to the disloyalty of the Spaniards to their Portuguese commander and comrades.

It is therefore through the eyes of Pigafetta that we must visualize almost all that is known of the last three years of Magellan's life, narrated in the Italian's *Journal* with more continuity and in greater detail than the events of the many years that Magellan had lived before setting out from Seville, in his native Portugal, in Africa, India and further East, then in Portugal and Morocco and finally in Spain. How had Antonio Pigafetta come to embark on this expedition with Magellan? Who was this young Italian *sobresaliente* who is nearly always named, in contemporary documents that refer to Magellan's expedition, merely as Antonio Lombardo, because he was a native of Lombardy?

Though we know that he was a scion of one of the patrician families of Vicenza, no record of his birth has yet been discovered and there is still some doubt about where he should rightly be placed in the genealogical tree of the Pigafetta family, where one finds several of his contemporaries who bear the same Christian name as he. It would appear, however, that he was probably born in 1486, to a father who was named Giovanni, though some scholars claim that he was the son of another Pigafetta, somewhat appropriately named Ulysses.

Around 1519, Antonio Pigafetta appears to have become a knight of the Order of Rhodes, which later became the Order of Malta. He may thus, before joining Magellan, have already fought the Turks in the Eastern Mediterranean; in fact, the arrows of the Brazilian Indians first encountered on Magellan's expedition reminded him of Turkish arrows. In 1523, a year after his return to Italy from Magellan's expedition, he is described by Sanuto, the Venetian diarist, on the occasion of a reception given to Pigafetta by the Republic's

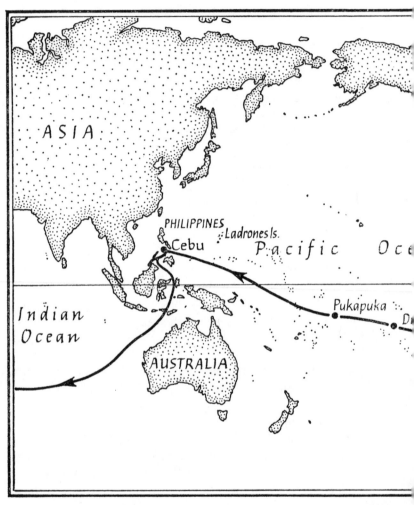

Route of the first voya

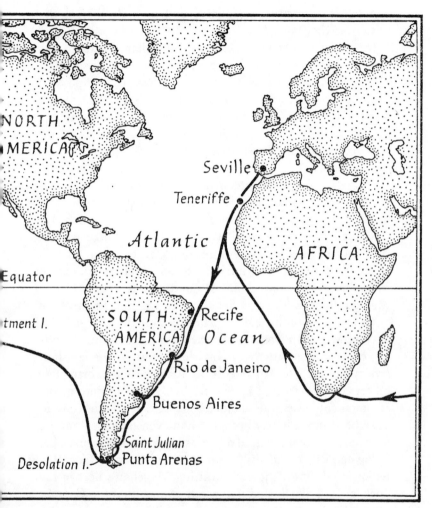

NORTH
AMERICA

Seville

Teneriffe

Atlantic

AFRICA

Equator

tment I.

SOUTH
AMERICA

Recife

Ocean

Rio de Janeiro

Buenos Aires

Saint Julian
Desolation I. Punta Arenas

nd the world

Senate, as a *cavaliere*, or knight, and as a Brother of the Order of Rhodes.

In 1519, when he embarked with Magellan, Pigafetta was still on the personal staff of a prelate of great distinction, Francesco Chiericati of Vicenza, who was then Apostolic Protonotary or Nunzio representing the Holy See at the court of the King of Spain, having previously represented it in England. There is no evidence, however, that Pigafetta had accompanied Chiericati on his earlier diplomatic mission to England.

In Spain, Pigafetta attended the Spanish court in Saragossa, Valladolid and Barcelona. It was in Barcelona that he first heard of the preparations for Magellan's expedition. He was immediately possessed with the desire to take part in such an unprecedented venture and was fortunate enough to obtain, through the Nunzio, letters of recommendation to Magellan. From Barcelona, Pigafetta hastened by sea to Malaga, then overland to Seville, which he reached in June 1519, three months before Magellan finally set sail. In Seville, Magellan was still experiencing difficulty in recruiting enough men, after so many desertions. In the constant rivalry and strife between the Spanish and Portuguese officers of his Armada, he was probably glad to find, at the last moment, a neutral Italian *sobresaliente*. Pigafetta seems to have been immediately accepted and even trusted, from the very start, with confidential duties as Magellan's personal aide.

Pigafetta's *Journal* dismisses in a few lines the lengthy, tedious and difficult job of outfitting Magellan's fleet in the dockyards of Seville and points out at once that the Captain General, from the very start, was unwilling to reveal to his men the course that he intended to take. The vastness of his enterprise, Magellan feared, might well dismay those who might realize what dangers it would entail. Besides, his captains hated and distrusted him: 'I don't know why,' Pigafetta guesses somewhat ingenuously, 'unless it were because he was a Portuguese and they were Spaniards.'

Magellan's order of the day, when his fleet left Seville, provided that his five ships would keep together day and night, and that his own ship would always take the lead at night. The fleet consisted of the *San Antonio*, 120 tons and over fifty men, the *Trinidad*, 110 tons and over sixty men, the *Concepción*, 90 tons and over forty men, the *Victoria*, 85 tons and some forty men, and the *Santiago*, 75 tons and some thirty men. Tonnage was still estimated by the number of 'tuns' or wooden casks of wine that a ship could carry. Such a 'tun' measured approximately 40 cubic feet, so that a ship of 120 tons, such as the *San Antonio*, would be registered, in modern terms, as being of about 145 tons.

Each one of Magellan's five *naos* had a single main deck leading up to a high forecastle at the prow and a similar sterncastle at the aft. Officers, *sobresalientes* and crew had very little space for their living-quarters and personal effects. Each ship carried a cargo of goods for sale or barter and ample stores for maintenance in addition to food, water and ammunition. Its stores of food often included livestock to be slaughtered for supplies of fresh meat, and the ships were always infested with rats. When the storage-space below deck was fully occupied by cargo, munitions and supplies for a long voyage, the crew could stow their sea-chests and other belongings only on the open deck, in the low waist of the ship between forecastle and sterncastle, which offered practically no protection from spray. In a storm, members of the crew who were not kept busy on deck could seek shelter in any available space in the storage rooms of the forecastle or, below the main deck, in a low-ceilinged gun deck, a kind of shelf that ran around the wide open hatch of the hold, which always contained bilge-water, either drained from the decks, which were easily washed by waves, especially when the ship was heavily loaded, or else accumulating from leakages in the ship's timbers, which had to be inspected constantly and kept watertight by frequent applications of pitch.

Magellan's order of the day included instructions concerning the lights or signals which would be used to communicate from one ship to another. At night, his own ship would display at its poop a large wooden torch, called a *farol*, which meant that the four other ships should follow him. Another light was a lantern; a third one was a wick of sparta-grass, soaked and beaten in water, then dried in the sun or smoked. Magellan's four other ships were to answer these signals, which varied according to the weather, so that he would know that they were all following him.

If he showed one other light, in addition to his torch or *farol*, the ships were to veer or correct their course, when the wind was not favourable; if he showed three lights, they were to lower their bonnet sail, a small supplementary sail which was fastened below the mainsail if the weather was suitable for sailing faster. The bonnet sail was always lowered in order to be able to furl the mainsail more easily in a sudden squall. If he showed four lights, they were to strike all the sails; after that, if he again signalled with only one light, it would mean that his own ship was standing still.

If he showed a greater number of lights or fired a mortar, it meant that he had sighted land or shoals. After this, four lights meant that he wished to have all sails set full, so that the other ships would follow in the wake of his torch or *farol*. If, after showing two lights to alter their course, he then showed one light, this meant that he wished to know whether the four other ships were following him, so that each one of them would now have to reply by also showing one light.

Magellan concluded his order of the day with instructions for three nightly watches: one at the beginning of the night, followed by a midnight watch, then by a third for the end of the night. All the men of each ship were thus divided into three shifts. The first shift was under the direct orders of the captain or his boatswain, who took night-duty in turns; the second, under the pilot or the boatswain's mate; the third, under the master.

Such an order of the day was not at all unusual. Because no navy yet had official articles of war or other rules or discipline, it was left to each commander to formulate his own and make them known to his officers and crews when they first set sail.

At last, on Monday morning of Saint Lawrence's day, August 10 1519, Magellan's fleet sailed from Seville, down the Guadalquivir towards the river's estuary. According to Pigafetta, there were 237 men aboard the five ships, 'counting those of every nationality'; other contemporary documents quote other figures, but never much larger or much smaller. 'Discharging many pieces of artillery', they held their forestaysails to the wind and sailed majestically but cautiously downstream, past the village of San Juan de Alfaraje, once an important settlement where the Moors had built a bridge across the river. Later, this bridge had been destroyed, but two of its columns still subsisted in midstream, beneath the water; pilots who knew the location of these columns were needed, to avoid striking them. They had to be passed when the estuary's tide was at its highest.

Further downstream, they sailed past Coria and other villages, till they reached the castle of the Duke of Medina Sidonia in San Lúcar de Barrameda, the maritime harbour of Seville. There they stopped until September 20, to obtain supplies which they had apparently failed to find in Seville.

Every day, they went ashore to hear Mass in the church of Our Lady of Barrameda. Before their departure from San Lúcar de Barrameda, Magellan required that all his men should confess; as if this were a vigil preceding a Crusade, he further forbade that any women be allowed aboard his five ships while they stood in San Lúcar.

When they sailed from San Lúcar, on Tuesday September 20 1519, they set their course by the south-west wind known in Spanish as the *garbín*, from the Arabic *gharb*, meaning 'west'. By September 26, they had already reached Tenerife, in the Canary Isles, which were a Spanish possession. They stopped there three and a half days, to obtain fresh supplies of water, meat and timber, after which they stopped again two days in Monte Rosso, on the same island, to replenish their supply of pitch.

The Portuguese historian Corrêa reports, in his *Lêndas da Índia*, written a few decades later, that, while Magellan was still in the Canary Isles, another Spanish vessel caught up with him, bringing him letters from his father-in-law, Diogo Barbosa. These warned Magellan that his Spanish captains had boasted to their friends and relations in Seville that they intended to mutiny and murder him, should he happen to rouse their anger. Corrêa also states that Magellan wrote back to Barbosa that he would give his captains no reason to carry out their threats. Whether good or bad, they had not been appointed by himself, but by the factor of the *Casa de Contratación*, and he could be relied upon to serve King Charles faithfully. Later, still according to Corrêa, Barbosa showed this reply to the directors of the *Casa*, who were pleased with it and praised Magellan. But Magellan meanwhile set sail from the Canary Isles, quite unperturbed, at midnight on Monday October 3.

Later historians suggest that Magellan experienced his

first open conflict with Juan de Cartagena and his two other Spanish captains soon after his fleet had sailed from the Canary Isles. Cartagena then appears to have questioned Magellan's course, suspecting him of planning to betray Spain's interests by sailing too close to the African coast, which was dotted with Portuguese forts and factories, or to the Cape Verde Islands, already Portuguese territory. But Magellan replied that their orders were to follow his flag by day and his *farol* by night; they had to obey him, for the time being.

Pigafetta reports that they sailed between Cape Verde and the islands that bear the same name, though without sighting either, then followed the coast of Africa as far south as Sierra Leone before striking west, across the Atlantic, to the coast of Brazil, which was also Portuguese. They may even have landed somewhere on the African coast of what was then called Guinea: one of Magellan's many biographers states that he tried and executed, off the African coast, a Genoese member of the crew of the *Victoria* who had been caught in the act of sodomy. The laws of most Christian nations, in those days, required the death-penalty for both parties to this act, if they both happened to be human and Christian. Because only one was condemned and executed in the present case, the other party to the act must have been an animal, a Moslem or a heathen African. But this incident, as well as Magellan's first open conflict with Juan de Cartagena and his other Spanish captains, remains obscure.

Magellan had to rely, for his course across the Atlantic, mainly on his knowledge of Portuguese charts of the recently discovered route to Brazil. He was therefore in considerable danger of encountering a Portuguese fleet, since there was already a brisk trade between Brazil and Lisbon in brazil-wood, from which a valuable red dye was obtained. King Manuel appears moreover to have sent out a fleet to intercept

Magellan, so that the latter had to waste three weeks in a game of hide and seek, deliberately sailing into the doldrums, an area of dead calm off the African coast, where the Portuguese would scarcely expect to find him.

During the storms experienced shortly before crossing the Equator, Magellan's men were often dazzled and comforted by the curious meteorological phenomena known as 'Saint Elmo's Fire' or 'The Holy Body', after a fourth-century Italian bishop and martyr, Saint Anselm or Saint Elmo, who had become the patron saint of sailors. Produced by humidity of the air, these fires are small electrical flames that leap around the mast-heads of ships. They were long believed by sailors to have been sent by the saint in order to assure them of his protection and announce the approaching end of the storm. Sometimes, on a three-master, there would appear three lights, one on each of the three mast-heads. They were then known as the Fires of Saint Anselm or Elmo, of Saint Claire and of Saint Nicholas. In antiquity, they had been known as the fires of Castor and Pollux.

Pigafetta reports that these fires 'appeared to us many times, among other times on a very dark night, in such splendour, like a blazing torch, at the top of the mainmast, and stood there some two hours or more with us, consoling us in our lamentations. When that blessed light wished to leave us, so dazzling was its brightness in our eyes, that we all remained for more than an eighth of an hour quite blinded and crying out for mercy, truly believing that we were dead. Suddenly, the sea became calm.'

Magellan had required, though not in his original order of the day and perhaps only after he had received Diogo Barbosa's warning in Tenerife, that every evening, before nightfall, the four other ships of his fleet should, in turn, come up close to his own, which stood still. Each captain

156

was then expected, according to a custom that appears to have been generally accepted in those days in the Spanish fleet, to greet the *Trinidad*: '*Dios vos salve, Señor Capitán General y Maestro, y buena compañía*'. If weather permitted, they were to confer with Magellan aboard the *Trinidad*, so as to report to him the day's incidents and receive his instructions for the morrow. Never did Magellan reveal to them the full course that he planned to follow.

It was most probably somewhere between Cape Verde and Sierra Leone that Juan de Cartagena, whose title of *veedor* signified that he must watch over the King of Spain's interests, first became suspicious of Magellan's course, because he was still steering south and dangerously close to the Portuguese possessions, instead of striking out due west across the Atlantic. To his anxious questions, Magellan gave no satisfactory reply, simply reminding all his captains of his original order of the day and of their duty to follow his flag by day and his *farol* by night.

Nothing further happened for the time being, though Juan de Cartagena may well have felt that he had been treated like a schoolboy and openly insulted in the presence of his peers or even his subordinates. One evening, however, some time later in mid-Atlantic, the *San Antonio* moved close up to the *Trinidad*. But the usual greetings were not uttered by Juan de Cartagena. Instead, he had delegated his quartermaster to report to Magellan, instructing him to greet Magellan only as '*Capitán y maestro*', not as '*Capitán general y maestro*'. This could only mean that Juan de Cartagena, as *veedor* or representative of his monarch's interests, no longer wished to recognize Magellan as his commanding admiral.

Magellan reacted to this affront by demanding that Juan de Cartagena salute him, in the presence of all his brother officers, as Captain General. The obstinate Spaniard replied that he had already sent the best of his men to bring his greetings to Magellan who, if he were not content, might prefer to be greeted by one of his page-boys! After this, instead of following Magellan's *farol*, Juan de Cartagena's *San Antonio* began to cruise on its own, sometimes circling the four other ships as if to taunt them, sometimes losing sight of them for a while and then catching up in a playful manner.

In such a crisis, which threatened to undermine his authority, Magellan needed to strike a blow that would reaffirm it fully. It is perhaps at this point chronologically that we must place the mysterious trial and execution of a crew member of the *Victoria* accused of sodomy. Solemnly, aboard the *Trinidad*, the culprit was to be tried in the presence of all five captains. The four other captains, when thus summoned by Magellan, may have interpreted this decision as marking a change in Magellan's policy of never consulting them.

Little is known of what actually happened when the five met aboard the *Trinidad*. Did Juan de Cartagena again question Magellan about the course he had chosen? Did Magellan again refuse to offer any explanation? Certainly, hard words were exchanged, and Magellan suddenly ordered his *alguazil* or provost marshal to arrest the *veedor*. The others were all taken by surprise. The *alguazil* was about to lead his prisoner to some tiny rat-infested cabin in the ship's hold, when Luis de Mendoza plucked up courage to request that he himself be allowed, on his word of honour, to watch over the captive *veedor*, night and day.

Magellan accepted this offer. In the presence of the other officers, Luis de Mendoza swore that he would keep his prisoner always at Magellan's disposal. That same evening, Antonio de Coca, a Spaniard, was already acting as captain aboard the *San Antonio*, and thereafter greeted Magellan in the proper manner.

VI

First Contacts with Americans: A bucolic interlude

Magellan's five ships first sighted the coast of Brazil near Pernambuco on November 29. But they landed only on December 13, Saint Lucy's day, probably near the future site of Rio de Janeiro. There Pigafetta relates that they took on ample supplies of poultry, sweet potatoes, 'very sweet pines' which appear to have been pineapples, as well as the meat of the tapir 'which tastes like beef', sugar-cane and other victuals. 'For a fish-hook or a knife', the natives, who had no knowledge of metals, would gladly offer five or six hens; 'for a comb, a brace of ganders; for a mirror or a pair of scissors, enough fish to feed ten men; for a bell or a sail needle, a whole basket of sweet potatoes, which taste like chestnuts and are as long as turnips'; for a king of diamonds from a pack of playing-cards, six hens, 'and felt they had thereby cheated you'.

When the Sun was at its Zenith, Magellan's men found the climate warmer here than on the Equator, though they were now, according to Pigafetta's erroneous reckoning, twenty-three and a half degrees north of the Antarctic Pole.

Brazil offered Pigafetta his first opportunity to reveal his gifts of observation as an anthropologist. Its natives, he points out, are not Christians, worship nothing at all and live according to the mere rules of nature. They can attain the age of one hundred and twenty-five or even one hundred and forty years; concerning their reputed longevity, he shared a belief widely accepted in his age. Both men and women went naked and all lived 'in certain long houses, which they call *booi*, and sleep in cotton nets which they call hammocks', fastened by each end, in these houses, to thick beams. Between these beams, they built their fires on the ground. In each one of their long houses, as many as a hundred men might live with their wives and children, all making a great deal of noise. They also carved their boats, 'which they call canoes', out of a single tree trunk with the use of stone axes, and 'employ stones as we do iron, since they have no iron'. As many as thirty or forty men could man a canoe, which they paddled 'with oars like fire irons'. Black, naked and hairless as their bodies were, they looked, when they paddled, like the inhabitants of the Stygian marshes of Inferno.

In these few lines of his *Journal*, Pigafetta was one of the first Europeans to describe in writing a sweet potato, indigenous to the Americas, as well as to make observations on some of the customs of a people still living in the Stone Age. He may also have been the first to use two American Indian words adopted later by most European languages: *hammock* and *canoe*.

The Brazilian Indians, he points out, 'are made male and female as we are, but eat the human flesh of their enemies, not because it tastes good to them, but because of a certain custom'. He fails to note, however, the high frequency of homosexuality among them, though this was widely observed and discussed only a few decades later by the horrified Catholic missionaries who first attempted to convert them to Christianity. On the subject of their cannibalism, Pigafetta proves, however, to be one of the first Europeans to understand its ritualistic rather than utilitarian nature. He attributes its origins to a legend related to him by João de Carvalho, the Portuguese pilot of the *Concepción* who had already spent four years in Brazil, some ten years earlier with João de Lisboa's expedition, and had even left there a son by a native Brazilian wife or concubine. Carvalho now chanced to meet his half-Indian son, who joined his father and remained, until they reached Borneo, with Magellan's expedition.

Pigafetta goes on to describe how the naked Indians, whether men or women, 'paint the whole body and the face in a wonderful manner with fire in various designs'. The men pluck their hairs and are beardless. When they dress, they adorn themselves with clothes fashioned of the feathers of parrots, with great wheels, made of the longer plumes, set around their buttocks, giving them a very comical appearance. Nearly all the men, but not the women and the children, have three holes pierced in the lower lip so as to adorn themselves with round stones, about one finger in length, which hang on their chins.

They are not entirely black, but of a dark olive colour, and do not cover their private parts, their whole body being naked and hairless. They call their chief a *cacique*, an American Indian word which the Spaniards and Portuguese soon adopted; even now, in the Portuguese colonies of Africa and of Timor, in distant Indonesia, the native chief of African and Indonesian villages are officially called *caciques*.

The natives of Brazil 'have an infinite number of parrots and gave us eight or ten of them for a mirror'. In Europe, parrots were still very rare pets which could be seen only in the most luxurious palaces. Pigafetta also notes that the Indians have 'the most lovely little yellow cats that look like lions', an animal which his later editors and commentators cannot agree to identify.

The Indians make round loaves of white bread 'from the marrow of certain trees', which does not taste very good, looks like fresh cheese and is found between the bark and the timber; Pigafetta is presumably describing here some kind of sago. He then goes on to describe a species of swine, now known as the peccary, 'which have their navel on their back', actually a scent gland under an opening in the skin on the ridge of the spine.

For an axe or a knife, the Brazilian natives would willingly sell one or two of their daughters as slaves, but on no account would they agree to sell their wives, who were all scrupulously faithful to their husbands, though they were reported never to have intercourse with them by day and only by night.

During the daytime, the women work outside the village and bring in their crops from the hills in baskets balanced on their heads, or slung on their backs with a line over the head. They go always accompanied by their husband, who is armed with a bow of brazilwood or black palmwood and a quiver full of cane arrows, because these husbands are all jealous. The women also carry their infants slung from their necks in a cotton net.

Magellan's crew celebrated Mass twice on shore among the natives, many of whom attended it on their knees 'with so great contrition and with clasped hands raised aloft', which 'was a very great pleasure to behold'. They built a house for Magellan and his men, expecting them to stay there for some time. When they saw that Magellan was about to leave, they cut a great quantity of brazilwood and gave it to him, knowing that this was the chief article of trade that Europeans already sought in that area.

Because they had remained some two months in drought and saw rain soon after Magellan's arrival, the Indians believed that the Europeans came from the sky and had brought the rain. Pigafetta concludes that they 'could be easily converted to the faith of Jesus Christ' and goes on to relate two anecdotes that reveal the simplicity of their minds.

At first, because they had seen the small boats lowered from the Spanish ships, the Indians thought that the latter were giving birth to them and later, when the boats were lying alongside the ships as if suckling, were nursing them. One one occasion, an attractive native girl came aboard Magellan's ship, perhaps only in search of adventure. She glanced in the direction of the master's cabin and saw there a nail of more than a finger's length. She took it and very adroitly and coquettishly inserted it 'through the lips of her nature'; after which she went off, bending forward to conceal the theft from Pigafetta and Magellan, who watched her with amusement. This is the only occasion when Magellan is recorded by an eye-witness to have been amused.

Magellan and his men spent thirteen days at the point of first landing, after which they sailed south to the Plata estuary, where, by a river of fresh water, they found 'men called cannibals and who eat human flesh'. One of these, 'tall as a giant', came to the flagship to make sure that the others could also come safely; 'he had a voice like a bull'.

While this giant was aboard Magellan's ship, his companions gathered up their possessions and fled inland, probably because they feared reprisals for having captured and eaten Juan de Solis and sixty of his men a few years earlier. Seeing them flee, Magellan landed a hundred men to try to palaver with them or to capture one by force. But they fled with such great strides 'that we, although running, could not catch up with them'.

In the Plata estuary, Magellan discovered seven small islands, on the largest of which precious stones could be found. This was near the headland earlier explorers had called Cape Saint Mary and beyond which they believed a passage might lead to the Pacific, though no ship was known to have sailed beyond this point. Magellan explored the whole estuary, until he found that its waters were no longer tidal or brackish but already fresh, at which point he knew that he was in the mouth of a river and not, as he had hoped, in a strait.

Sailing further south along the coasts of what is now Argentina towards the Antarctic Pole, he discovered, around the 47th latitude south, islands densely peopled with penguins and seals, which Pigafetta describes and calls 'geese and sea-wolves'. Magellan's men killed and ate a great quantity of penguins. Towards the end of February they suffered a great storm, in the course of which they were comforted by appearances of the 'three Holy Bodies', Saint Anselm, Saint Nicholas and Santa Clara, in the form of electrical discharges of lights around their mast-heads.

When they reached the 49th latitude south of the Equator, 'because it was winter, our ships entered a good haven' to spend the winter there. They called this haven Saint Julian and remained there from March until August 1520, five months in all, for the first two months 'without seeing a single soul'. Then one day there appeared a Patagonian Indian, 'of the stature of a giant', who stood there naked, by the shore of the haven, dancing, singing and casting dust on his head. Magellan sent a man ashore, ordering him to mimic the native's actions as a sign of peaceful intentions, after which the Patagonian was brought by boat to a small island where Magellan had established his winter quarters. There the giant expressed great astonishment and, raising a finger to the sky, communicated his belief that Magellan and his men must have come from there.

He was so tall 'that we reached only up to his waist', but he was well proportioned. He had a huge face, painted red, but with yellow around the eyes and two hearts delineated in the middle of his cheeks. His scanty hair was dyed white. His clothing consisted of the skins of beasts, very cunningly sewn together. These beasts have 'a head and ears as big as a mule's, the neck and body like a camel's, the legs of a deer and the tail of a horse; they also neigh like a horse and are very numerous in that land'—which adds up to a fairly exact description of the guanaco, a ruminant similar to the llama.

The Patagonian giant's feet were shod in stockings of the same animal's skin, covering them like shoes; in one hand, he carried a short but thick bow with a cord somewhat thicker than that of a lute, made of the gut of the same animal, and he also had a bundle of short arrows of cane, 'feathered like ours'. Instead of iron heads, these arrows were pointed with black and white flints, fashioned by means of another stone, 'in the manner of Turkish arrows'.

Magellan ordered food and drink for his Indian guest and showed him, among other things, a large steel mirror. When the giant saw his own face reflected, he was overcome with fear and jumped back, 'throwing three or four of our men to the ground'. Then Magellan gave the giant some bells, a mirror, a comb and a few rosaries, and sent him ashore in the company of four of his own men. One of the giant's companions, who had not dared come aboard, saw him return with these Europeans and ran off to fetch more of the natives, who came naked and in single file to meet the strangers. As soon as Magellan's men joined them, they began to dance, raising one finger to the sky and offering a white powder, which they made from the roots of a vegetable and kept in earthenware pots to eat when they lacked anything else. Magellan's men made them understand by signs that they were to come aboard the ships and that they themselves would help them carry their possessions; but the Indians merely picked up their bows, leaving their women, loaded like asses, to carry the rest.

These women, Pigafetta notes, were not as tall as the men, but very much fatter: 'when we saw them, we were greatly astounded'. Their breasts hung very low and were half an arm's length, and they were painted and dressed, if at all, exactly like their husbands, except that they wore a small piece of animals' fur to cover 'their natural parts'. They were leading four small guanacos, harnessed with thongs like a halter. Pigafetta relates that the Patagonian Indians, when they wish to catch a wild guanaco, tie one of its young to a thornbush; the big ones then come to play with it, so that the Indians, who are lying in wait, can shoot them with their arrows. Magellan's crews led eighteen native men and women to the ships and set them to work on both shores of the harbour to catch guanacos for them.

Before a party of Magellan's men, sent ashore to collect firewood, another giant appeared six days later, painted and dressed like the others and likewise armed with bow and arrow. Approaching the strangers, he first touched his own head, face and body, then did the same to them, after which he raised his hands to the sky. Informed of all this, Magellan ordered his men to bring him this new giant in a small rowboat; and the giant was brought to the islet in the harbour where Magellan's men had built, as their winter quarters, a house for their smiths and for the storage of supplies unloaded from the ships.

The new giant was even taller and better proportioned

than the others and as tractable and friendly. He jumped up and down as he danced and, at every leap, his feet sank a palm's breadth in the earth. He remained many days with his new friends, long enough for them to baptize him and name him John. He could pronounce the words Jesus, *Pater Noster, Ave Maria* and his own name 'as clearly as we', but with a truly stentorian voice. Magellan gave him a shirt, a cloth jerkin, cloth breeches, a cap, a mirror, a comb and other gifts before sending him back to his people. He went his way quite happy and content and, the next day, returned with a live guanaco, which he gave to Magellan, obtaining many more gifts in return, so that he might bring other such animals. But that was the last they saw of him; they even feared that he might have been killed, for having conversed with them, by other giants of his tribe.

A fortnight later, presumably in June 1520, Magellan's men sighted four more giants who were unarmed, having concealed their weapons in the thornbushes, as the two they later captured revealed. Magellan decided to capture two of them, the youngest and best proportioned, and take them back to Spain. The men of his age indeed felt no moral qualms about thus kidnapping exotic human specimens to display at home, much as we might bring mere artifacts as souvenirs of our travels. The courts of the Portuguese and Spanish monarchs were particularly well provided with odd or rare human specimens, such as the monsters whom Velasquez later depicted.

To succeed, Magellan had to use trickery; for the Patagonians might easily have killed one of his men. He therefore deceived them by first giving them many knives, scissors, mirrors, bells and glass beads. When they had their hands full of gifts, he had two pairs of iron fetters brought to him, of the kind that were generally fastened to a prisoner's ankles, and made as if he would give them as presents. Because they were of metal, the fetters delighted the Indians, but they did not know how to carry them and were sorry to leave them behind as they had no place to put so many gifts and needed to use their hands to hold their robes of skins wrapped around them. Magellan would not allow the other two giants to help them. Instead, he offered by signs to have the fetters fitted to the ankles of those whom he had chosen to capture, so that they would be able to carry them away. They nodded assent and Magellan immediately had them both fettered at the same time. Only when the crossbolts were being driven home did the captive giants begin to suspect a trick; but Magellan reassured them and they stood still.

Later, when they realized that they had been tricked, they raged like bulls, calling aloud upon Setebos, their god, to come to their aid. Only with great difficulty were Magellan's men able to bind the hands of the other two Indians and bring them ashore with a party of nine sailors, whom they then guided to the wife of one of the two captives, because her young husband had expressed by signs his great grief at being parted from her. On their way, one of the Indians managed to free his hands and escape, running off with such speed that his captors soon lost sight of him. He went where his companions had been, but failed to find the one he had left there with the women, so he wandered off to seek him and tell him what had happened. Meanwhile the other Indian captive, whose hands were still bound, continued to do his best to free himself. To prevent this, his captors struck him and wounded him on the head, which angered him very much; nevertheless, he led them where the women were waiting. João Carvalho, who was in charge of the party, decided not to bring back to the ships the wife of the captive whom they had left there in fetters, because it was already too late in the day. Instead, he decided to spend the night there, presumably to try his luck with the native women.

Meanwhile, the giant who had managed to free his hands returned with another. Seeing their companion with a head-wound, they said nothing for the time being, but the next morning spoke to the women in their own language, after which they all ran away, the smaller ones running even faster than the big ones, though leaving all their belongings. From a distance, two of the giants began shooting arrows at the party of Europeans, one of whom was wounded in the thigh and died on the spot. Seeing that he was dead, the Indians fled.

Though armed with crossbows and flintlocks, the Europeans were never able to strike any of the Patagonian giants because, in combat, the latter were constantly leaping and dodging aim. Magellan's men therefore buried their dead companion and set fire to the goods the Indians had left behind. Pigafetta remarks here that the Patagonians run faster than a horse and are very jealous of their wives; this last remark may well have been suggested to him by their reactions to Carvalho's attempts to seduce their women.

Pigafetta goes on to describe many beliefs and customs of the Patagonians. When they are sick, instead of taking any medicine, they swallow an arrow that is about two feet long and then vomit bile mixed with blood. This bile is green because they sometimes eat thistles. If they have a headache, they cut a gash across their brow, and other wounds in their arms and legs, so as to draw blood from several different parts of the body. One of the two Patagonians whom they captured explained later to Pigafetta, on whose ship he was kept prisoner, that the blood was unwilling to remain in any part of the body where one felt pain.

The Patagonians cut their hair, tonsured after the fashion of Catholic clergy, but not so short. Around their brow, they wear a string of cotton behind which they tuck their arrows when they go out hunting. Because of the great cold, they bind their penis close to their body. When one of them dies, ten or twelve of them appear disguised as demons and dance merrily around the corpse. The chief among their gods or demons is called Setebos; they call the other demons Cheleulle. In sign-language, the captive Patagonian explained to Pigafetta that he had actually seen demons, with two horns on their heads, long hair covering their body down to their feet, and breathing and farting fire!

Magellan himself coined the name whereby these Indians and their native land are still known: 'Patagonians' and 'Patagonia' are words derived from a Portuguese slang expression for a man who has huge feet. They may have earned this name from the animal skins that they wrapped round their feet, so that these appeared even larger than they were. Pigafetta points out, in conclusion, that they wear only the skins of the guanaco, are nomads like European gypsies and have no houses, only tents made of guanaco skins that they carry with them in their wanderings, and that they eat raw meat and a sweet root that they call *chapal*. The two giants who had been captured could eat a whole basket of ship's biscuit at a single sitting and drink half a bucket of water in a single draft. They even ate the ship's rats, skin and all.

Though Pigafetta lived in an age that had no generally accepted phonetic alphabet for notations of this kind, his vocabulary of close on a hundred words of the language of the Patagonian Indians includes ten which have been identi-fied by modern scholars as still being used four centuries later by the Tcheulchi tribe. He compiled his vocabulary while conversing with the captive giant aboard his ship: 'When he saw me write down these words', for bread and water, 'asking him pen in hand for other words, he understood me. Once I made a Cross, showed it to him and kissed it. Suddenly, he cried out *Setebos* and explained to me by signs that, if I made a Cross again, *Setebos* would enter my body and make it burst. Later, when he was ill, he asked for a Cross and embraced and kissed it fervently. He wanted to become a Christian before dying. We called him Paul. When these people want to kindle a fire, they rub a pointed stick against another piece of wood until the fire catches in a certain pith, between the two sticks.' Pigafetta's observations of the customs, language and beliefs of the Indians of Brazil and Patagonia are among Western man's earliest attempts to describe objectively an entirely alien and much more primitive society. In many respects, this young Italian humanist was thus one of the unconscious founders of the modern science of cultural anthropology.

VII

Misgivings and Mutinies

Pigafetta's *Journal* devotes more attention to descriptions of encounters with the Indians of Brazil and with Patagonian giants than to any other aspect of the life of Magellan's men during their first months in the Southern hemisphere. He thus misleads his readers into believing that this part of their expedition remained in other respects relatively uneventful. But it was in the Bay of Saint Julian, while they were wintering there, that Magellan's Spanish captains finally mutinied against him.

The accounts of their mutiny are confused and contradictory. Pigafetta reports briefly that the captains of all four ships mutinied. From other sources we know that the captain of the *Santiago* remained neutral. Even the available log-books of Magellan's pilots fail to agree on the length of the fleet's stay in the Bay of Saint Julian, though it seems likely that it wintered there from the end of March to the last week of August. Nor can one reliably reconstruct the actual events of the mutiny from reading these log-books.

Most of Magellan's biographers have moreover neglected to interpret the valuable evidence contained in the third volume or 'Decade' of the *Asia* of João de Barros. A relative of Duarte de Resende, who was Portuguese factor in Ternate, in the Moluccas, when the *Trinidad* returned there much later and its crew was arrested, João de Barros had access to documents found by Resende aboard the *Trinidad*, including the journal and other papers, now lost, of Magellan's astronomer, Andrés de San Martín. Barros quoted from them extensively in his account of Magellan's expedition.

San Martín apparently began to have misgivings about Magellan's course when the fleet was still in the Bay of Rio de Janeiro. Somehow, his astronomical observations no longer tallied with what the tables of the famous astronomer Regiomontanus, which he consulted daily, led him to expect. As the fleet progressed further south, his observations became increasingly divergent from those predicted in these otherwise reliable tables. Were there misprints in the tables? They had been printed by a reputable printer and San Martín could scarcely believe it. Diligently, he noted his observations and his misgivings.

No astronomer had yet voyaged so far south or made astronomical observations of this kind so close to the Antarctic Pole. Based on a meridian that passes through Seville, San Martín's observations could not possibly tally with those of contemporary tables because all the astronomers of his age, like all the geographers, still believed the world to be a smaller sphere than it is. Since it is a sphere, its circumference along every meridian that passes through both poles must necessarily be equal to its circumference at the Equator. Because contemporary estimates of this latter circumference were too small, those of the Earth's circumference along any meridian were just as inaccurate. The astronomical tables of Regiomontanus, like those of Zacuto and all other mediaeval and Renaissance astronomers, were founded moreover on a Ptolemaic theory of concentric heavenly spheres, representing the orbits of the Moon, the Sun and the visible planets, with the Earth itself as the innermost sphere and centre of the whole system. On the basis of a great number of astronomical observations of recurrent phenomena made over several centuries, mainly in Mediterranean Europe and North Africa, tables predicting the positions of a number of heavenly bodies for every day of the year and for as many as four years ahead had been worked out by mathematicians and astronomers. San Martín checked his own daily observations against these tables in order to estimate the fleet's position in terms of latitude from the Equator and longitude from the Seville meridian. San Martín's tables thus told him where he should expect to see his guiding heavenly bodies throughout the year, if the Earth were truly as small as Regiomontanus and other mathematical geographers believed and if San Martín were now as close to the Antarctic Pole as his whole system erroneously led him to believe.

But the sphere of the Earth was larger and the divergence between these tables and San Martín's observations increased daily as Magellan's fleet sailed further away from the area where Regiomontanus and other reputable astronomers had made their observations. Because his angle of observation was no longer where the authors of his tables led him to expect, San Martín therefore kept on noting changes of degree which puzzled him so much that he soon gave up astronomy and fell back on astrology.

João de Barros reports that San Martín communicated his misgivings to Magellan and his other companions. The Spanish captains were worried in any case, even before they reached the Bay of Saint Julian, by the increasing roughness of the seas. To their objections, Magellan replied that the seas around Iceland and Norway are as easily navigable in summer as those around Spain. Here in the Southern hemisphere, one had every reason to expect the same seasonal differences in corresponding latitudes. They would therefore winter in a suitable bay and wait for the seas to become more easily navigable in summer.

But they were further from the Antarctic Pole than they believed and they no longer knew where they really were. Even Magellan had begun to lose faith in Ruy Faleiro's astronomical system of estimating longitudes by means of tables based on the Ptolemaic system of astronomy and on an incorrect estimate of the Earth's circumference both at the Equator and along any meridian. From now on and until he finally reached the Philippines, Magellan consulted San Martín more and more often to find out where they were. In his perplexity, the astronomer gave him replies that were only astrological predictions, since astronomy had failed him. But the astronomer's perplexity was shared by all the Spanish officers of Magellan's fleet. Were they being led by a madman or a traitor? João de Barros quotes a rumour, prevalent among the Spaniards, that Magellan planned to lose them all and then, with his few surviving Portuguese officers and men aboard his flagship, to return to Portugal and make his peace with King Manuel.

The frightened Spanish officers therefore mutinied, on the night of Easter Sunday, the first day of April 1520. Magellan had become increasingly taciturn and uncommunicative, perhaps to conceal his own perplexity and misgivings. To the questions and objections of his officers, he had long ceased to give satisfactory replies, either remaining silent or answering them in a dogmatic and schoolmasterly manner, as if they were ignorant children. His argument about the seas around Iceland and Norway might well seem logical, but any experienced sailor knows that one cannot extrapolate knowledge of weather conditions, winds and currents as freely as that; what one observes in a given area of the Northern hemisphere need not be true of the corresponding area of the Southern hemisphere. Now that they had lost confidence in Magellan, San Martín's perplexities, which he certainly discussed with the pilots and other officers who had some experience of navigating by the stars, could only increase their general distrust of Magellan's whole venture.

But it was from now on that Magellan, in the face of such odds, proved to be a man of truly unusual qualities. The enormity of his basic misconception, founded on a tangle of geographical misinformation and fallacies which were common to his age, now began slowly to dawn on him. First, he had failed to find a strait where he expected it to be; now, he discovered that America continued to extend into what he had expected would be the Antarctic region. (Later, the Pacific Ocean proved to be several thousand miles broader than he believed it to be.) Throughout the last months of his life, Magellan suffered disappointments and hardships that might have broken any less tenacious man. In spite of everything, he stuck to his purpose, to reach the Far East from the West. With the exception of Pigafetta, who watched him with admiration, and perhaps a couple of his more loyal Portuguese friends, Magellan was the only man of his whole fleet who never yielded to despair.

Antonio de Coca, the Spaniard whom Magellan had appointed captain of the *San Antonio* in Juan de Cartagena's stead, had now been replaced, perhaps while the fleet was still in Rio de Janeiro, by Álvaro de Mesquita, a Portuguese officer who is reported to have been a relative of Magellan, perhaps even his first cousin. Magellan's excuse for this change of command was that Antonio de Coca's responsibilities as *contador*, accountant or paymaster of the fleet, conflicted with his new duties as captain of a ship. In addition, Juan de Cartagena, still a prisoner, was no longer entrusted to Luis de Mendoza, another Spaniard, but to Gaspar de

Quesada, captain of the *Concepción* and Bishop Fonseca's personal protégé.

The increasing inclemency of the weather, as they sailed south from Rio de Janeiro into the Antarctic winter, their repeated disappointments as they searched for a passage that might lead to the Pacific, the uncertainty of their future course and Magellan's own taciturn and dogged manner, all these exerted great pressures on the morale and patience of his officers and crews.

Magellan himself must have soon realized how worthless was the information on which he and Faleiro had founded their hopes of finding the strait which would lead to the Pacific. Yet he refused to admit defeat and, in spite of what he had said in Valladolid to Bishop Las Casas, no longer mentioned his alternative plan of turning back across the Atlantic and following the Portuguese course to the Indies, round the Cape of Good Hope. Obstinately, he insisted on pursuing his course further south, perhaps only because of the excitement of always discovering new lands and seas that he was the first European explorer to view and chart, but perhaps also because he still believed in the ancient geographical theory that all continents are islands set in one vast surrounding ocean, so that sooner or later he would inevitably find, even in an apparently endless American continent, a point where the Atlantic joined the Pacific beyond it. Magellan also sensed that it would be madness to sail into the Antarctic winter, into blizzards and seas infested with ice-floes. As we have seen, on one of the last days of March, they fortunately discovered another uncharted bay that appeared to be relatively well protected against winds and heavy seas, and in this place, which they called the Bay of Saint Julian, Magellan announced that they would spend the winter. But this half of their expedition had already lasted much longer than he had planned. The rest could be expected to last at least as long, when they would finally find their way into the Pacific, much further south than Magellan had expected, since they would then have to sail that much further north again. Rations must therefore be reduced. Magellan ordered his men to hunt and fish rather than rely on their supplies of ship's biscuit and other stores; their low stores of wine would be distributed to them only on Sundays and holidays.

The bleak landscape, almost on the 50th parallel south, is discouraging: a rocky grey shore rising from equally grey but foam-flecked seas and adorned only with sparse yellow grasses and a few stunted trees that have been tortured and twisted by the vicious winds. There is not a living creature, animal or man, in sight, except sea-birds that utter their lugubrious cries like ominous warnings as they circle round the mastheads.

Easter in 1520 happened also to be April Fool's Day. Magellan invited his four captains to attend an Easter Mass aboard his flagship and to share his table afterwards. But they refrained from accepting his invitation, so that Magellan found himself sharing his meagre fare only with Álvaro de Mesquita and Duarte Barbosa. Darkness falls early in that season in regions so close to the Pole. That night, a couple of row-boats left the *Concepción* silently and approached the *San Antonio*. Juan de Cartagena, the deposed *veedor* of the fleet, had been liberated from custody, and was perhaps in command, accompanied by Quesada, Coca and some thirty armed men, among them a certain Juan Sebastian del Cano, who later became captain of the *Victoria*, after Magellan's death and that of Barbosa and Serrano, and after Carvalho had been deposed. It was del Cano who finally brought the *Victoria* safely back to Seville and on whose testimony rested much of the evidence in the subsequent official enquiry into the mutiny of Saint Julian's Bay and the other questions concerning the fate of Magellan and his missing ships and men.

The mutineers boarded the *San Antonio* without meeting any resistance. Nobody stood watch on its deck, off this deserted coast where they had not yet encountered any natives. Cartagena and Coca made their way to the Captain's cabin and, before he was able to offer resistance, arrested Álvaro de Mesquita and placed him in fetters, together with his pilot Mafra. But the armed men following Cartagena and Coca had failed to muffle the clanking of their armour and weapons, and members of the *San Antonio*'s crew, roused from their sleep, now rushed on deck. The ship's master, Juan de Eloriaga, was their leader; by the faint light of a lantern, he recognized Quesada and challenged his presence aboard the *San Antonio* at this hour. Quesada's only reply was to strike him, according to some witnesses, as many as six times in the breast with a dagger. Eloriaga died on July 15, more than three months later, of the wounds received that night.

All the Portuguese officers and men aboard the *San Antonio* were arrested. To the rest of the crew, an extra ration of biscuit and wine was immediately distributed, to put them in a good mood. The next morning, all five ships were peacefully at anchor in the late grey dawn, as if nothing had happened overnight. How could Magellan guess that Álvaro de Mesquita was no longer in command of the *San Antonio*, but a prisoner replaced by Juan Sebastian del Cano, who had remained aboard together with Quesada, while Cartagena and the rest of the mutineers had returned to the *Concepción*?

Fairly late that morning, Magellan happened to send from his flagship a boat, taking orders to the *San Antonio*. The quartermaster in command was told bluntly that the *San*

Antonio no longer accepted orders from Magellan's flagship, but only from Quesada, now considered to be in command of the whole fleet. The boat then turned back to report the news to Magellan, after first obtaining similar replies from the *Concepción* and the *Victoria*. Only the tiny *Santiago*, captained by Serrano, had remained faithful to Magellan.

But the mutineers were perhaps already afraid of the consequences of their initiative and, in any case, had not yet agreed on how to proceed. Should they attack the *Trinidad*, arrest Magellan and return to Spain with him as their prisoner? Should they still attempt reconciliation? They chose the latter course and, around noon, sent a messenger from the *Concepción*, bearing a letter from Quesada to Magellan. Instead of the ultimatum that the Captain General may well have expected, he found himself reading a respectful and almost humble plea. His mutinous Spanish officers listed their grievances, assured him that they would continue to follow his orders if only he would offer them some satisfaction, and requested that he consult them in future and treat them according to the instructions given him by the King, their common Lord.

Magellan immediately sensed, in Quesada's carefully worded plea, the disunity and indecision it concealed, and decided to act forcefully, though in a manner that would puzzle his adversaries and take them by surprise. First, he arrested the crew of the boat that had brought him Quesada's plea: this already weakened the forces of the mutineers. Then, aboard the same boat, he sent five men commanded by Gonzalo Gonzalez de Espinosa, the *alguazil* or captain of arms of his fleet. Ostensibly, Espinosa bore a written message in his hand. The boat first approached the *San Antonio*, then circled it and proceeded towards the *Victoria*, which lay at anchor further away. The *alguazil*, followed by four of his five men, climbed aboard the *Victoria* and handed Magellan's message to Luis de Mendoza. While Mendoza was reading it smilingly, as later chronicles based on eye-witness reports aver, Espinosa stabbed him with a dagger in the throat and one of Mendoza's sailors struck Espinosa's head. Mendoza fell, but the alarm had been given and the sixty men of his crew rushed to his rescue.

The *alguazil* and his four men were soon surrounded and on the defensive. But Duarte Barbosa, commanding fifteen armed men from Magellan's flagship, had meanwhile approached the *Victoria* in another row-boat, quite un-observed. Clambering aboard, these men now attacked Mendoza's crew from the rear. Not knowing how many attackers might yet join Barbosa's men, the crew of the *Victoria* soon accepted his offer of a full pardon if they surrendered immediately. Barbosa then took command of the ship, ordered the crew to lift anchor, unfurl their sails and prepare their artillery for action. While the officers and men aboard the two other ships of mutineers, the *San Antonio* and the *Concepción*, were still wondering what might have happened aboard the *Victoria*, the latter moved past them and joined the *Santiago* so as effectively to block the entrance to the bay.

Magellan, aboard the *Trinidad*, now found himself in command of three ships, against the mutineers, whose remaining two ships were blocked in the bay and threatened by his artillery. So far from home, the mutineers may well have hesitated, at this point, to engage in a bloody naval battle against their compatriots, with so few chances of success. Yet later accounts affirm that Quesada was found fully armed on the deck of the *San Antonio*, sword in hand and exhorting his frightened men to fight, when a boat from the *Trinidad* came to accept their inevitable surrender.

Magellan was not as ruthless as might have been expected, in the light of the customary naval discipline of his age. The Spanish captains and many of the men of their crews had obviously mutinied. In the legal enquiries subsequently held in Spain, the court decided that forty officers and men had been guilty. Magellan had thus every right to have them tried and executed on the spot. Yet only one mutineer was immediately tried and beheaded, though there is confusion in the various contemporary accounts about the identity of the victim.

It appears likely that Mendoza's corpse, after he had died of wounds, was first taken ashore, drawn and quartered on April 4, while a solemn judgement condemning him post-humously as a mutineer or traitor was read aloud to the assembled officers and crews. One manuscript affirms that it was Juan de Cartagena who was drawn and quartered; but there is good reason to believe that he suffered instead another and no less dramatic fate, in being left, together with a mysterious priest who has never been indisputably identified, to starve on the inhospitable Patagonian coast, 'some days later', as Pigafetta states, 'for plotting another betrayal'. Pigafetta adds (though the various existing manu-scripts of his *Journal* confuse Cartagena and Quesada) that Magellan was unwilling to have his prisoner beheaded because of the rank to which he had been appointed by the King of Spain; he was after all *veedor* and, as *coniuncta persona*, in some respects Magellan's equal. Magellan may also have hesitated, when handling this mysterious last conflict with Cartagena, to execute a priest who had again plotted with the indomitable *veedor*.

The only mutineer who was actually tried and condemned by a court martial, presided over by Álvaro de Mesquita aboard the *Trinidad*, was finally beheaded on April 7. It is almost certain that the victim was Quesada; some sources state that his equerry, Luis de Molina, who had stood beside him and assisted him in the murder of Eloriaga aboard the *San Antonio*, was offered a pardon, as his accomplice, if he agreed to perform the duty of executioner, and that Molina accepted. When Sir Francis Drake had Thomas Doughty court-martialled on the shore of the Bay of Saint Julian in 1578 for plotting a mutiny, he offered him the choice between being beheaded, like Quesada, or abandoned there like Cartagena. Doughty chose to be beheaded, and Drake later claimed that he was executed on a blood-stained block which they had found there and which had already been used when Magellan executed the leader of those who had mutinied against him.

Other mutineers may well, for a while, have been kept prisoners, in fetters or in stocks. For them, confined as the whole fleet was in its winter quarters on these bleak shores, it must have been a 'prison within prison', like Samson's blindness as a prisoner in Milton's *Samson Agonistes*. Of the morale of Magellan's crews and of their experiences during the long months of their sojourn in Saint Julian's Bay, little is said in the log-books, in Pigafetta's *Journal* or in the testimony of survivors on their return to Seville. When the Patagonian native giants began to appear a few weeks after the mutiny had been quelled, they certainly provided, with their antics, a welcome comic relief to the despair and boredom of Magellan's officers and men. Even the unidentified Genoese pilot, generally so laconic and matter-of-fact in his notations of strictly navigational details, allows himself in his log-book more space to expatiate on the Patagonian giants and their customs than on any other incident of the whole voyage. The Genoese pilot's brief narrative also offers valuable testimony on the events that took place in the Bay of Saint Julian. He makes it quite clear that Magellan was aided, in quelling the mutiny, mainly by the 'foreigners' in his fleet, that is to say by the Portuguese, Italians and others whom he had been careful to concentrate aboard his own flagship, perhaps because he already suspected the Spaniards aboard the other ships of plotting a mutiny; he also reports without any ambiguity that Luis de Mendoza was stabbed and killed by the *alguazil* or captain of arms aboard the *Victoria*, and that Gaspar de Quesada was later tried, beheaded and quartered.

The Patagonian natives served another purpose which explains the enthusiasm with which they are described: they provided Magellan's men, whose supplies were already running low, with occasional extra rations of the meat of the guanaco, and also taught them to prepare and eat some of the unknown edible plants of this inhospitable coast where the Europeans found no familiar sources of supply.

During the dreary winter months, Magellan would send out one of his ships, when weather permitted, to explore the coast further south. On one such occasion, the scouting *Santiago* met with disaster. Pigafetta notes that all its crew was saved 'by miracle, not even having to swim ashore'. When they reached the shore in their lifeboats, they sent two men up the coast to report the loss of their ship to Magellan in his winter quarters, which they reached only after suffering great hardships on the way. Magellan sent back a party with supplies of ship's biscuit for two months. The crew of the *Santiago* remained near the wreck until they had finished salvaging usable supplies and other valuables as they continued to be washed ashore. Again and again, food had to be taken to them overland, across rough country infested with thornbushes. The men who went on these expeditions spent four days on the road, sleeping at night among the bushes; on their way, they found no drinking water, only ice.

When they were finally able to leave these inhospitable winter quarters, Magellan's crews erected a Cross on the highest point of the shore at the Bay of Saint Julian, 'as a sign that it belonged to the King of Spain', and named this point Monte del Cristo. On August 24, Magellan decided to move to other winter quarters further south. With only four ships, he entered the estuary of the Rio Santa Cruz, where they at least had a good supply of fresh water. During the two months that Magellan spent here, his Portuguese chief pilot Estevão Gomez roused some officers again to urge Magellan to abandon his search for a strait leading through to the Pacific and to sail east instead, across the South Atlantic and round the Cape of Good Hope, to the Moluccas. Magellan refused to follow their advice. On October 18, after all his men had confessed and communed 'like true Christians', Magellan left these final winter quarters.

VIII

Eureka

At fifty-two degrees south, Magellan's fleet discovered, on October 21, a cape which he named, after that day's Saints, the Cape of the Eleven Thousand Virgins, and on sailing into what might well have been but another estuary, he and his men discovered that it was the strait that they had so long and despairingly sought. Pigafetta describes it as 'surrounded with very high snow-capped mountains'. It was impossible, in its deep waters, to find bottom for anchoring: instead, they had to attach their prows to shore-anchors with ropes of twenty-five to thirty yards. Pigafetta writes that, 'Had it not been for the Captain General, we would not have found this strait, because we all thought and said that it was surrounded by land on all sides. But the Captain General knew that he had to navigate through a very well-concealed strait, because he had seen it, in the King of Portugal's Treasury, in a map made by that excellent man Martin Behaim.' Of course, Martin Behaim's globe, as we know it, depicts no such strait as far south as the one that now bears Magellan's name. But Magellan insisted so firmly that he knew where he was sailing that Pigafetta and many of his men, when they at last found a passage to the Pacific, now believed that this unknown strait was known to Magellan even before they had sailed from Seville.

Why did Magellan now claim that he owed to Behaim his

knowledge of the existence of this unknown strait? After having so stubbornly insisted that he knew where he was leading his officers and men, it would have been difficult for him to lose face in their eyes by showing surprise at finally discovering the strait, and because his captains knew all the up-to-date charts of the Reinels and of other reputable cartographers, he could attribute his own secret knowledge only to an unknown foreigner.

Still, he was not yet sure that they had actually found the passage which they were seeking. He therefore sent the *San Antonio* and the *Concepción* ahead to explore the narrows, while the *Trinidad* and the *Victoria* waited all night for their return in a great storm that lasted until noon of the next day, forcing them to lift anchor and drift in the bay, so as not to be driven against the rocky shore. The two ships that had been sent ahead to explore were unable to double a cape formed by the bay almost at the end of the strait, because the stormy seas and winds drove them back when they tried to return. Fearing that they might be driven aground, they therefore approached the end of the bay and, when they thought they were about to be wrecked, suddenly discovered a small opening which appeared at first to be only another sharp turn. In desperation, they hauled into it and thus discovered the passage quite by chance. When they now saw that, instead of a bay, they had found a strait, they sailed ahead and found another bay, then another strait and finally a bay that was greater than the first two. In their joy, they turned back and hastened to inform Magellan of their success.

Because of the storm's violence and of the two whole days they had been gone, and especially because of the smoke signals sent up when two of their men were set ashore to light fires, Magellan and the men of the two ships which remained behind believed that both the *San Antonio* and the *Concepción* had been wrecked. But now these two ships returned in triumph, with full sails and banners flying to the wind. As they approached their companions, they fired their mortars while all the men on their decks burst into cheers.

After solemn celebration of Mass to thank God and the Virgin Mary, all four ships then sailed into the newly discovered strait, where they found two openings, to the southeast and the south-west. Magellan sent the *San Antonio* and the *Concepción* ahead to find out whether the first of these two openings led into the Pacific Ocean. Without waiting for the *Concepción*, the *San Antonio* sailed ahead and never returned.

Failing to sight the *San Antonio*, the *Concepción* sailed hither and thither at random while the *Trinidad* and the *Victoria* explored the other opening towards the south-west, sailing through the narrows till they reached a river which they named after the sardines that abounded in its mouth. There they waited four days for the return of the *San Antonio* and the *Concepción*. But they also sent ahead a boat, with sufficient supplies, to explore the waters beyond the cape that lay ahead of them. Within three days, this scouting party returned and reported that it had rounded the cape and sighted the open sea. Pigafetta here describes for the first time an expression of real emotion in Magellan, who wept for joy and named this last cape, because it had been desired so long, Cape Deseado.

They turned back in search of the missing ships, but found only the *Concepción*, whose captain, Juan Serrano, reported that he had lost sight of the *San Antonio* entering the bay. The three remaining ships then searched for it in every nook and corner of the strait, as far back as the opening where the missing ship had vanished. Magellan even sent the *Victoria* all the way back to the eastern entrance of the strait, but all in vain.

The *San Antonio* was Magellan's largest ship, carrying over sixty men and a good share of the fleet's supplies, especially stores of food, of which, while crossing the Pacific, they would begin to [feel an acute shortage while still carrying abundant supplies of bells, mirrors and other barter-goods. Magellan was more disconcerted by the loss or desertion of the *San Antonio* than by the mutiny of Saint Julian's Bay or the earlier wreck of the *Santiago*. For the first time, he openly showed signs of indecision. He consulted the astronomer, Andrés de San Martín, who, from a study of horoscopes but perhaps also from private knowledge of secret plans that had leaked to him, concluded that there had been a mutiny aboard the *San Antonio* and that it had sailed back to Spain.

Magellan is also said to have issued, on November 21, an order of the day of which an approximate text has survived, a copy of one of the documents seized when the *Trinidad*, his former flagship, was seized by the Portuguese in the Moluccas after his death. The document suggests that he had anticipated that charges would be brought against him in Spain by the officers and men of the *San Antonio*, and that, to counter them, he had consulted his remaining officers for the first time, asking them for written statements of opinion as to whether or not they should pursue their westward course to the Spice Islands.

The authenticity of this document, as a word-for-word text of Magellan's original order of the day, is in many respects dubious. It is addressed, to begin with, only to Duarte Barbosa, captain of the *Victoria*, and to its pilots, masters and quartermasters, but not to the officers of Magellan's two other remaining ships. Magellan describes himself, in consulting his officers for the first time, as a man who never rejected the opinion or counsel of anyone, 'but rather all my affairs are discussed and communicated generally to all, without any person being affronted by me', and he then goes on to accuse Barbosa and the officers of the *Victoria*, because of 'what happened in the port of Saint Julian with respect to the death of Luis de Mendoza, Gaspar de Quesada, and the banishment of Juan de Cartagena and Pero Sanchez de Reina, the priest', of failing through fear to tell him and counsel him 'in all that may appear to you to be in the interest of his Majesty and of the safe conduct of this fleet'.

All this reads as if it were later concocted by Magellan and Barbosa, his relative by marriage, to neutralize whatever charges might be brought against him in Spain by Estevão Gomes and the officers and men who deserted aboard the *San Antonio*. Magellan may have carefully preserved the original of this document among his own personal papers aboard his flagship, the *Trinidad*, instead of leaving it among the papers of Barbosa, who captained the *Victoria*. It is certainly unlikely that Magellan would actually have read to his officers and crews an order of the day that conflicted so flagrantly with their long experience of his taciturn habit of never consulting anyone or accepting any advice.

Magellan appears to have made his own decision known on November 23. Swearing solemnly, by the habit of the Knights of Saint James of Compostella which he wore for this occasion, to continue his voyage into the vast and unknown ocean ahead, he is said to have declared: 'Even if we have to eat the leather thongs on our masts and yards, I will still go on to discover what I promised.' These words now sound, however, somewhat suspect, as if culled by a later narrator from Pigafetta's description of how Magellan's crews actually tried to eat these leather thongs as they nearly starved on their voyage across the Pacific.

Pigafetta's *Journal* and the Genoese pilot's log-book both refrain from reporting on the spot either this dramatic oath or the whole incident of Magellan's consultation of the fleet's astronomer and of his subsequent order of the day. Instead, they both report that Magellan ordered the *Victoria*, if it failed to find any trace of the *San Antonio* in its search of the whole strait, to plant a banner on the summit of some conspicuous hill by the shore and to bury beneath it, in an earthen pot, a letter instructing the *San Antonio* concerning the course that the rest of his fleet would now follow.

Two such banners were indeed planted, together with letters of instruction: the first on a hill above the shore of the first bay as one enters the strait from the east, the second on a small rocky island in the third bay, 'where there are many sea-wolves and large birds'. Magellan waited meanwhile for the *Victoria*'s return near an unidentified river 'which meanders between high snow-capped mountains and empties into the sea near the River of Sardines'. There, on an island, he also set up a cross. Pigafetta concludes his reports of the whole episode of the discovery of the strait by affirming that, 'if we had not discovered this passage, the Captain General was determined to go as far south as seventy-five degrees towards the Antarctic Pole'.

Pigafetta goes on to describe the short polar summer nights and equally short winter days. In October, for instance, the night lasted only three hours. He describes the straits as abounding in safe havens, good fresh water and timber of all kinds but cedarwood, also in fish, sardines and shellfish, while a kind of sweet cress grew plentifully around the springs, though a more bitter kind of cress was also found: 'We ate of it for many days, for we had nothing else. I believe that there is not a more beautiful or better strait in the world. . . .'

Pigafetta is describing here the southern shore of the Strait of Magellan—that of the island known as Tierra del Fuego. But he never mentions its primitive inhabitants, with whom Magellan and his men appear to have had no contact. Only in Maximilian of Transylvania's later account of Magellan's voyage, written for Charles the Fifth on the basis of the oral testimony of the survivors, do we find any reference to the fires observed on this shore and to which Tierra del Fuego still owes its name: 'One night, a great number of fires were seen, mostly on their left hand, from which they guessed that they had been sighted by the natives of that region. But Magellan, seeing that the country was rocky and bleak with eternal cold, thought it useless to waste many days exploring it.' Maximilian adds that Magellan and his men thought, quite correctly, that the shores of Tierra del Fuego, on their left, were those of islands, 'because sometimes on that side they heard on a still more distant coast the rumbling and roaring of the sea', where the waves dash on the rocky islands north-west of Cape Horn. In view of this testimony, printed and published in Rome as early as 1523, it is surprising that cartographers continued for several decades to depict Tierra del Fuego on their maps as a northern promontory of their still imaginary Antarctic continent, separated from South America only by the narrow straits that Magellan had discovered. Later explorers revealed that the fires sighted by Magellan on the shores of Tierra del Fuego were those that its natives kept burning permanently in hollow logs placed on mounds of earth. Even more primitive than the Patagonians who could at least light a fire by rubbing two sticks of wood together, these stone-age Indians had not yet learned to produce a new fire and merely kept alive what natural fires they chanced to find.

*   *   *

The documents preserved in Seville in the Archives of the Indies reveal a somewhat confused story of the return of the *San Antonio* to Spain. According to the witnesses heard in the course of the enquiry instigated by the charges made against Magellan by Estevão Gomes, the *San Antonio* had returned well ahead of time from its mission in the misty strait to its agreed meeting-place with the *Concepción*. Álvaro de Mesquita, who was still in command as its captain, lit bonfires on a nearby hill, to signal its presence in the agreed manner; he may even have left some documents for Magellan, though this seems unlikely, as another testimony states that he proposed to rejoin the Captain General's flagship without awaiting the *Concepción*. If he left any documents there, they were probably not intended for Magellan but for the captain of the *Concepción*, to inform him of his decision and movements, much as Magellan left similar instructions in earthen pots, beneath banners placed on hillocks, for the vanished *San Antonio*.

But the officers of the *San Antonio* rejected their captain's proposal and mutinied during the following night. After wounding him and placing him in irons, they sailed back to Spain, which they reached six months later. On their way, they stopped in the Bay of Saint Julian and tried to find Juan de Cartagena and the priest whom Magellan had marooned there. According to one dubious report, they were successful and brought them back to Spain; but this seems unlikely, since there is no testimony of Cartagena in the ensuing enquiries and no further record of his life and activity in Spain.

The Portuguese pilot Estevão Gomes and a clerk named Guerra, recently promoted by Magellan to the rank of treasurer, appear to have instigated the mutiny of the *San Antonio*. In his *Journal*, Pigafetta reports that Gomes had long been jealous of Magellan because, 'before this expedition had been planned, he had gone to the Emperor and asked to be given some caravels in order to go out on a voyage of discovery; but His Majesty, when our Captain General also came, did not grant his request'.

On its way back to Seville, the *San Antonio* stopped again on the Guinea coast of Africa for water and supplies. It reached Seville on May 6 1521 and, six days later, its responsible officers sent to Bishop Fonseca, as president of the Council of the Indies, a detailed report in which Magellan was accused of a great number of errors, irregularities and crimes. His cousin, Álvaro de Mesquita, the *San Antonio*'s deposed captain, was imprisoned; he was accused of having been the first to use weapons in the conflict aboard his ship and even of having advised Magellan to maroon Juan de Cartagena and the priest Sanchez de la Reina on the Patagonian coast.

Bishop Fonseca was puzzled and disturbed by the jealous Portuguese pilot's accusations. Orders were given to the police of Seville to watch Magellan's wife and child in order to prevent their possible escape to Portugal. Mesquita, Gomes and Guerra were sent separately under armed guard to Valladolid, as witnesses in the official enquiry. The mutineers were acquitted and, in October 1521, Estevão Gomes was even allowed to set out on another expedition, but the *Victoria* then returned at last, in September 1522, from its circumnavigation of the Earth. On the testimony of its few survivors, Mesquita was finally released and Gomes was imprisoned in his stead. In his subsequent report on

Magellan's whole expedition, Peter Martyr sums up his opinion of Gomes as 'a man of vain and frivolous imagination'. This did not prevent Charles the Fifth, in 1534, from knighting him 'for having discovered the strait in the course of his duties as chief pilot'.

Pigafetta's *Journal* reports that Magellan named the strait that he had discovered 'the Strait of Patagonia'. He is reported elsewhere to have named it 'the channel of All Saints'. Other names suggested for it are the Strait of Victoria, after the ship that first sighted it, the Strait of the Mother of God and even, much later by nineteenth-century German nationalists, the strait of Martin Behaim. Nobody has ever suggested that it be named after Estevão Gomes.

IX

The Only People in the World

When Magellan's fleet, reduced from five to three ships, sailed at long last, on November 28 1520, into the unexplored Pacific Ocean, it had spent a full month voyaging the three hundred and sixty miles of the strait that now bears his name, exploring its many bays before finding the right issue. At this point in his *Journal*, Pigafetta formulates a mysteriously correct hypothesis: 'When we came out of this strait, if we had continued due west, we would have been able to sail all the way round the world without sighting any land until we returned to the Cape of the Eleven Thousand Virgins, which is at the other end of the same strait.' If one now looks at a map of the world, one sees that he was right. But how could he have guessed, in an age when such vast areas of the Southern hemisphere were still unexplored, when the very existence of Australia and the Antarctic continent was still unknown to Western cosmographers and mariners, that only a few unimportant islands are scattered in the Oceans that lie between the longitude of the southern tip of South America and that of the most northerly coasts of the Antarctic continent?

Magellan had celebrated his discovery of the passage to the Pacific, which Balboa had claimed some years earlier for the King of Spain, by firing many mortars. Now, before embarking on its waters, he had a priest bless his ships while his crews chanted a solemn *Te Deum*. To his officers assembled on the deck of the flagship, Magellan delivered a speech, reminding them that they were about to steer into waters where no ship was known to have sailed before: 'May we always find them as peaceful as this morning. In this hope, I shall name this Sea the Pacific.'

Pigafetta pauses here in his *Journal* to make some astronomical observations, borrowed perhaps from the fleet's astronomer San Martín, about the night-sky in the Southern hemisphere, where 'the Antarctic Pole does not have the same stars as the Arctic Pole'. He notes the presence of the Southern Cross, already observed off the shores of Africa by Portuguese mariners even before Diaz had rounded the Cape of Good Hope. But Pigafetta also describes 'many small stars clustered together'—those distant galaxies which Amerigo Vespucci had already observed but which are now known as 'Magellanic clouds', as if they had first been sighted during Magellan's expedition. Pigafetta or San Martín must have been gifted with unusually sharp eyesight to be able to perceive, without any special instruments, that these nebulous lights, almost like luminous vapours, actually consist of clusters of countless stars.

Pigafetta also notes how Magellan now observed quite correctly that the deviation of the compass, caused by the Antarctic magnetic pole in the Southern hemisphere, is greater than that caused, in the Northern hemisphere, by the Arctic magnetic pole. He warned his pilots to take this phenomenon into account. From what earlier explorers, one wonders, had Magellan acquired this information? And if he was the first to note it, with what instruments was he able to observe it?

Magellan could dispose of no reliable information about the great stretch of the Pacific Ocean, with all its islands and its vast landless wastes of water, that lies between the western coast of South America and the distant Moluccas, situated in the heart of the East Indies. No European had yet explored this part of the globe, and no maps, charts or planispheres that Magellan might have studied in Portugal or in Spain could offer him anything but fanciful interpretations of Marco Polo's vague geography of whatever lay east of China.

Because his men had suffered so long under the rigorous sub-antarctic climate, Magellan decided to enter a more temperate zone as fast as possible, by following the coast of Chile to the north and north-west until his fleet crossed the Equator, after which he planned to sail due west. Most maps illustrating the course of Magellan's voyage make him strike out across the Pacific too soon. Had he truly followed this course, one wonders how he could have failed for so long to sight any of the numerous inhabited and fertile isles of Polynesia, in the South and Central Pacific, where he would have found badly needed supplies of water and fresh food and encountered relatively friendly natives. He must have crossed the Equator somewhere between 120 and 140 degrees West longitude, instead of about 165 degrees, as some maps and biographers suggest. Having crossed the Equator, however, Magellan then sailed nine hundred miles north before heading due west towards the Philippines. But he certainly knew that the Moluccas, his ultimate goal, are situated further south, along the Equator. It would thus appear that Magellan, misled by Martin Behaim's or Schöner's hypothetical geography of the Pacific, expected to encounter, when he first began to strike due west, the southern tip of Cipangu or Japan, if not the legendary archipelago of Septem Ciudades or the equally legendary Cape Cattigara; this was still believed to be the southernmost point, somewhere in the vastly reduced Pacific Ocean, of the mainland of Asia, where it was generally described, as in Ptolemy's geography, as curving down, to the north of Canton, to reach even further south than the Malay peninsula, which had often been confused with it but was now generally known as the Golden Chersonese.

Both Behaim and Schöner placed Zipango, Zipagri or Japan close to the Equator and, in the case of Schöner's slightly less fanciful globe, closer to the Pacific coast of the Americas, still represented by Schöner as four huge islands, than to the coasts of China. Magellan may therefore have believed that he could obtain supplies in Japan or elsewhere in the Pacific Ocean before reaching the Moluccas; he may even have planned to establish in some such friendly territory a base from which, should he find Portuguese forces from Malacca already occupying the Moluccas, he could attack them more easily and, if necessary, force them to respect Spanish claims founded on his interpretation of the imaginary line of the Treaty of Tordesillas. Pigafetta's *Journal* thus mentions that their ships must have sailed close to Cipangu and to Sumbdit Pradit, which some scholars have tried to identify as the legendary archipelago of Seven Cities or Septem Ciudades, both of which Pigafetta describes as 'very rich'. He also states, however, that they were heading towards Cape Gaticara; but he places Cipangu or Japan on the 20th latitude south of the Equator, Sumbdit Pradit on the 15th, and Cape Gaticara, 'to correct the cosmographers who have drawn maps but never seen it', towards the 12th latitude north of the Equator, all of which is sheer geographical fantasy.

According to an old mediaeval legend, the Islands of the Seven Cities were those to which the Christian Visigothic Bishops of Portugal had fled with their followers, in the

Atlantic, under pressure of the Arab invasion. But how could these islands be situated so far from Portugal in the Pacific Ocean? Even in Magellan's time, a particularly picturesque area of the Azores was already believed to be the site of these legendary Seven Cities. In recent decades, some late Roman coins, of a kind still in currency or hoarded in Visigothic Spain and Portugal, have been discovered in the Azores, where they may well have been brought by these vanished Christian refugees or by other unidentified mariners from the moribund Roman Empire. Pigafetta's Sumbdit Pradit would therefore appear to be more probably a corruption of a Hindu or Malay name derived from the writings of Marco Polo or from the reports of some other voyager who had brought back to Europe vague information about areas east of modern Singapore.

Be that all as it may, Magellan's reduced and starving fleet sailed for two whole months in the Pacific without sighting land, and even then found only two unidentified desert isles 'where we found nothing but birds and trees, for which we called them the Unfortunate Islands. They are two hundred leagues apart. We found no anchorage there, but near them saw many sharks.' Pigafetta locates these islands on the 15th and the 9th latitudes South. Two of the pilots' surviving log-books locate them somewhat differently, and various scholars have sought to identify them as San Pablo Island, south-west of Puka-Puka in the Paumotu archipelago, or as Wostok Island, north of Flint Isle in the Manihiki group. After sighting these two islands, Magellan sailed another month through watery wastes without finding any other island where he could obtain supplies.

Though Magellan's Genoese pilot never mentions the expedition's sufferings and Francisco Albo's log-book limits its comments almost exclusively to navigational technicalities, Pigafetta describes in eloquent detail the privations suffered by Magellan's starving men: 'We were three months and twenty days without obtaining any kind of fresh supplies. We ate ship's biscuit that was no longer biscuit, but crumbs swarming with worms, for these had already devoured whatever was good. Besides, it stank powerfully of the urine of rats. The water we drank was yellow and had long been putrid. We were reduced even to eating certain pieces of leather that had been placed on the top of the mainyard to prevent it from chafing the ropes. From exposure to sun, rain and wind, this leather had become very hard, so that we let it macerate for four or five days in the sea then placed it for a while on the embers and thus ate it. Often too we ate sawdust from the ships' timbers. Rats were sold for half a ducat a piece if we could catch any. But the worst of all our misfortunes was the following: the gums of both the lower and the upper jaws of some of our men began to swell so much that they could no longer eat at all and consequently died. Nineteen of them died of this disease, as well as the other Patagonian giant and one Indian from Brazil. In addition, some twenty-five or thirty more men fell ill of other diseases, in their arms, legs or parts, so that very few remained well. I myself, by the grace of God, suffered however no sickness.' Pigafetta may have kept fit mainly because of his habit of supplying himself with fresh fish that he caught from the sea.

Magellan had aptly named the Pacific Ocean on first sighting it. Its waters remained peaceful throughout the three months and twenty days of his voyage across it. Pigafetta adds: 'Had not Our Lord and his Blessed Mother aided us by granting us such calm weather, we would all have died of hunger on that very vast sea.' He estimates that they sailed some four thousand leagues, keeping an average of fifty, sixty or even more leagues a day, depending on the winds.

On March 6 1521, they finally sighted a small island to the north-west and two others to the south-west. One of these islands appeared to be larger and to rise higher above sea-level than the other two. Magellan decided to land there in order to seek supplies. But this proved impossible when a crowd of natives began to swarm around them and to board their ships, stealing everything they could lay their hands on. Too weak and sick with scurvy and other ailments, Magellan's crews were incapable of protecting themselves and their belongings. The natives even stole the small boat that was moored to the poop of the flagship.

Roused to fury by this thieving, Magellan rounded up enough able-bodied men to send a punitive expedition ashore and burn fifty native huts as well as many native canoes; they even killed seven natives while recovering their own stolen boat. Some of Magellan's sick men begged the members of the punitive force to bring back the entrails of any men or women they might kill, believing that to eat them would cure them of their ills. This was still a common superstition among Europeans, but Pigafetta neglects to note whether any such medicinal cannibalism actually occurred among Magellan's men. As usual, however, he expressed wonder and pity when he observed the apparent innocence of these primitive natives: wounded by the shafts of the European crossbows that pierced their loins or their breast from side to side, the islanders looked at the shaft with great astonishment and drew it out by pulling on it 'now on this and now on that side', thereby losing so much blood that they died, 'which moved us to great compassion'.

After thus punishing the thieving islanders, Magellan ordered his ships to set sail again. But the islanders followed the fleet aboard their canoes or catamarans, swarming around the ships in over a hundred of their own craft and offering fish which they feigned to be bringing as gifts. They pelted the ships with stones and then fled, steering their craft very skilfully between the ship that was under full sail and the small boat that followed it, moored to its stern. From the decks, Magellan's men watched this improvised regatta with delight. In some of the native craft, there were women who wept and tore their hair, presumably mourning the men who had been killed.

In spite of the brevity of their stay in these islands, which long continued to be called Ladrones or Isles of Thieves, as Magellan had named them, Pigafetta was able to note some curious observations about the customs of the natives of the island, which we presume to have been Guam, in the archipelago now known as the Mariannas: 'Each one of these people lives according to his own will, for they have no chief. They go naked and some of them are bearded, with black hair that reaches down to the waist in tresses. They wear hats woven of palm-fronds, like the Albanians, and they are as tall as we and well built. They worship no God and have an olive-coloured complexion, though they are all born white. Their teeth are red and black, which they consider very beautiful.' It would appear that Pigafetta mistook for a cosmetic the consequences of their addiction to chewing betel-nut.

He reports that the women of Guam went naked, 'except that they wear a strip of palm-bark thin as paper, to conceal their nature', in fact a kind of tapa-cloth such as is still produced by the natives of most Pacific islands. He found these native women beautiful and delicately formed, with lighter complexions than the men, and very black hair falling loose down to the ground: 'These women never work in the fields, but stay in the house, weaving mats, baskets and other household utensils, all made of palm-leaves. The islanders all anoint their bodies and their hair with coconut oil and oil of *giongioli*,' which may be beniseed-oil or seseli-oil. Their diet consisted mainly of coconuts, yams which Pigafetta calls potatoes, birds, bananas which he calls 'figs of the length of a man's palm', sugar-cane and flying fish. They built their huts of timber, roofed with boards which were then thatched with what he calls fig-leaves, meaning those of the banana-tree. These huts had doors and windows, and the rooms within and the beds were decorated with beautiful palm-leaf mats. Their beds were upholstered with very soft and fine palm-straw.

Their only weapon was a kind of spear that bears a sharp fishbone at its point. Though ingenious and thievish, they were poor and believed, according to the signs that they made, 'that there were no other people in the world but themselves'. Their sport, for both sexes, consisted in wandering from island to island in their catamarans or outriggers, which Pigafetta describes in detail, comparing their palm-leaf sails to a lateen sail and the boat itself to the swift *fucelere* of the Venetian lagoon: 'For rudders, they use a wooden blade like the shovel of a baker's oven with a wooden handle. They can change stern and prow at will, and their craft leap in the water like dolphins from wave to wave.' Obviously, Pigafetta was among the fifty men who were fit enough to take part in Magellan's punitive expedition, but he seems to have wasted very little time on merely trouncing the thieving islanders.

X

First Men Round the Earth

Between Guam and the Philippines, the next islands that Magellan's fleet sighted fifteen hundred miles further west, the winds must have been very favourable, for this great distance was covered in less than ten days, in spite of the weakness of the sick and starving crews. Pigafetta reports that they discovered, at dawn on March 16, an island that rose high above the sea; it was Samar, south-east of Luzon in the central Philippines. Because it appeared to be inhabited, Magellan preferred not to land there, if only to avoid further conflicts between unfriendly or thieving natives and his weakened men. Instead, he landed next day on another island, off the coast of Leyte, which appeared to be uninhabited when they sighted it to the west of Samar.

Here they found supplies of water and prepared to rest on land, where Magellan had two tents set up for the sick and ordered that a sow be slaughtered to provide them with fresh meat. It would appear that the sow was wild and that some of the abler men had trapped it on a successful hunting expedition.

Magellan and his men had been on land only one day when, in the afternoon of March 18, they saw a boat approaching them with nine men aboard. As a precaution, Magellan ordered that none of his men should move or utter a word without his permission. When the strangers landed, their leader came immediately to Magellan, 'showing himself pleased at our arrival'. This would suggest that Magellan's expedition was not the first within living memory to have reached the northern and central Philippines from the outside world. Magellan's Genoese pilot even notes, in his logbook, that the natives reported that they already welcomed in their isles other foreign navigators whose skins were of a lighter hue than their own. The Genoese pilot guesses that these other light-skinned navigators must have been 'Mongolians or Chinese', a fact now proved by archaeological excavations in Luzon, where Chinese ceramics of the Ming and Sung dynasties have been found. Five of the more richly adorned natives remained with Magellan, while the rest were sent to fetch others, who were fishing offshore.

When Magellan understood that these natives were 'reasonable' and friendly, he ordered food to be set before them and offered red caps, mirrors, combs, bells, ivory, linen cloth and other gifts. In return for these courtesies, the natives gave fish, a jar of palm-wine, plantains, bananas and two coconuts, having nothing else to offer. But they explained by sign-language that they would return in four days with rice and many other kinds of food.

Within a short time, Magellan and his men had established friendly and familiar relations with these natives, who soon taught them a few words of their language as well as the names of some of the islands that could be seen from where they were. The natives came from Suluan, one of the smaller islands south-west of Samar. To impress them, Magellan invited them aboard his flagship and showed them samples of the spices that he had come to seek: cloves, cinnamon, pepper, nutmeg and mace, and also gold and all the goods that he could offer in exchange. When he afterwards ordered a few salvoes fired from his cannon, the natives were so scared that they wanted to jump overboard. But Magellan's attempts at obtaining information were successful: the natives recognized the sample spices he had shown and explained by signs that they indeed grew in the islands which were the expedition's goal and which could no longer be very far away, since they were already known in this area. Before departing, the natives took leave with great courtesy and cordiality, promising to return as agreed.

Pigafetta reports that the island where they had elected to land was known to the natives as Humunu, which is Homonhon, but that Magellan's men named it 'the watering-place of good omen', because they found there two springs of very clear water and the first traces of gold that they discovered in this region. As for the whole archipelago, they named it after Saint Lazarus, having first landed there on this saint's day, March 17.

The natives kept their promise and returned four days later, on Friday March 22, in two boats loaded with coconuts, sweet oranges, palm-wine, and a cock, to show that they had poultry in their land. Magellan paid for all these supplies and the natives were very content and friendly. Their chief was an elderly man, heavily tattooed or painted, and wearing gold ear-rings; the others wore many gold bracelets and wore kerchiefs tied as turbans around their brows. Magellan's slave was able to converse with their chief who, unlike the others, could speak several languages, including a dialect presumably of Malayan origin.

Magellan stayed eight days in Homonhon. Every day, he landed from his flagship to visit the sick and tend them with his own hands, offering them coconut-milk, which appeared to have excellent medicinal effects on their scurvy. At noon on Monday March 25 in Holy Week, as they were about to set sail, Pigafetta went aboard ahead of the others in order to fish. On his way down to the armoury, he slipped on a wet cable and fell overboard, without any of his companions witnessing his plight. As he was about to drown, he was fortunate enough to find one of the ropes of the mainsail dangling overboard and hung on to it while he cried for help until a boat was sent to rescue him.

After he had been rescued, the fleet sailed westward, passing between four small islands that lie between Leyte and Mindanao. On Thursday March 28, having seen fires at night on an island, they sailed close to its shore and met a native craft, with eight men aboard. It came close to Magellan's flagship and his slave Enrique began conversing from a distance with its native crew. The men aboard the native craft could understand his speech and came closer to the ship, but refused to come aboard. When Magellan saw that they remained distrustful, he threw them a red cap and some other gifts, all carefully tied to a board, which they joyfully accepted, after which they went off to inform their king. Some two hours later, Magellan's men saw two long native craft approach their fleet, both full of men. In the larger of these two boats a native king was seated beneath a canopy of woven mats.

When the King's boat reached Magellan's flagship, Enrique greeted it and was immediately understood by the King because, as Pigafetta explains, 'in those parts the Kings know more languages than the others'. The King then ordered some of his men to go aboard the flagship while he remained in his boat that stood by until they returned, after which the King and his followers departed.

Magellan entertained lavishly all those who had come aboard, loading them with gifts, in return for which the King, before departing, gave Magellan a large bar of massive gold and a basketful of ginger, which Magellan graciously declined to accept. One wonders why he accepted the gold, but refused the ginger. Later that afternoon, the fleet came closer to the shore and anchored near the King's palace.

The next day was Good Friday. Magellan sent his slave Enrique, acting as his interpreter, ashore in a row-boat to ask the King if he could supply provisions to the fleet and to assure him that he would obtain satisfaction for all services thus rendered, 'for we had come to his island as friends and not as foes'. One of Magellan's pilots reports in his log-book that Enrique celebrated his return to a land where his mother-tongue could at long last be understood by allowing himself a drunken spree as soon as he set foot on shore. The King returned to the flagship in the same boat, together with six or eight of his men, and came aboard. After embracing Magellan, he offered him three porcelain jars, presumably of Chinese craftsmanship, covered with a design of foliage and full of raw rice, also two very big fish and other gifts. In return, Magellan gave the King a coat of red and yellow cloth cut in the Turkish fashion and a fine red cap; to the King's companions, he gave knives and mirrors, after which he offered them refreshments and explained to them, through Enrique, that he wished to become the King's blood-brother, according to the Malay ceremony of *casi-casi* whereby the wrists are slashed so that the blood of both parties can mingle as it flows. The King agreed to become Magellan's blood-brother, after which he was shown cloth of various colours, linen, coral ornaments and a great deal of other goods as well as the ship's cannon, which were fired in his honour. Some of the visitors were terrified by the salvoes.

Magellan then ordered one of his men to wear his full armour while three others surrounded him and struck him with swords and daggers all over his body. The King was dumbfounded by this display and Magellan had Enrique explain to him that one such armoured man was worth one hundred of his own native guards, with which the King readily agreed. To impress him even further, Magellan bragged that he had two hundred such armoured men aboard each one of his three ships; after which he showed the King a great number of breastplates, swords and small round shields and had some of his men give a display of swordsmanship.

Having impressed the King and his companions with this show of military strength, Magellan showed him his sea-chart and ship's compass and explained how he had discovered the strait in order to come here and how long they had voyaged without sighting any land. The King expressed great wonder at all this. In conclusion, Magellan asked him to allow two men to accompany him ashore so as to show them in turn some of his possessions. The King agreed to this suggestion and Pigafetta was one of the two envoys who went ashore as guests. Though the second envoy is nowhere named, one presumes that Pigafetta was accompanied by Magellan's slave Enrique as interpreter.

They were received cordially and with great honours. After being feasted on the royal barge and again in the King's palace, which Pigafetta describes as a kind of hay-loft or barn because it was built on piles, they spent the night there and returned the next day to their ships, accompanied by a 'brother' of their host, the King or rajah of a neighbouring island. Pigafetta began to compile lists of native words; his hosts expressed admiration for his ability to write.

As usual, Pigafetta gives detailed descriptions of native customs and costumes, housing and foods. When Magellan's envoys parted from their host, for instance, the latter kissed their hands, a gesture that Pigafetta and his companion promptly reciprocated. Pigafetta also observes that the King or rajah of each principality they subsequently visited was, 'according to their custom', the handsomest man among his subjects.

On Easter Sunday, the last day of March, Magellan sent a priest ashore, early in the morning, to perform Mass on land in the presence of the natives. Enrique accompanied the priest, to explain that Magellan's men were not coming ashore to converse with the natives, but to attend Mass. The King promptly offered them two slaughtered swine, perhaps because he expected them to perform some sacrifice to their gods. When the hour came for Mass, some fifty men came ashore to attend it, wearing no armour but still carrying their usual weapons. Before they landed, six salvoes were fired from the ship's cannon, as a sign of peaceful intentions. Magellan himself, before the Mass began, sprinkled both of the native Kings with perfumed water. When the time came for the collection, the Kings came up to the Cross, together with Magellan and his men, and kissed it, but offered no alms. When the host was raised, the Kings knelt with the faithful and joined their hands as they worshipped, while the fleet fired its guns offshore. After Mass, all received communion.

The religious ceremonies were interrupted by a display of fencing, which Magellan ordered his men to offer as an entertainment for the Kings, who enjoyed it greatly, after which a Cross, adorned with nails and a crown of thorns, was brought forward. The Kings followed the example of the party of Christians and bowed before these symbols. Through his interpreter, Magellan explained to them that these were the insignia of the Emperor, his sovereign, who had ordered him to place them wherever he went, so that any other ships that might come later from Spain would see them and know that Magellan had been there; such ships would then leave the natives in peace. Should any Spaniards take prisoners from among the natives, these would be released as soon as the Cross was shown to their captors. The Cross must therefore be placed on the summit of the highest hill, where they would all be able to see it every day and worship it, so that they would no longer suffer harm from thunder, lightning or storm.

A charismatic change appears to have occurred in Magellan's character; it was revealed repeatedly during the next six weeks in his behaviour and his utterances until the moment of his death. His crossing of the Pacific, from the straits he had triumphantly discovered to the Philippines, which he was the first European explorer to visit, appears to have been not only a period of physical trial but also of intense spiritual solitude, soul-searching and doubt, leading to a consolidation of religious faith and fervour now that he could hope to see his great venture at long last crowned with success. Earlier, in Brazil and in Patagonia, he had known moments, in his brief relations with Guarani and Patagonian Indians, of missionary zeal of a kind not recorded in reports of his earlier activities in India, East Africa, Malacca or Morocco. True, he had converted his slave Enrique; but this was common practice among Catholic owners of household slaves and may have been dictated by mere convenience on his return from the Orient to Portugal, where the Inquisition no longer tolerated the presence of Moslems, Jews or heathens. From now on, however, Magellan conducted such a conscious and successful campaign to christianize those areas of the Philippines he visited that one begins to wonder, as one reads Pigafetta's reports of his missionary exertions and even of a miraculous cure he appears to have accomplished, why he has never been proposed in Rome as a candidate at least for beatification.

One asks inevitably whether Magellan was inspired, in his missionary zeal, by mere considerations of imperialist expediency, believing that a christianized population, in these newly discovered territories, would be more likely to remain loyal to the King of Spain than the populations of other recently acquired colonies which were merely exploited or enslaved. Had his earlier experiences in India, under the Viceroy Almeida, convinced him of the more lasting nature of peaceful penetration, as opposed to the reign of terror imposed by Albuquerque all the way from Aden to Malacca? Did he feel that the presence of an unsuspected Indian Christian population had facilitated Portuguese penetration of the Malabar Coast, and now hope, by christianizing these other Orientals in the Philippines, who appeared less primitive and more accessible than the stone-age natives of Brazil, Patagonia and Guam, to establish a similar bridgehead for future Spanish imperial expansion in the Far East? Had he always been, as his humane treatment of Enrique suggests, a believer in the minority views of the Dominicans who, in Spain and Portugal, had long been protesting against the enslaving of Africans and whose indignation at Spanish treatment of the American Indians was so forcefully expressed, a few years later, by Bishop Bartolome de Las Casas? Had Magellan perhaps been converted to these views by his brief meeting with this 'Apostle of the Indies' at the Spanish court in Valladolid? Pigafetta, in his *Journal*, offers no clue to the motivations that may have directed Magellan's missionary zeal and contents himself with reporting its manifestations.

In his dealings with native rulers and their subjects, Magellan was careful from now on to impress them not only with the military power and wealth of the King of Spain but also with the miraculous spiritual power of the Cross. Again and again, he demonstrated military power by firing salvoes from his cannon and by displays of superior armour, weapons and fighting skill in peaceful tournaments. The King's wealth was also demonstrated, in the eyes of the natives, by Magellan's lavish distribution of rare and exotic gifts. The power of the Cross, on the other hand, was suggested by the fervour of repeated religious ceremonies in which all Magellan's officers and men participated with as much pomp as possible.

Magellan's propagandistic and missionary efforts were everywhere crowned with a success that, after brief landings on Leyte and other smaller islands, culminated, on the rich island of Cebu, in the mass conversion to Christianity of its ruler and of a great number of his subjects.

Everywhere, Magellan, through his interpreter, questioned the native rulers, to find out whether they and their subjects were 'Moors or Gentiles'—Mohammedans or heathens. When he gathered from two kings of Mindanao that they worshipped no idols but prayed, with joined hands raised to the sky, to a Being they called 'Abba', he expressed great satisfaction. Had he perhaps already heard this word, which means 'Father' in Syriac and Aramaic, pronounced on the Malabar Coast by Indian Christians? Did he believe that he had discovered, in the distant Philippines, some remnant of those legendary Noachites who inherited the faith of the patriarch Noah but never heard of Moses or Christ and were said by some Talmudists, as well as by some Christian theologians, to be admissible to the Kingdom of Heaven if they lived as just men according to their primitive standards of right and wrong? Magellan even offered to place his armed men at the disposal of these two friendly kings, should they need military aid to combat their enemies. They in turn supplied Magellan with pilots to guide his fleet to Cebu, which they indicated to him as the most important commercial harbour in that area. At first, in exchange for the pilots they loaned, Magellan offered to leave one of his own men as a hostage with these friendly rulers, but one of them now proposed to accompany Magellan in person as his pilot, if Magellan would only delay his sailing two more days so as to allow him to make the necessary preparations.

It is far from easy to reconstruct, from the various manuscripts and editions of Pigafetta's *Journal*, the route Magellan followed, from his first landing in the Philippines until he reached Cebu. Pigafetta's memory of the names of the islands and harbours where they landed, and the order in which these were discovered, seems sometimes to have failed him. He thus mentions Butuan and Calagan as if they were islands; they are harbours on the island of Mindanao. He seems to confuse the islands of Leyte and Mindanao, which is not surprising since Magellan had no charts of this area which he was discovering as he went, with no possible idea of the general conformation of this confusing archipelago. What is definite is that around noon on Sunday April 7 Magellan sailed in state into the harbour of Cebu, accompanied by one of the friendly native rulers of the islands where he had already landed. It was here, on the small island of Mactan off the shore of Cebu, that he was destined to die, a few weeks later, at the height of his triumph.

XI

Conquistador and Holy Man

Today, four hundred and fifty years afterwards, a curious visitor to Cebu can still find reminders of Magellan's brief but dramatic passage on the island and on nearby Mactan. In the city's Church of the Augustinian Convent, one is shown a Flemish image of the Virgin that Magellan is supposed to have donated to the local ruler's wife on the occasion of her conversion and baptism. In a square near the centre of the old city, a huge wooden cross is also displayed, beneath a canopy of masonry erected later to protect it. This is the Cross Magellan is reported to have raised here, as he had raised others elsewhere in the Philippines, to mark his passage and to protect friendly natives from the possible violence of later Spanish or Portuguese invaders. In this case, the Cross may even be the one he raised to consecrate a Christian burial-ground.

On the island of Mactan, a Spanish monument was erected, over three hundred years later, on the site where Magellan is believed to have been killed. In recent years, Filipino nationalists have now built, facing it, a much more important monument to commemorate Si Lapulapu, the vassal of the King of Cebu whom Magellan had set out to conquer but who is now honoured as the first hero of Filipino anti-colonialist resistance because he defeated and killed Magellan. Only these four monuments, two of them erected much later, now testify to Magellan's passage through the Philippines. Elsewhere in Portugal, in Spain, in India, East Africa, Morocco, Brazil, Patagonia, Tierra del Fuego or Guam, Magellan left even less trace of his presence, only his last will and testament and a few other scattered documents, most of which are of minor significance. Few great men, in modern history as opposed to antiquity, have left us so faint a trail of their passage among their contemporaries.

Indeed, Magellan's undistinguished appearance and taciturn and uncommunicative manner were not of a nature that could impress his contemporaries, especially in an age that tended so much to stress all display that can immediately impress. His character was of a kind that reveals its greatness only in adversity. His self-confidence and his firmness of purpose were such that he rarely felt the need to explain his actions or to convince the men whose fate was in his hands. Had he failed in his venture, had his last three ships only reached Guam and no survivors then returned to Europe, he might now have been no more famous than those two unfortunate Portuguese navigators, the Cortereal brothers, whose ships appear to have reached Labrador but then disappeared off the North American coast in 1501 and 1502.

Magellan's whole life thus appears to be summarized in one great action of epic proportions, for which the thirty-nine years that preceded it may well have been a slow preparation. He had already revealed, on occasion, rare qualities of presence of mind, of endurance, of courage, of wisdom and of dignity, in Malacca for example and when he was shipwrecked on the shoals of Padua, off the Malabar coast of India, and later in Morocco and in his difficult relationship with the King of Portugal. But the context of all these other occasions had not allowed Magellan to stand out from the crowd of other adventurous Portuguese officers of his age and generation in such a manner as to impress contemporary witnesses with his unusual character. Only on his great expedition did these qualities begin to make themselves manifest to his more perceptive companions. His handling of Cartagena's display of rebellious independence, off the coast of Africa, already revealed his genius for leadership and cunning, which was proved even more brilliantly by the way in which he later mastered the mutiny in the Bay of Saint Julian.

But it was now, in his actions and his bearing in the Philippines, that Magellan displayed, to all who saw him, a kind of greatness of which he himself appears to have been aware, if only as the apostolic representative, in these distant lands, of the Christian Church and of the King of Spain. As he sailed, 'passing many villages where we saw houses built on piles', into the harbour of Cebu, at noon on Sunday, April 7 1521, Magellan ordered his ships to unfurl all their banners and to lower their sails, as if for battle, and fire all their cannon. This show of force immediately caused a panic in the population of the city, but Magellan then sent ashore as his 'ambassador', together with an interpreter, a young man whom Pigafetta mysteriously describes as the Captain General's 'pupil' or 'foster-son', probably meaning that he was Magellan's page.

When they landed, the young delegate and his interpreter found a large crowd of natives gathered around their ruler, expecting the worst after Magellan's display of his artillery. The interpreter explained to them that such was the custom of Magellan's fleet, whenever it entered a harbour like that of Cebu, and that the firing of all their cannon expressed their friendly intentions and their respect for the local ruler. Reassured, the King of Cebu asked Magellan's envoy the purpose of their visit; it was explained to him that the Captain General had come as the representative of the world's most powerful monarch and that the Spice Islands were the ultimate goal of his expedition. Because of the good that Magellan had heard of the King of Cebu from the ruler of a neighbouring isle, he had come here solely on a visit and to replenish his stores of food, in exchange for some of the merchandise he carried.

The King offered his welcome, adding however that it was the custom that all ships entering his harbour should pay him tribute. Only four days earlier a junk laden with gold and slaves had come from Siam and paid this tribute. To prove his point, the King introduced a merchant who had remained after the junk's departure to sell its cargo. Magellan's envoy replied through his interpreter that their Captain, because he represented so great a monarch, paid tribute to no other ruler throughout the world. If the King of Cebu wished peace, he would have peace; if war, he would have war. A Moorish merchant, perhaps a Malayan or Javanese Moslem, interrupted the conversation to warn the King: 'Be careful, Lord, these are the people who have already conquered Calicut, Malacca and all of India. If you treat them well, you will gain thereby. But if you treat them badly, you will fare badly and worse at their hands, like the rulers of Calicut and Malacca.'

The interpreter understood all this and explained to the Moor that the King of Spain, being Emperor of all Christendom, was even more powerful, in terms of ships and armed men, than the King of Portugal. If the King of Cebu now rejected the King of Spain's friendship, the latter would send another expedition with so many men that they would destroy him, all of which the Moorish merchant now repeated to the native monarch, who replied that he would consult his advisers before sending Magellan an answer on the morrow. Meanwhile, he ordered that a plentiful feast be brought, served in porcelain dishes and with a great quantity of wines. After the meal, the envoys returned aboard their flagship, to report to Magellan. Another native ruler, who had accompanied Magellan, then went ashore to convince the King of Cebu of Magellan's 'great courtesy'.

On the Monday morning, the fleet's notary was sent ashore with the interpreter and was met there, in the main square, by the monarch, accompanied by all his chief officials. Magellan's envoys were invited to be seated beside the King, who asked them if there were more than one captain aboard their ships and whether Magellan expected him, the King of Cebu, to pay tribute to the King of Spain. He was reassured when Magellan's envoy stated that this was not expected. The Captain General only wanted to trade some of his goods here rather than elsewhere.

The King seemed satisfied and suggested that Magellan send him some blood from his arm, in order to celebrate the Malayan ceremony of blood-brotherhood, for which he too would send Magellan some of his own blood. To this, Magellan's envoy agreed. In addition, the King stated that all captains who came to his land followed the custom of exchanging gifts with him, so they should suggest to Magellan that he also observe this custom. Again, Magellan's envoy agreed, but suggested that the King of Cebu make the first move and offer Magellan a gift, after which Magellan would certainly do his duty.

The following morning, the native ruler who had come to Cebu with Magellan returned aboard the flagship, accompanied by the Moorish merchant and bearing greetings from the King of Cebu, who was busy collecting as many provisions as possible to send as gifts to Magellan. Later in the day, the King of Cebu planned to send one of his nephews, with a delegation of men of rank, to conclude a peaceful agreement.

Again, Magellan had recourse to tactics of intimidation, perhaps because his memories of the unfortunate first Portuguese expedition to Malacca had left him little faith in Malayan expressions of friendliness. To impress the King of Cebu's envoys, he therefore ordered one of his men to don full armour and then explained, through an interpreter, that all his men went into battle thus armed, a boast which appeared to dismay the Moorish envoy considerably. Magellan reassured him, however, by stating that the weapons of his force were gentle to his friends and sharp only to his foes: much as a linen kerchief can wipe away a man's sweat, so could the arms of the Spaniards mop up and destroy all the enemies of their faith and those who wished it ill. Pigafetta adds in his *Journal* that Magellan was at great pains to impress this Moor with his power, since he knew that he was more intelligent than the natives of Cebu and would repeat it all to their King.

Later in the day, the King's nephew returned with the other native ruler, the Moorish merchant, the governor of the city, the captain of the local forces and other officials. Their purpose was to conclude the formal peace treaty. Magellan received them in a thronelike red-velvet chair, surrounded by his chief officers, seated on leather chairs, while the rest sat on mats on the deck. Magellan begun by asking them whether it was their custom, on such occasions, to make their formal declarations in secret council or by public proclamation, and whether the King's nephew had been granted powers to conclude a peaceful agreement. They replied that he had the necessary powers and that the ceremony should be public.

Acting as host aboard his flagship, Magellan assumed the

responsibility of initiating the public ceremonies by delivering a long speech on the benefits of peace, after which he pronounced a prayer this earthly peace be confirmed by the Almighty in Heaven. All this was interpreted to the native envoys, who were delighted with it and exclaimed, according to Pigafetta's report, that they had never heard such thoughts and arguments uttered. Seeing that he had such a willing audience, Magellan continued his speech, encouraging them to accept the Christian faith.

After a while, he asked who would inherit the King of Cebu's throne after his death. He was told that the King had no sons, only several daughters, but that his nephew was married to the eldest of these daughters and was therefore the heir to the throne. But it was not their custom to await the death of a ruler. In their country, parents who became old were always set aside or deposed by the son who then assumed command.

Magellan resumed his speech by explaining how God had created the Heavens, the Earth, the Seas and all things that are in the world and had ordered that each man should honour and obey his father and his mother, so that whoever neglected this commandment would be condemned to the eternal fires of Hell. He also expounded many other particulars concerning the Christian faith, all of which they heard willingly, asking him to leave two of his men among them to guide them in the Christian faith.

Magellan replied that, in present circumstances, he could spare none of his men to grant such a request. But, should these people truly wish to become Christians, his fleet's priest would baptize them, and he himself would later return to Cebu with priests and preachers who would teach them the Christian faith. They answered, however, that they wished to consult their King before becoming Christians.

Pigafetta reports that Magellan's men wept with joy as they witnessed the good will of these natives, and that Magellan recommended to them that they should not become Christians out of fear of the Spaniards or to ingratiate themselves with them, but their conversion should come truly from their hearts and from their love of God. Should any of them prefer to continue to live by their own laws, no harm would be done to them, though those who became Christians would of course be granted preferential treatment. As with one voice, the natives cried out that they were not inspired by fear or by a wish to please in their desire to become Christians, and Magellan then promised them, should they indeed be converted, that he would leave them the weapons that Christians use, since such had been his orders from the King of Spain. Finally, the native envoys stated that they no longer knew what to reply to Magellan's good words and promises, but that they placed themselves in his hands for him to use them as if they were his servants.

Magellan concluded the ceremony by rising from his chair to embrace them with tears in his eyes. Taking the native ruler and the young prince by their hands, he declared to them solemnly, by the faith he had in God and the loyalty he bore to the King of Spain as well as by the costume of a Knight of the Order of Saint James of Compostella he was now wearing, that he promised them a lasting peace with the King of Spain. The young prince and his retinue replied with a similar promise.

Magellan then offered refreshments to his guests, who presented to him, on behalf of the King of Cebu, generous gifts of rice and meats, while apologizing for the simplicity of these gifts as unworthy of their recipient. In exchange, Magellan offered the prince some fine cloth and a great quantity of glassware, including a cup of gilded crystal of a kind particularly prized in the Orient. To all the members of the prince's retinue, various gifts were also offered, and Pigafetta and another officer were sent ashore with gifts for the King of Cebu: a robe of yellow and purple silk, cut in Turkish style, a fine red cap and some crystal ware, together with a silver platter and two gilded drinking-glasses.

On reaching the city, Pigafetta and his companion found the King of Cebu awaiting them in his palace, where he was seated on a palm-leaf mat, surrounded by his whole court. Pigafetta describes the King as being naked except for a loin-cloth 'that concealed his shameful parts', a fine silk-embroidered linen turban on his head, a heavy gold chain round his neck and gold ear-rings mounted with precious stones. He was short and stout and had designs branded on his face. As he sat on the floor, the King was eating tortoise-eggs out of porcelain bowls and drinking palm-wine through sugar-cane straws from four different vessels.

After bowing before him, Magellan's two envoys offered him the gifts they bore while their interpreter explained that these were not offered as compensation for those the King had already sent but as an expression of Magellan's love for him, after which the King's envoys reported to him Magellan's professions of peace and exhortations to become Christian. The King had meanwhile donned his new silken robe and red cap and, after accepting the other gifts as well, invited Magellan's two envoys to partake of a feast. They declined, however, and withdrew to the house of the King's nephew, where they were entertained by four girls to a concert of native music on instruments which Pigafetta found strange but soft in sound. Later, they danced with these and other girls, some of whom wore only loin-cloths from the waist to the knees while others, according to one manuscript of the *Journal*, were quite naked. These amusements were followed by a repast, after which Pigafetta and his companion returned to their ship.

That night, one of their men died. The next morning, Pigafetta and the interpreter were sent back to the King to petition for a place of burial. Their request was granted: 'If I and my vassals are ready to be those of your Lord and Master, our land and country must likewise be his.' It was then explained to the King that they planned to consecrate the burial-ground according to their ritual and raise a cross on the grave. The King expressed his satisfaction and declared that he would likewise worship this cross.

The dead man was buried in the middle of the square, perhaps on the spot where one can now see the Cross Magellan is believed to have raised in the centre of the city of Cebu. The same evening, they had to bury another of their men, many of whom had not yet recovered from their hardships. They also unloaded from their ships a great quantity of goods which they stored in a house in the city, to be disposed of by sale or barter. Four men were left ashore to guard and handle these goods, under the protection of the King.

Two days later, Magellan's men began to display their goods in the new store, much to the amazement of the natives, who were willing to give gold in exchange for baser metals and iron tools, and rice or cattle in exchange for the lighter goods. For fourteen pounds of iron, they gave ten of their weights of gold, each one of which Pigafetta estimated as worth two and a half ducats. But Magellan forbade his men to accept large quantities of gold, lest the sailors be tempted to sell their personal property too cheaply in their greed and thus bring down the value of goods he hoped to dispose of more profitably.

On the Saturday, Magellan ordered a platform erected in the square, which had already been consecrated. This platform was decorated with tapestry hangings from the ships and with palm fronds. The King had promised to accept baptism on the coming Sunday. Magellan told him that he need not fear if the cannon were then fired, as it was their custom to fire such salvoes, without cannon-balls or stones, on all holidays.

On the Sunday morning, forty of Magellan's men came ashore, two of them fully armed at their head as they followed the flag bearing the arms of the Spanish King and Emperor. As they landed, the ships fired their cannon and the people fled in all directions in panic. Magellan met the King; they embraced and went to the platform which had been erected for the baptismal ceremony. There they sat in two chairs, one upholstered with red velvet, the other with purple, while the chief officers and members of the royal retinue sat on cushions or mats, each according to his custom.

Magellan explained to the King that the royal banner of the King of Spain was never displayed on land unless it were accompanied by fifty men in armour, such as he himself wore, and fifty other men bearing firearms. As an exception, however, and out of friendship for the native monarch, he had landed today with a much smaller escort. With so many sick men still aboard his ships, it would indeed have been difficult for Magellan to muster up, out of his reduced crews, one hundred able-bodied armed men for the customary escort which he now claimed for such occasions; but Magellan was still intent, by the use of such bluff, on dazzling the King of Cebu.

With the help of his interpreter, Magellan began to prepare the King for his ceremonial conversion to Christianity. First, he gave grace to God for having inspired this conversion, and assured the King that, after his baptism, he would vanquish all his enemies more easily than before. The King then reaffirmed his wish to become a Christian, but added that some of his chiefs refused to obey him, claiming to be his equals. Magellan therefore summoned all the King's chiefs and declared to them that, if they failed to obey their ruler, he would have them executed and would confiscate their property and give it to the King. To this threat they all replied by swearing that they would obey. To the King, Magellan now explained that, should he himself complete his voyage and return to Spain, he would later return to the Philippines with so much power that he would make the King of Cebu the most powerful monarch in this part of the world, because he had been the first to wish to become a Christian.

Raising his hands to heaven, the King thanked Magellan and begged him to leave some of his men there in order to instruct him and his people in the Christian faith. The Captain General now agreed to leave two of his men in Cebu, but added that he wished to take back to Spain two of the King's sons in order that they learn Spanish and, on their return home, explain to the rest of the population all that they had seen and learned in Europe. Such exchanges of hostages, as a precautionary measure, were customary in that age, in most dealings between Europeans and native rulers.

A great cross was now raised in the centre of the square. If they wished to become Christians, Magellan explained to the King and his retinue, they would have to destroy all their idols and raise such crosses in their place. Every day, each convert would have to worship on his knees before the Cross, with hands joined and raised to the sky. Magellan also showed them how each day they should make the sign of the Cross.

After this brief and summary instruction, the King and his retinue confirmed their desire to be baptized. Leading the King by the hand on to the platform, Magellan told him that he would be baptized with the name of Charles, in honour of the King of Spain, and the other native King with the name of John, while one of the chiefs was named Ferdinand, after Magellan himself, and the Moor, who declared his willingness to abandon Islam and become a Christian, was named Christopher. The other converts were likewise baptized with new Christian names. In the course of this one Mass, Pigafetta reports, five hundred men were baptized.

After the ceremony, Magellan invited the King and his retinue to dine aboard his flagship, which they declined, though they accompanied him to the shore, where they all embraced him as they parted. To conclude the celebrations, the fleet fired salvoes from all its cannon.

Later that day, Magellan's priest went ashore again, accompanied by several others, to baptize the Queen and forty of her ladies. They were all led on to the platform, where they remained seated on cushions while the priest donned his vestments. He then showed them a carved wooden figure of the Madonna bearing the infant Jesus and a Cross. It had a quasi-miraculous effect on the ladies of Cebu, who were overcome by contrition and, in tears, begged to be baptized. The Queen was named Joanna, after the daughter of Ferdinand and Isabella who was the mother of the King of Spain. The Queen's daughter was named Catherine and the wife of the other native King was named Elizabeth.

In the course of this second ceremony, some three hundred more natives were baptized; Pigafetta concludes that eight hundred men, women or children were thus baptized in one day. He goes on to describe the beauty of the Queen and the crown of palm-leaves, shaped somewhat like a papal tiara, which she wore. She asked to be given the image of the Virgin and the infant Christ, in order to keep it where she had previously kept her idols. In 1565, when the second Spanish expedition landed in the Philippines, this image was recovered in Cebu, where it had meanwhile been replaced by an idol; it is now carefully preserved in the church of Cebu's Augustinian monastery as a relic of the first conversion of its people to Christianity.

After the Queen's baptism, the whole court accompanied the priest and his party down to the shore. Magellan ordered his fleet to fire many salvoes in their honour, both of light and heavy artillery. Within the next week, the whole population of Cebu and of some of the neighbouring isles was baptized. Humaubon, Rajah of Cebu, now renamed Charles, and Magellan called each other brothers and co-operated in the task of proselytization. One village indeed was destroyed by fire, for refusing to obey the King, and was thus christianized by force: 'We raised a Cross there,' Pigafetta explains, 'because these people were Gentiles. Had they been Moors, we would have raised a column there as a symbol of greater severity, because Moors are somewhat more difficult to convert than Gentiles.'

In spite of the destruction of this one village, Magellan's penetration of Cebu appears to have been achieved relatively peacefully, with a minimum of violence and a great deal of persuasion in addition to some sheer bluff. In this respect, it contrasts strongly with the atrocities committed by the Portuguese under Albuquerque in their penetration of India and with those that Spanish conquistadors perpetrated in the Americas. Nor is Magellan's insistence on peaceful proselytization the only remarkable aspect of his policy: for Pigafetta had recorded on at least two occasions Magellan's unwillingness, unlike other conquistadors, to accept gold, whether in the form of gifts or in exchange for the goods that he offered.

During the days that followed these solemn baptisms, Magellan appears to have been completely carried away by his sudden success in his newly acquired apostolic vocation. Missionary work now appears to have become Magellan's main preoccupation, to the extent of obsession. Every day he went ashore to attend Mass with his numerous new converts and to instruct the King in the Christian faith. One day, the Queen came with great pomp, with all her ladies in waiting. After paying her respects to the altar she sat on a silken cushion. Before the service began, Magellan came and sprinkled scented water over her and her attendants.

On another occasion, before the daily service began, Magellan summoned the King and the chief men of the city. He made the latter take an oath of loyalty to their King, whose hands they had to kiss; after which, the King had to swear that he would always obey the King of Spain and be loyal to him, which he agreed to do. Then Magellan drew his sword and, standing before the image of the Virgin Mary, declared to the King that, after giving this oath, he should be more ready to die than ever to break it. The King repeated his oath, swearing loyalty before the Madonna.

Magellan rewarded him with the gift of one of his throne-like chairs of red velvet, explaining that he should have it carried before him wherever he went, as a symbol of his power. In exchange, the King offered Magellan a costly replica of his own regalia of gold and gems, including earrings and bracelets for arms, and ankles, which he had ordered to be made and would give him as soon as they would be ready.

Not content with friendly and pious declarations, Magellan appears also to have spent some time checking the religious practices of his recent converts, with an eye for relapses from their newly acquired faith into their older heathen practices. One day, he asked the King and his retinue why they had not burned all their idols, as they had promised to do now that they were Christians, and why they still offered sacrifices of flesh to them. They replied that they did not make these sacrifices for themselves, but for a sick man, in order that the idols should grant him health. For the last four days, the sick man had already been too weak to speak. He was the prince's brother and the wisest and bravest man of the whole island.

The Captain General insisted that they burn their idols and place their faith in Christ. If the sick man were baptized, he would immediately recover his health. If this failed to happen, they would be free to behead him, Magellan, immediately. The King agreed to follow Magellan's instructions, since he himself truly believed in Christ. They accordingly went in procession from the great square to the sick man's house. They found him already unable to speak or to move and baptized him then and there, together with his two wives and ten maidens. Magellan then asked the sick man how he felt. Suddenly, he spoke and declared that, by the grace of God, he already felt better. Pigafetta was present at this scene and declares, in his *Journal:* 'This was a most manifest miracle accomplished in our times.' When Magellan heard the sick man speak, he gave thanks to God, after which he offered him a drink of almond-milk, which he had specially prepared for him, and sent him later a mattress, a pair of sheets, a blanket of yellow cloth and a pillow. Until he was fully recovered, Magellan continued to send him daily gifts of almond-milk, rose-water, rose-scented oil and some sweetmeats. Less than five days later, the sick man was already able to walk and ordered the burning of an idol which some old women had kept concealed in his house. This was done in the presence of the King and of all the people. He also ordered the destruction of a great number of heathen shrines that were along the sea-shore and in which it was their custom to eat consecrated sacrificial meats. With loud cries of 'Castille! Castille!', the people destroyed them, declaring that, if God would lend them life, they would continue to destroy whatever idols they found, even in the King's palace.

Pigafetta now interrupts his account of Magellan's crusade against heathen practices in order to devote several pages of his *Journal* to various native customs that he had observed. A description of the idols destroyed in the zealous campaign of Christian iconoclasm leads him to name the main towns or villages of Cebu and their various princes or chiefs, then to describe in detail the ritual of their heathen sacrifices of swine—how the flesh is prepared and ceremoniously eaten. Finally, he offers some curious descriptions of native sexual customs. The men, he observes, all have their penis pierced or infibulated with a metal instrument that makes it impossible for them to penetrate a woman or to withdraw from her while in a state of erection. They have this custom, he declares, because the men 'are weak by nature', presumably meaning that, like many other peoples of the Far East, they are endowed with a somewhat small penis. The women, on the other hand, are specially trained from early girlhood, 'by opening their nature' at the age of six, to cope later with a penis that has thus been artificially enlarged. Though each married man has a chief wife, the men are polygamous and marry as many wives as they wish. But Pigafetta also reports that the women of Cebu soon showed a remarkable predilection for the men of Magellan's fleet, which may well have been a leading cause of the troubles that soon ensued.

In spite of Magellan's catechistic successes on the island of Cebu, Christianity did not make such remarkable progress on the smaller neighbouring island of Mactan. On Friday April 27, a delegation came from there to Magellan, sent by Zula, one of Mactan's two chiefs, bringing him the tribute which had been promised, but with apologies for delay, caused by the stubbornness of Mactan's other chief, Si Lapulapu, who refused to recognize the authority of the King of Spain as his new overlord. Pigafetta and most of Magellan's biographers refer to this chief as Celapulapu or Silapulapu; they have failed to understand that the particle *Si*, added as a prefix to his name, is only a Malay title, meaning *Lord*, which was borrowed from Arabic. Si Lapulapu, it would seem, was actively attempting to prevent Zula from communicating with Magellan. In fact, Zula begged Magellan to send him, during the following night, a boat full of armed men to aid him in combat against Si Lapulapu.

Encouraged by his recent successes, Magellan now took a decision that very soon proved to have been surprisingly unwise. Had he not, only a few days earlier, wagered his own life and then won his bet by accomplishing a miracle? With the overconfidence of the hero of an ancient Greek tragedy, he ignored the warnings of his officers, who begged him not to accompany this minor expedition, and set out for Mactan at the head of three boatloads of armed men.

They departed at midnight, sixty armed men, wearing breastplates and helmets with visors. 'Like the good shepherd,' Pigafetta adds, Magellan 'did not wish to abandon his flock'; and the author of the *Journal* of course accompanied him, like the shepherd's faithful dog. They were also accompanied by the Christian King of Cebu and a fairly large retinue of his chiefs and native warriors. They reached Mactan three hours before dawn. Magellan was unwilling to fight at once. Instead, he sent a 'Moorish' interpreter, perhaps the Moor who had only recently abjured his faith and accepted baptism, to announce to the chiefs of Mactan that Magellan was ready to be their friend if they were willing to obey the King of Spain, to recognize the Christian King of Cebu as their immediate suzerain and to pay tribute. If they refused, however, they could expect to see how well Magellan's men's lances could strike.

They replied that they had good lances of bamboo and sharpened stakes, well hardened by fire, but wished not to be attacked at once, only later by day, when they would be more numerous. This request, however, was only a ruse intended to entice Magellan to attack at once, in the dark: between their houses, they had dug deep man-traps into which they hoped that Magellan's men would fall.

Magellan, however, waited until dawn, when some fifty of his men disembarked into the shallow offshore waters that reached up to their thighs and had to wade 'more than two crossbow flights' before reaching land. Because of the rocks, their boats could not bring them nearer to the shore. Eleven men remained aboard to guard the three boats.

When they reached the land, they found more than fifteen hundred armed natives awaiting them, divided in three combat groups which charged upon them at once, two groups at their flanks and one at their front, all uttering loud war-cries. Magellan immediately reorganized his small force in two groups as the battle began.

For the first half-hour, his musketeers and crossbow-men shot in vain, from too far away. Magellan ordered them to cease firing, but was not heeded. When the natives saw that their shields could withstand the shots of the European weapons, they redoubled their war-cries and still stood firm, only leaping about, behind their shields, to dodge the aim of their enemies. Meanwhile, they showered so many arrows, bamboo spears—some tipped with metal—and pointed stakes, together with stones and mud, at Magellan and his men that the latter could scarcely defend themselves.

Magellan therefore sent a part of his men to set fire to the houses in order to start a panic. But the fire only increased their rage. Two of the incendiaries were killed on the spot, but some twenty or thirty houses were set on fire.

Then the natives charged Magellan's men so as to engage in closer combat. Magellan himself was soon wounded in the right leg by a poisoned arrow and ordered a slow retreat towards the shore. But his men took to flight, except six or eight of them, including Pigafetta, who remained close to their wounded leader.

The natives aimed only at their legs which, because they had been forced to wade to land from their boats, were bare and unprotected. Pelted with arrows, spears and stones, the retreating men could offer no resistance. From their three boats, their mortars could not cover their retreat with effective fire, being too far away. Still fighting up to their knees in the water, they continued their retreat while the natives pursued them, picking up their spears as they advanced and hurling them again and again. Recognizing Magellan, they now attacked him now in such large numbers that they knocked his helmet twice off his head. But, like Orlando and his paladins in the poems of Boiardo and Ariosto with which Pigafetta was perhaps familiar, Magellan and the few who surrounded him still stood firm.

Refusing to retreat any further, they fought a full hour,

knee-deep in the water. One native warrior then hurled his spear at Magellan's face. But Magellan struck him with his own lance, which he left in the native warrior's body. Seizing his sword, he was able to draw it only half-way, being already wounded in the right arm by a bamboo spear.

When the natives saw Magellan thus unarmed, they all threw themselves on him. One of them wounded him in the left leg with a large scimitar. Magellan fell face downward in the water. Immediately, the natives rushed upon him with their spears and scimitars, 'until they slaughtered our mirror, our light, our comfort and our true leader'.

While they were still striking him, Magellan turned several times to see whether his men were managing to escape. The last of them, including Pigafetta, seeing that their leader was dead, retreated as best they could to the boats, which were already pulling away. The Christian King of Cebu would willingly have intervened in the battle, but Magellan had ordered him, before landing, not to leave his boat and to watch the battle from offshore. He wept when he heard that Magellan was dead.

Pigafetta adds here, to his account of the battle in which he himself was wounded, a final and very touching tribute to the character of his hero: 'Had it not been for our poor captain, not a single one of us would have been saved in the boats, for the others were able to withdraw to them while he was still fighting. I hope . . . that the fame of so noble a captain will never be effaced in our times.'

The battle occured on Saturday, April 27 1521. Magellan had chosen to fight on a Saturday, believing that this day of the week was always particularly propitious in his life. Eight of his men were killed with him, besides four recently baptized natives who had tried to come to their rescue but been shot by the mortars firing from the three boats to cover

Magellan's retreat. Of the enemy, fifteen were killed, but many of Magellan's men now returned wounded to Cebu. Si Lapulapu, of whom nothing else is recorded in history, earned himself in this one day, as a vassal who had rebelled against the King of Cebu, an immortal glory as the first hero of Filipino resistance to foreign colonial penetration.

During the summer of 1971, a news-item from the Philippines was widely publicized in the world press. In the course of excavations on the island of Mactan, some human remains had been discovered. The available evidence suggests that they are some four hundred and fifty years old, and the structure of one skull, in particular, reveals that it is that of a European. It was of course claimed that Magellan's skull had been discovered, but it may just as well be the skull of one of his companions who was also killed and buried in Mactan, since we have no knowledge of Magellan's features and no way of identifying his skull.

Conclusion

The Survivors Return Yesterday

Deprived of their leader, the survivors of Magellan's expedition succumbed almost immediately, in Cebu, to the same kind of confusion as a colony of termites on the death of its queen. Unlike other conquistadors, Magellan had imposed on his men, at all times, a strict discipline to restrain their adventurous rapacity, whether for gold or for women, in their dealings with the natives of the lands that they visited. Now they could give full rein to their greed, without considering whether they would thereby offer to the recent converts of Cebu a less edifying picture of Christian civilization.

Later on the fateful day of Magellan's death, the Christian King of Cebu, after consultation with the surviving Spanish and Portuguese officers, sent an envoy to Mactan, offering its chiefs any quantity of goods in exchange for the bodies of the dead. Though haughty, Si Lapulapu's reply suggests an implicit acknowledgement of Magellan's greatness: 'They would not give up such a man, as well we might think, nor would they give him up for all the greatest riches in the world, but they wished to keep him in order to remember him.' Magellan's corpse was then so carefully kept that his remains have never been found. The monument that commemorates him on the island of Mactan rises far from the shore where he actually died; nor can it be proven that he was ever buried there.

As soon as Magellan's death was known in Cebu, the four men to whom he had entrusted the care and the sale or barter of the expedition's goods in the city began to load them aboard their ships. Were they afraid of being forced to exchange them unprofitably for their lost leader's corpse? Were they expecting his survivors to sail immediately for the Spice Islands, without any further delay in the Philippines? Or did they now intend to disregard Magellan's instructions not to accept gold in payment, but henceforth to sell only smaller quantities against gold and for personal profit? Whatever the reason, their actions did not remain unnoticed and began to undermine the confidence that Magellan had managed to inspire among the natives of Cebu.

Meanwhile, the expedition's survivors could not expect to reach their ultimate goal in the Spice Islands and then return to Spain without a leader. As usual, there were rivalries between Spaniards and Portuguese. Finally, a compromise was reached by electing two leaders, a Portuguese, Duarte Barbosa, a relative by marriage of Magellan, and a Spaniard, Juan Serrano, who had captained the *Santiago* until it was wrecked off the coast of Patagonia. Portuguese historians have claimed that Serrano was a native of Portugal and had previously served Portugal in India; in his report to King Manuel on the preparations for Magellan's expedition, the Portuguese Consul in Seville, Sebastião Alvares, indeed referred to Serrano as Portuguese, confusing him perhaps with Magellan's friend or relative Francisco Serrão. But Pigafetta states clearly that Serrano was a Spaniard and it seems unlikely that the surviving Spanish officers of Magellan's expedition would have accepted, in the present emergency, to serve under two

Portuguese leaders. Serrano may, of course, have been originally of Portuguese extraction, but he had certainly lived several years in Seville and it is known that he had a Spanish wife.

Magellan's slave Enrique was among the wounded who returned from Mactan, where Magellan's personal page or *sobresaliente*, Cristovão Rebêlo, a native of Oporto, had been killed. Enrique appears to have been quite overcome by the death of his master; though not seriously wounded, he lay all day aboard the *Trinidad*, wrapped beneath his cloak or blanket, and refused to go ashore any longer as the expedition's interpreter. Duarte Barbosa lost his temper with the grieving slave and reminded him that, though Magellan was dead, he himself had not thereby become a free man but, on their return to Spain, would become Magellan's widow's slave. If Enrique continued to refuse to do his job as interpreter ashore, Barbosa threatened to beat him.

Enrique knew that Magellan had promised, in his last will and testament, to free him on his own death. Feigning not to heed Barbosa's threats, he went ashore secretly and reported to the King of Cebu that the expedition was planning to sail away very soon, but that it would still be possible by trickery to gain control of its ships and store of goods. A plot was therefore devised whereby the crews would be deprived of all their officers.

From other sources than Pigafetta's *Journal*, we also know that various native chiefs were already exerting considerable pressure on the King of Cebu to get rid of the invaders. Si Lapulapu, for instance, offered to make peace with him if he joined an alliance of native chiefs to drive out the foreigners; if he refused to join them, they threatened to fight him too.

An Italian survivor of the expedition reported moreover, on his return to Europe, that the natives of Cebu were jealous of their wives, so many of whom, as Pigafetta had also noted, already showed a marked preference for Magellan's men. Now that Magellan was no longer there to restrain his men in their amorous relationships with native women, it is indeed very probable that many of them followed the example of Carvalho, whose propensity for such exotic loves had already been proved on his earlier expedition to Brazil, where he had fathered a son by a native Indian mother, and again, under Magellan's captainship, in Brazil and in Patagonia.

While the plot was being hatched in Cebu, Enrique returned aboard the *Trinidad*, where he became less sullen and more serviceable, since the success of the plot depended to a great extent on his efficiency as interpreter.

On Wedneaday morning, May 1, the King of Cebu invited the commanders of the ships to a festive meal in the course of which he promised to hand over to them the jewelry which he had ordered to be made as a gift for the King of Spain. Twenty-four officers thus went ashore, including the expedition's astronomer, San Martín. They were accompanied by Enrique as their interpreter. Pigafetta's face was still inflamed from the poison of the arrow that had wounded it in Mactan, and this fortunately kept him aboard the *Trinidad*. Two of the officers, Carvalho and Espinosa, the provost marshal or constable of the fleet, soon returned, however, as they suspected treachery.

Scarcely had these two explained their reasons for returning when a great outcry reached the ships from the city of Cebu. In order to be ready for any emergency, the three ships weighed anchor, probably on orders from Carvalho and Espinosa, and began firing from their mortars at the houses on the waterfront as they drew in closer to the shore. While they were still firing, Serrano appeared on the strand, wounded, unarmed and in his shirt, in fact bound as a prisoner, and cried out to them to cease firing as the natives would otherwise kill him.

When they asked him, from the ships, whether the others, including Enrique, had already been murdered, he replied that only he and the interpreter had been left alive. He begged them to redeem him from his captors by offering some of their goods. But Carvalho, Espinosa and their friends would not allow a boat to be sent ashore to save Serrano. Pigafetta adds significantly: 'in order that they might remain masters of the fleet'. It would thus appear that Carvalho and Espinosa may have been party to the whole plot, and now remained deaf to Serrano's desperate entreaties. There is every reason to believe that Serrano was promptly killed in Cebu; Enrique, however, may have found his way back from there to his native land and have thus been the first man to circumnavigate the whole Earth.

At a distance of eighteen leagues from Cebu and off the island of Bohol with its curiously rounded brown hills that look like chocolate puddings, the three Spanish ships came to a drastic decision. Twenty-two men had just been lost in Cebu, so that they had only one hundred and fifteen men left to man their ships. After agreeing to allow Carvalho and Espinosa to replace Barbosa and Serrano as their leaders, they chose to sacrifice the *Concepción*, the least seaworthy of their ships, and stowed away the best of its cargo and equipment aboard the *Trinidad* and the *Victoria* before setting fire to it.

The next six months were devoted to aimless wanderings and near-piracy, in the course of which they often faced starvation. Instead of sailing due south to the Moluccas, Carvalho and Espinosa chose to wander off towards the west. They landed in Palawan, the westernmost island of importance in the Philippines, and then in Brunei, a Moslem sultanate on the northern coast of Borneo.

In Palawan they were well received by the native chiefs; and at first the same happened in Brunei. Pigafetta gives us enthusiastic descriptions of the magnificence of this city, built like Venice on canals, of the reception at the Sultan's palace, of the Sultan's elephants and jewels. At long last, he was beginning to see some of the legendary splendours of the Orient. But Carvalho suspected treachery and attacked some of the Sultan's ships that were actually sailing out of the harbour on a military expedition against a neighbouring heathen ruler. In the course of this skirmish, prisoners were taken, though Carvalho later released some of them against ransom, which he pocketed in secret. In retaliation, the Sultan kept as hostages some of the men of the Spanish ships who happened to be on shore. Negotiations for an exchange of prisoners were only partly successful. When Carvalho lost patience and decided to set sail, he left in Brunei, as a hostage, his own young son by a Brazilian Indian mother. Described in surviving contemporary documents as 'Joãozito' or 'Niñito', this child was certainly the first American to go to the Far East. Nothing is known of his subsequent fate.

Returning from Borneo to Palawan, the two ships kidnapped a friendly chief and extracted from him a considerable ransom. In the course of such piratical ventures, Carvalho appears to have thought mainly of lining his own pockets and supplying himself with a floating harem of native women. Pigafetta's accounts of these wanderings and explorations offer us an unusual but somewhat reticent firsthand report of the kind of activity in which an increasing number of Portuguese privateers, deserters or renegades and other European riffraff were already engaging throughout Asia, but especially along the eastern shores of the Bay of Bengal. At its best, this kind of activity, when it consisted of relatively honest coastal commerce conducted between

Asian ports, was soon known as 'country trade'; at its worst, it degenerated very easily into mere piracy.

Carvalho revealed himself, in this respect, quite unscrupulous. After stopping among some smaller islands off the northern coast of Borneo to caulk and mend their ships with timber obtained with great difficulty and hardship from the tropical forest, the crews mutinied, under Espinosa, against Carvalho, who was tried for his irregularities after having been replaced by Sebastián del Cano. Later, in the Moluccas, when the King of Tidore asked them to leave a few men with him as hostages or representatives of Spain as they were about to depart, Carvalho was one of the few chosen to remain there. Though he had been involved in the mutiny in the Patagonian Bay of Saint Julian, del Cano, a Spaniard, was a man of greater will and discipline than Espinosa. Within the next few months, he proved, on the long and hazardous return voyage to Spain, a truly great leader and pilot.

At first, however, del Cano appears to have hesitated. Perhaps he had lost his bearings and no longer really knew where they were. After failing to find the course to the Moluccas, the two battered ships sailed back to the Philippines, where they picked up native pilots who finally guided them to their goal. At long last, on November 6 1521, they sighted four mountainous islands that rose high above the sea. These were the famed Spice Islands, legendary goal of their whole expedition. They had reached them, according to Pigafetta's carefully kept log-book, 'twenty-seven months less two days' after sailing out of Seville. To express their joy they fired all their cannon and rendered to God prayers of thanks.

They finally landed on the island of Tidore on November 8. The next day, they were well received by the island's monarch, who had been warned of their coming in a dream.

Although Mohammedan, he declared his readiness and that of his people 'to be the most loyal friends and vassals to our King of Spain'. But, on entering the ship and departing from it, 'he would not stoop' and 'would never bend his head'. Pigafetta describes him as well built, having 'a royal presence' and being an excellent astrologer. His name like that of many another Moslem Sultan, was Almanzor or El-Mansur.

His eagerness to curry favour with the King of Spain can be explained by the fact that his old enemy, the Sultan of the neighbouring island of Ternate, was assured of Portuguese support, should war ever flare up again between them. In 1511, Magellan's friend or cousin Francisco Serrão had already reached Ternate from Malacca and established himself successfully there as Grand Vizier or adviser of the local Sultan, even managing to negotiate a peace with Tidore, whose Sultan was forced to accept the ruler of Ternate as his overlord. But Serrão had died in Ternate some eight months earlier.

Pigafetta's account of the political situation in these otherwise fortunate and fabulously wealthy islands is full of curious insights and details. Serrão had been the 'Captain General' of the King of Ternate in his wars against Tidore and conducted these so successfully that he had forced the ruler of Tidore to give one of his daughters in marriage to his victorious enemy as well as most of his sons as hostages. Some years after this humiliating peace, Serrão had come on a visit to Tidore, whose King availed himself of this opportunity to poison him with doctored betel-leaves offered after a sumptuous feast. On his return to Ternate, Serrão expired.

But a small Portuguese force, coming from Malacca at Serrão's request, had already established regular links with

Ternate, so that the survivors of Magellan's Spanish expedition could no longer hope to obtain control, with their weakened forces, of all the Spice Islands for the King of Spain. From Tidore and the neighbouring island of Bacchian, however, with the help of Sultan Almanzor, they obtained at very advantageous prices, in exchange for their own goods, the valuable cargo of cloves and other spices with which, on their return to Spain, they still hoped to finance the huge cost of the expedition. With typically Italian insight, Pigafetta soon understood that the friendly Sultan hoped to use the Spanish expedition and its artillery to serve his own political ambitions: 'He wished us to give him a seal of the King of Spain and a royal banner, because he had decided that henceforth his own island and that which is named Ternate (and of which one could crown his nephew Colonoghapi as King) would both come under the dependency of the King of Castille. For the honour of his Suzerain, he was ready to fight until his own death, and should he no longer be able to resist or defend himself, he would sail off to Spain aboard a junk, with all his retinue. After which, he begged us to leave some of our men with him in order, at all times, to remind him all the better of his obligations to the King of Spain.'

Dynastic ambitions and entanglements were the main occupation of the wealthy monarchs of the five Spice Islands, of which Ternate was the largest and wealthiest. Less than two weeks after Serrão's death by poisoning, it was his monarch's turn: the King of Ternate had already driven his own son-in-law from the throne of the neighbouring island of Bacchian or Batjan, but was now frustrated in his imperialist ambitions by his daughter who avenged her husband by poisoning her father while pretending to have invited both husband and father to a feast that would lead them to a peaceful solution of their conflicts. Two days later, the poisoned monarch died, leaving no less than nine sons as legitimate heirs, to say nothing of other sons by his numerous concubines.

One of these sons now came on an official visit to Tidore, to meet the captains of the two foreign ships. In his retinue, he brought, as interpreter, an Indian Christian named Manuel, the servant of a Portuguese, Pedro Alfonso de Lorosa, who had come to Ternate, after Serrão's death, from a Portuguese trading-station on the island of Banda, in the southern Moluccas, where the Portuguese had been established ever since 1512.

Pedro Alfonso de Lorosa was now invited by letter to come to Tidore without fear. A few days later, he complied with the invitation. For the survivors of Magellan's expedition, this was their first contact with another European since they had left the Canary Islands just over two years earlier.

Lorosa had already spent sixteen years of his career in the Portuguese Indies, at first in India and now, for the past ten years, in the Moluccas. But he was well informed and received information and instructions regularly from Banda and Malacca. Though they had now been trading directly with the Spice Islands for the past ten years, in fact ever since Serrão had discovered them and settled in Ternate, the Portuguese kept this a secret, most probably because their manpower shortages prevented them from establishing new bases beyond Banda. They were therefore very anxious that Spain, if Magellan's expedition proved to be successful, should not establish bases in the other islands ahead of them.

The most important news from Europe Lorosa brought to Magellan's survivors in Tidore concerned themselves. Lorosa knew that the King of Portugal, to intercept Magellan's expedition on its departure from Europe, had sent out two fleets, one to await its arrival near the Cape of Good Hope, the other near Cape Saint Mary, south of the Plata estuary in South America. Neither of these fleets had managed to sight Magellan's fleet. Later, the King of Portugal had been informed, probably by his spies in Seville when the *San Antonio* returned, that the rest of the Spanish fleet had passed 'by another sea' and was well on its way to the Spice Islands. Immediately, he had instructed Diogo Lopes de Sequeira, who commanded his forces in India, to send six ships to the Moluccas. But Sequeira, hard pressed by threats of a new Turkish attack on his Indian bases and on Malacca, had been unable to spare these ships. Instead, he had sent all his available ships to attack the Turkish fleet in the Red Sea, off Aden and Jeddah.

The Venetians were still urging the Sultan of Turkey to help them wrest the spice trade from the Portuguese, and Suleyman the Magnificent, during the early years of his reign, continued to harass Portuguese shipping, with varying success, throughout the northern part of the Indian Ocean. On this occasion, however, Sequeira's Portuguese fleet failed to contact the enemy and had to content itself with burning a few Turkish galleys stranded in dry dock on the shore of Aden. On his fleet's return to India, Sequeira felt less immediately threatened and then sent a galleon, accompanied by two smaller ships armed with cannon, to intercept Magellen in the Moluccas. But they encountered reefs, adverse currents and winds in the straits between Singapore and Sumatra and were forced to turn back to Malacca. From there, however, a caravel and two junks had reached Ternate and Batjan only recently, to collect a shipment of spices and obtain news of Magellan. After acquiring cloves in Batjan, this Portuguese expedition had been forced to return hurriedly to Malacca, without loading its precious cargo: the seven Portuguese officers of its two junks—the rest of their crews being composed of native Asian seamen— had molested the women of the royal entourage, though they had been warned not to apprach them, and had been captured and killed, after which the caravel had set sail without further ado, leaving its cargo of cloves as well as enough merchandise to purchase more spices by barter.

These were the cloves which the King of Tidore was now offering in Batjan to the Spanish fleet, instead of his own cloves which, he said, had not yet been harvested or properly dried. From the reports of Lorosa, Magellan's men were moreover able to gather that the Spice Islands exported their valuable crops quite regularly aboard native junks to Malacca. These junks could sail from the northern Moluccas in three days to Banda and from there in fifteen days to Malacca. Without having yet established a base in the northern Moluccas, Portugal had thus been secretly controlling, via Malacca, most of their valuable exports for the past ten years. But the quarrelsome Kings of these rich islands were so deeply involved in dissensions and dynastic intrigues that they were now quite willing to shift their loyalties overnight to Spain and even welcomed the arrival of a Spanish fleet as a strong bargaining point in further dealings with the Portuguese.

These Kings of Tidore, Ternate, Mothir, Machian, Batjan and nearby Gilolo seem moreover to have had other reasons to welcome the Spaniards in their area. On the one hand, they had already experienced Portuguese rapacity, both in wresting the spice trade from the Moslem merchants of Malacca who had formerly controlled it and in their predatory attacks on native women and equally predatory attempts to extort gold; on the other hand, they were well aware of the blind hatred of Islam that the Portuguese displayed wherever they established themselves, all the way from Morocco to the Indian Ocean and Malacca.

Of the Spaniards, however, these Moslem rulers had no knowledge and could reasonably hope, since these too were enemies of the Portuguese, that they could become useful allies. How could they have heard, in an age when no established trade-routes existed across the vast Pacific Ocean, of the atrocities that the intolerant Spanish conquistadors were already committing in the Americas? Because they already felt threatened from Portuguese bases in Malacca and Banda, they revealed a touching willingness to ally themselves with Spain and to rely on the Spaniards to defend their vested interests.

Pigafetta's *Journal* records numerous incidents that illustrate this faith and these hopes. Under Sebastian del Cano's leadership, the officers and crews of the expedition appear moreover to have recovered some of the discipline Magellan had imposed on them but which they had forgotten in the panic that followed his death and during the long months of near-piracy into which Carvalho had led them. In their dealings with the various rulers of the Spice Islands and with their subjects, they were now scrupulously ceremonious and honest, though at times hesitant, apprehensive or distrustful.

The native rulers in their turn all appeared anxious to establish friendly relations with Spain on a permanent basis. Not only did they offer at advantageous prices far more spices than the two ships could load, but they promised to reserve for them, for their return from Spain, whatever they could not load at once as well as all future crops. Clearly, they were unwilling to continue trading with the Portuguese. Even the Portuguese agent in Tidore, Pedro Alfonso de Lorosa, turned up one day in Ternate, with his native wife and all his goods, and asked to be transported back to Spain.

At the last moment, however, the departure of the two ships was delayed by an ominous mishap. They had almost run out of goods to distribute as gifts or to exchange in barter for spices, so that the officers and men alike were reduced to the bare necessities of life in their eagerness to obtain, in exchange for any surplus clothing, weapon or other personal property, as large a private store of valuable spices as possible, so as to sell them profitably on their return to Spain. Both ships were thus as heavily loaded as they had ever been, with all their stores and arms, when they had first set out from Spain, but no longer at all as seaworthy. As they were about to set sail, the *Trinidad* sprang a mysterious leak, which could not be located in its hull. Even the most expert divers, summoned by the friendly King of Tidore, were unable to find its source. Pigafetta describes with admiration how they remained under water a whole hour, which scarcely seems possible, while they repeatedly explored the whole hull, allowing their long hair to float loosely in the sea so that it would be drawn by the suction to the spot where the water might be penetrating the damaged timbers.

Finally, it became clear that the *Trinidad* needed to undergo extensive repairs before it could be expected to undertake the long voyage back to the nearest Spanish port. It was therefore decided that the *Victoria*, captained by Sebastian del Cano, would set forth alone for Seville, while the *Trinidad*, captained by Espinosa, would remain in Tidore for repairs and then cross the more peaceful waters of the whole Pacific Ocean so as to reach a Spanish port in Darien, on the isthmus of Panama, and thus avoid being buffeted, in its precarious condition, by the stormy seas which could be expected while rounding the Cape of Good Hope. From

251

Darien, its precious cargo would have to be transported overland to the Gulf of Mexico, and taken aboard another ship across the Atlantic to Spain.

Fortunately for himself as well as for posterity, Pigafetta was able, at the last moment, to abandon the *Trinidad*, on which he had sailed so far because it was Magellan's flagship. He now boarded the *Victoria* so as to complete his circumnavigation of the Earth by returning to Seville under Sebastian del Cano. With him, he brought his precious *Journal*, but all of Magellan's papers as well as those of the fleet's late astronomer, San Martín, remained aboard the *Trinidad* and were subsequently lost.

Leaving the *Trinidad* to be repaired in Tidore, where the King promised to supply all the necessary timber and labour and to keep its officers and crew, while the repairs were being undertaken, under his personal protection, the *Victoria* set out at long last, on its hazardous return voyage, on Saturday December 21 1521.

Its officers and men were fully aware of the dangers that they faced. Though heavily loaded with its precious cargo of spices, the *Victoria* no longer had sufficient stores of trade-goods to obtain more than the barest necessities for supplies and repairs. Besides, its reduced crew was neither powerful enough nor well enough armed to be able to defend itself against the attacks of Portuguese ships encountered along the sea-lanes, between the East Indies and the Canary Islands, that were policed by Portuguese fleets which had been warned from Lisbon to intercept Magellan at any cost. Sebastian del Cano chose very wisely to avoid all those routes, through the Straits of Malacca and across the Bay of Bengal and the northern part of the Indian Ocean, which had already been explored and were now regularly used by Portuguese navigators. Instead, he trusted to his own sea-

manship and to the experience he had acquired in sailing
unknown seas by unfamiliar stars under Magellan. Charting
an entirely new south-westerly course, at first with the help
of native pilots, the *Victoria* thus sailed from the Moluccas
towards Amboyna and Timor, then passed south of Java so
that they just missed discovering Australia, still an unknown
continent.

For nearly two months, the *Victoria* skirted the southernmost string of islands in the East Indies, stopping from time
to time, whenever del Cano felt safe from Portuguese
attacks, to obtain supplies of fresh water or foodstuffs, or to
caulk his ship. Pigafetta was then able to observe, among the
natives of islands that Hinduism and Islam had not yet
penetrated, many curious customs that he describes in his
Journal with his usual alacrity.

But his account of the course actually followed is confused
by additional information he obtained from hearsay about
other areas of the Far East which the *Victoria* never even
approached. His *Journal* thus offers us facts and fables about
China, the Malayan peninsula, even Burma and India,
including some sketchy details about the latter's caste-
system. He reports as facts some ancient legends, such as that
of the gigantic *garuda* bird from which the Indonesian
national airline today derives its name. His lists of names of
the islands they actually passed or about which they heard
as they went has left modern scholars so perplexed that the
Victoria's exact course cannot be traced on any map.

Nor was its progress easy. Long before reaching the vast
landless stretches of the Indian Ocean, its crew was already,
on several occasions, in danger of starvation or of shipwreck.
During one particularly heavy storm, the terrified men of
the *Victoria* promised, should they survive and return safely
to Spain, to undertake a collective pilgrimage to Our Lady

of Antigua. According to the log-book of the pilot Francisco Albo, some of the men even mutinied or deserted on the island of Timor. At last, on February 11 1522, the *Victoria* left behind it these thousands of Indonesian islands and sailed into the great expanse of the Indian Ocean.

To avoid encountering Portuguese ships, they passed far to the south of Madagascar and, steering clear of the coasts of Africa, set out to round the Cape of Good Hope so far south that they were buffeted for nine whole weeks, with their sails hauled down, by adverse Antarctic storms. According to Francisco Albo, they sighted in the Indian Ocean an island, perhaps Amsterdam Island, where they tried in vain to land for supplies. Many of the men lost all hope as the *Victoria* was leaking badly and, because of the cold and the shortage of food, begged to be landed in the Portuguese settlement of Mozambique. Their rations were already reduced to rice and water; their stores of meat, for lack of salt to preserve them, had putrefied while they were crossing the Indian Ocean. But the majority, 'more anxious for their honour than for their life', preferred not to risk becoming prisoners of the Portuguese. Nevertheless, they decided to risk sailing closer to the Cape of Good Hope and finally, on May 6, rounded it at a distance of five sea-leagues from the shore. 'Had we not come so close to it,' adds Pigafetta, 'we would never have managed to round it.' But even the date of their rounding of the Cape remains obscure: Francisco Albo's log-book states that they passed from the Indian Ocean into the Atlantic on May 19.

For two months, they continued to sail up the western coast of Africa without daring to land for fresh supplies of food and water. Again, as on its crossing of the Pacific under Magellan, the crew suffered near-starvation and was decimated by disease. Twenty-one men, according to Pigafetta, died aboard the *Victoria* during those two months: 'When we cast their corpses into the ocean, the Christians sank to the bottom with their face turned upward while the Indians always sank with their face turned downward. If God had not granted us favourable weather, we would all have died of hunger.' This is the last reference, in Pigafetta's *Journal*, to Asian passengers or members of the *Victoria*'s crew; it would thus seem that they all died before reaching their next haven.

The plight of the *Victoria* was so serious that, in spite of the danger, it was forced to stop, on Wednesday, July 9 1522, at the island of Santiago, in the Cape Verde archipelago, already a Portuguese possession. Here del Cano sent a boat ashore with merchandise in order to obtain provision by barter. But he also had recourse to stratagem: instead of admitting to the Portuguese that they had come with spices from the Moluccas, his men were told to claim to be on their way back from the Americas, but to have been isolated from the rest of their fleet by losing their foremast 'under the equinoctial line' whereas they had actually lost it while rounding the Cape of Good Hope. According to this story, their captain general had already returned to Spain with two other ships while the *Victoria* had been delayed by having to restep its foremast.

The Portuguese at first believed del Cano's men and were friendly enough to provide two boatloads of rice in exchange for the goods they offered. But one of the sailors unwisely showed, in a boastful mood, some of his own valuable spices, so that the Portuguese, who had a monopoly of the spice-trade along these sea-lanes, at once understood that the *Victoria* was on its return to Spain from the Far East. Some contemporary Portuguese documents give another version of this story: the men sent ashore from the *Victoria* for a third boatload of rice were foolish enough to offer spices instead of money to the harbour slaves who helped load the rice and pump the bilge-water out of their boat.

Whichever version of this indiscretion is correct, the Portuguese reacted promptly to their discovery of the real identity of the *Victoria* and its crew. The Governor of Santiago arrested the thirteen men who were on land and sent word to the rest of the crew of the *Victoria* that they should surrender at once. But the *Victoria* had fortunately just prepared to sail closer to land; instead, while ships were now being sent out to surround it, it turned about swiftly and sailed off.

It was during their brief stay in Santiago that the men aboard the *Victoria* made a discovery that puzzled them greatly and continued for a long while to puzzle others when they finally landed, nearly two months later, in Seville. The men sent ashore in Santiago on Wednesday July 9 had been instructed by del Cano to check the date with the Portuguese, who informed them that it was already Thursday July 10. This surprised Pigafetta in particular: 'We could not understand how we had made a mistake, as I, who had never been ill, had never ceased to keep a journal every day, without any interruption.'

Though an Arab astronomer, Malek Abulfeda, had already calculated, some two centuries earlier, that one would gain a day, in theory, if one could circle the Earth while following the Sun, this phenomenon was not yet generally known nor could it be fully understood until it had now been observed empirically. But all this was satisfactorily explained to Pigafetta and the survivors of Magellan's expedition only later in Seville, after astronomers and navigators had debated the matter at great length.

Meanwhile, the crew of the *Victoria*, when it escaped from the Cape Verde islands, was reduced to a handful of survivors. 115 members of the expedition's original crews had sailed, aboard three ships, from Cebu. When they reached the Moluccas, after the losses suffered in Brunei and elsewhere, they had already been reduced to 101 men, without counting native pilots and other captives. Fifty-four had then been left in Tidore while sixty men of the original crews sailed from there aboard the *Victoria*. After the mutiny that occurred in Timor, several men had been executed and others had deserted. Twelve men, besides all the Indonesians who accompanied them, died of scurvy or of other diseases between their last landing in Indonesia and the Cape Verde Islands, where another thirteen men were seized by the Portuguese, who sent them later as prisoners to Lisbon.

On Saturday, September 6 1522, the battered *Victoria* entered at long last the Bay of San Lúcar, with only eighteen men left aboard. On Monday September 8, they cast anchor off the quay of Seville and fired all their guns. The very next day, barefoot and wearing only their shirts, they visited the shrines of Santa Maria de la Victoria and of Santa Maria of Antigua, each of them holding a lighted candle as they passed in procession through the streets of the city.

According to Pigafetta's reckoning, they had sailed fourteen thousand four hundred and sixty leagues. They were the first men known to have circumnavigated the Earth. As for their cargo of spices, it sold in Seville for ten thousand times what it had cost in the distant Moluccas, in fact for a sum sufficient to cover all the expenses of Magellan's whole fleet for three years and even to leave a profit to the King of Spain and to Magellan's financial backers.

Only much later was it known that the *Trinidad* suffered even greater hardships, when it was finally able to leave Tidore after undergoing repairs and then attempted to cross the Pacific again to reach Darien. Not yet knowing how to avoid the adverse trade-winds by steering a more northerly course on the eastward crossing, it was forced to turn back to the Moluccas, for lack of provisions, before reaching its destination. When it finally landed in Ternate, in November 1522, it was captured by a Portuguese force which had recently established itself there from Malacca after overpowering Carvalho and his token force that still represented Spain in Tidore. Only four members of its crew ever returned to Europe; the rest of them died in the course of their unsuccessful attempt to cross the Pacific or else, after their return to the Moluccas, in Portuguese prisons in the Far East, in India or in East Africa.

Thirty-five survivors of Magellan's expedition had already returned to Seville aboard the *San Antonio*. Eighteen now returned aboard the *Victoria*. Captured by the Portuguese in the Cape Verde Islands, thirteen were sent back to Lisbon as prisoners; four straggling survivors of the *Trinidad* returned much later from the Far East. Only seventy men are thus known to have survived the whole expedition and returned alive to Europe.

But the news of the return of the *Victoria* was soon widely discussed throughout Renaissance Europe and Islam. The survivors of the expedition were immediately summoned from Seville to the Spanish court in Valladolid, to report to the King, who ordered an extensive enquiry into the whole history of the expedition. In the course of this enquiry, Magellan's name was at last cleared of the accusations brought against him two years earlier by the deserters who had returned aboard the *San Antonio*. Sebastian del Cano was awarded the highest honours. Pigafetta became, for a while, a welcome guest of honour wherever he went, but soon lapsed into obscurity after rewriting his whole *Journal* and dedicating it to the Grand Master of the Order of the

Knights of Malta. For many years, claims were fought in Spanish courts by crew-members suing for back-pay, by persons who claimed to be Magellan's heirs and by the private backers who had helped finance his expedition. And, after much haggling, it was finally proved that the Moluccas are situated in the area which, according to the imaginary line of the Treaty of Tordesillas, was a Portuguese and not a Spanish sphere of interest.

Bibliography

Until the publication of the Visconde de Lagôa's monumental two-volume critical biography of Magellan which also contained a Portuguese translation of Pigafetta's Journal, *Fernão de Magalhãis, a sua vida e a sua viagem* (Lisbon, Seara Nova, 1938), the great navigator's biographers, including such serious historians as Lord Stanley of Alderley, author of *The First Voyage around the World by Magellan* (London, The Hakluyt Society, 1874) and such popular writers as Stefan Zweig, author of *Magellan: Pioneer of the Pacific* (London, translated by Eden and Cedar Paul, Cassell and Company Ltd., 1938), had all tended to rely on much the same documents and other historical sources. Many of these, however, had not yet been subjected to a thorough critical examination according to the best principles of modern historical science. The Visconde de Lagôa's work has thus proved to be a veritable landmark in its field, although most English or American writers who have concerned themselves with Magellan since 1938 have unfortunately neglected to consult it, either because it is available only in Portuguese or else because it is out of print and can now be found only in very few libraries.

I have been fortunate in acquiring a copy of this rare work, so that I was able to consult it at all times while writing *Magellan of the Pacific*.

A bibliographical recapitulation of all available manuscript documents, in Lisbon's Torre do Tombo National Archives, in Seville's Archives of the Indies and elsewhere, or of the more traditional published source-books that other biographers have been able to consult, would scarcely come within the scope of the present volume. In spite of occasional inaccuracies and typographical errors and of its somewhat chaotic listing of authors and titles in an order that is neither alphabetical nor chronological, one of the best and most up-to-date bibliographies is the one appended to Léonce Peillard's critical edition, in modern French, of the sixteenth-century French translation of Pigafetta's Journal: *Premier voyage autour du monde par Magellan* (Paris, Union Générale d'Editions, 1964).

In addition to a number of other works listed by Peillard or by other biographers of Magellan, the following have provided valuable information and insights for the writing of the present volume:

BIBLIOGRAPHY

ALBERI, EUGENIO: *Relazioni degli Ambasciatori Veneti al Senato*, Florence, 1839–63, 15 vols.

AZEVEDO, PEDRO de: 'A Inquisição em Ceuta e Tanger no Principio do Seculo XVII', pp. 398–471 in *Academia das Sciencias de Lisbôa, Boletim da Secunda Classe, Fasciculo no. 1, Nov. 1916–Marco 1917.*

BAGROW, LEO: 'The Maps from the Home Archives of the Descendants of Marco Polo', in *Imago Mundi*, Stockholm, 1918.

BARRADAS, LERENO ANTUNES: 'Embarcações europeas em pinturas rupestres no extremo sudoeste africano: navegações pre-henriquinas', in *Monumenta: Bol. da Commissão dos monumentos nacionais da Provincia de Moçambique*, Lourenço Marques, 1965.
'O Sul de Moçambique no Roteiro do Piloto Ahmad ibn Madjid', pp. 157–76, in *Rev. da Universidade de Coimbra*, vol. XXII, 1967.

BARROS, JOÃO de: *Asia de João de Barros*, edited by Hernani Cidade, Lisbon, Agencia Gera das Colonias, 1945–46, 4 vols.

BARROS, JOÃO de, and COUTO, DIOGO de: *Decadas da Asia*, Lisbon, na Regia Officina Typographica, 1777–1778, 24 vols.

BENSAUDE, JOAQUIN: *L'astronomie nautique au Portugal à l'époque des grandes découvertes*, Bern, Akademische Buchhandlung von Max Dreschel, 1912.

BOXER, C. R.: *The Portuguese Seaborne Empire, 1415–1825*, London, Hutchinson, 1969.
Portuguese Society in the Tropics: The Municipal Councils of Goa, Macao, Bahia, and Luanda, 1510–1800, Madison, Univ. of Wisconsin Press, 1965.

BRÉHIER, EMILE: *La Philosophie du Moyen Age*, Paris, Albin Michel, 1971.

CASTANHEDA, FERNÃO LOPES de: *Historia do Descobrimento e Conquista da India pelos Portugueses*, Lisbon, Tipographia Rollandiana, 1833, 7 vols.

CORRÊA, GASPAR: *Lêndas da India*, Lisbon, 1858–64, 4 vols.

CORTESÃO, ARMANDO: *Cartografia portuguesa antiga*, Lisbon, Com. Exec. do Quinto Centenario da morte do Infante D. Henrique, 1960.
'Curso de Historia da Cartografia', pp. 140–90, in *Bol. do Centro de Estudios geograficos*, Coimbra vol. 3, nos. 20–21, 1963.
'Do Ambiente cientifico em que se iniciaram os descobrimentos portugueses', pp. 1–20, in *O Instituto*, Coimbra, 1961.
History of Portuguese Cartography, Coimbra, Junta de Inv. do Ultramar, vol. 1, 1964.
Portugaliae Monumenta Cartographica, Lisbon, Imprensa de Coimbra, vols. 1–6, 1960.
'Cartographic indications of otherwise unknown Portuguese voyages', pp. 111–16, in *Actas do Cong. Int. da Historia dos Descobrimentos*, Lisbon, vol. 2, 1961.
The Nautical Chart of 1424, Coimbra, 1954.

CORTESÃO, JAIME: 'O Descobrimento das Canarías', pp. 256-58, in *Bol. da Segunda Classe da Academia das Sciencias de Lisboa*, vol. 19. Coimbra.

'Os Descobrimentos Pre-colombinos dos Portugueses', in *Obras Completas*, vol. 8, Lisbon, Portugalia Editora, 1966.

COUTINHO, Admiral GAGO: *A Nautica dos Descobrimentos*, Lisbon, Agencia Geral do Ultramar, 1951, 2 vols.

FARIA E SOUSA, MANUEL de: *Asia Portuguesa*, Tradução de Isabel Ferreira do Amaral Pereira de Matos e Maria Vitoria Garcia Santos Ferreira, com uma Introdução por M. Lopes d'Almeida, Oporto, Livraria Civilização, no date, 5 vols.

GODINHO, VITORINO MAGALHÃES: *Os Descobrimentos e a Economia Mundial*, Lisbon, Editora Arcadia, 1963.

L'économie de l'Empire portugais aux XVème et XVIème siècles, Paris, Imprimerie Nationale, 1969.

'Fontes quatrocentistas para a geografia e a economia do Saará e Guiné', pp. 47-65 in *Revista de Historia*, ano IV, no 13, Sao Paulo, 1953.

'O Mediterraneo Saariano e as caravanas do ouro: Geografia economica e social do Saará ocidental e central do Seculo XI ao Seculo XVI', pp. 59-108, in *Revista de Historia*, ano VI, no. 24, Sao Paulo, 1955.

HAMMER-PURGSTALL, JOSEPH von: *Geschichte des Osmanischen Reiches*, Pesth, 1827-35, 15 vols.

HOWELL, WARREN R.: *100 Rare Books, Autograph Letters, Manuscripts, Maps*, San Francisco, John Howell Books, 1970. (No. 64 in this catalogue describes *Eine schöne Newe Zeytung*, Augsburg, 1522, containing the first printed account, reproduced in the present volume, of Magellan's voyage. A number of historians and bibliographers have all too easily confused this very rare pamphlet with another, equally rare, *Copia der Newen Zeytung*, Augsburg 1520, which reports on 'Presilly Landt', meaning Brasil, and of which a copy is preserved in the John Carter Brown Memorial Library at Brown University, Providence, R.I.)

JONG, M. de: *Um roteiro inedito da Circunnavegação de Fernao de Magalhães*, Coimbra, Faculdade de Letras, 1937.

KAHLE, P. *Die verschollene Columbus-Karte von 1498 in einer türkischen Weltkarte von 1513*, Berlin–Leipzig, 1938.

KAMAL, Prince YOUSSOUF: *Monumenta Cartographica Africae et Aegypti*, vol. I., Cairo, 1926.

KHALIFA, HAJI: *The History of the Maritime Wars of the Turks*, translated from the Turkish by James Mitchell, London, 1831.

KONYALI, IBRAHIM HAKKI: *Topkapy Sarayinda Deri Üzerine Yapilmis Eski*

BIBLIOGRAPHY

Haritalar (Old parchment maps preserved in the Top Kapy Palace Collections), Istanbul, 1936.

LELEWEL, J.: *Géographie du Moyen Age*, Bruxelles, 1852.

MARCONDES DE SOUSA, T. O.: *A viagem de Fernão de Magalhães e Amerigo Vespucci*, Sao Paulo, 1961.

MARTYR D'ANGHIERA, PETER: *De Orbo Novo Decades*, 1530.

MORAIS E SOUSA, Vice-admiral L. de: *A sciencia nautica dos pilotos portugueses nos seculos XV et XVI*, Lisbon, 1924.

MORISON, Admiral SAMUEL ELIOT: *The European Discovery of America: The Northern Voyages*, A.D. *500–1600*, New York, Oxford University Press, 1971.

NAVARRETE, MARTIN FERNANDEZ de: *Colección de los Viajes y Descubrimientos, que hicieron por Mar los Españoles desde Fines del Siglo XV*, Madrid, Imprenta Real, 1825–37, 5 vols.

NORDENSKJÖLD, A. E.: *Facsimile Atlas*, Stockholm, 1889.

Periplus, Stockholm, 1897.

PIGAFETTA, ANTONIO: *Magellan's Voyage: A Narrative Account of the First Circumnavigation*, translated and annotated, with an Introduction, by R. A. Skelton, New Haven, Yale University Press, 1969, 2 vols.

The Voyage of Magellan, translated by Paula Spurlin Paige, New York, Prentice Hall, 1969.

Il primo viaggio intorno al Mondo, e il 'roteiro' d'un pilota genovese, edited, with an introduction and noted, by Camillo Manfroni. Milano, Istituto Editoriale Italiano, no date.

RAVENSTEIN, E. G., Fellow of the Royal Geographical Society: *Martin Behaim, his Life and his Globe*, London, George Philip and Son Ltd., 1908. (The line illustrations in the present volume, which depict old navigational instruments, are all reproduced from Ravenstein's remarkable and very rare work, which has all too often been neglected by Magellan's biographers.)

REIS, KATIP SEYDI ALI BEN HUSSEIN: *O Bahr-i-Mohit, ou Espelho dos Mares*, pp. 3–55, in *Boletim da Sociedade de Geografia de Lisboa*, 1958.

REIS, SIDI ALI (same as above): *The Travels and Adventures of the Turkish Admiral Sidi Ali Reis*, translated by A. Vambery, London, 1899.

REIS, PIRI: *Bir Turk Amirali*, Istanbul, 1937.

SANDERLIN, GEORGE: *First around the World*. London, Hamish Hamilton, 1966.

STILWELL, MARGARET BINGHAM: *The Awakening Interest in Science during the First Century of Printing, 1450–1550*, New York, The Bibliographical Society of America, 1970.

TAYLOR, E. G. R.: 'Imaginary Islands: a Problem solved', pp. 105–109, in *The Geographical Journal*, London, 1964, vol. 130, No. 1.

BIBLIOGRAPHY

'Some Notes on Early Ideas of the Form and Size of the Earth', pp. 65–68, in *The Geographical Journal*, 1935, vol. 85, No. 1.

'Imago Mundi', pp. 78–80, in *The Scottish Geographical Magazine*, Edinburgh, 1931, vol. 47, No. 2.

TAYLOR, E. G. R. and RICHEY, M. W.: *The Geometrical Seaman: a Book of Early Nautical Instruments*, London, Hollis and Carter, for The Institute of Navigation, 1962.

TOUSSAINT, AUGUSTE: *History of the Indian Ocean*, Chicago, University of Chicago Press, 1966.

Index